This Is Not Civil Rights

THE CHICAGO SERIES IN LAW AND SOCIETY
Edited by John M. Conley and Lynn Mather

This Is Not Civil Rights

Discovering Rights Talk in 1939 America

GEORGE I. LOVELL

THE UNIVERSITY OF CHICAGO PRESS   CHICAGO AND LONDON

George I. Lovell is associate professor of political science at the University of Washington. He is the author of *Legislative Deferrals*.

The University of Chicago Press, Chicago 60637
The University of Chicago Press, Ltd., London
© 2012 by The University of Chicago
All rights reserved. Published 2012.
Printed in the United States of America
21 20 19 18 17 16 15 14 13 12   1 2 3 4 5

ISBN-13: 978-0-226-49403-6 (cloth)
ISBN-13: 978-0-226-49404-3 (paper)
ISBN-13: 978-0-226-49405-0 (e-book)
ISBN-10: 0-226-49403-9 (cloth)
ISBN-10: 0-226-49404-7 (paper)
ISBN-10: 0-226-49405-5 (e-book)

Library of Congress Cataloging-in-Publication Data

Lovell, George I.
    This is not civil rights / George I. Lovell.
        pages — (Chicago series in law and society)
    ISBN-13: 978-0-226-49403-6 (cloth : alkaline paper)
    ISBN-10: 0-226-49403-9 (cloth : alkaline paper)
    ISBN-13: 978-0-226-49404-3 (paperback : alkaline paper)
    ISBN-10: 0-226-49404-7 (paperback: alkaline paper)
    [etc.]
        1. Civil rights—Language. 2. Civil rights—United States—Cases. 3. Citizen suits (Civil procedure)—Language. 4. Citizen suits (Civil procedure)—United States—Cases. 5. State action (Civil rights)—United States—Cases. 6. United States. Dept. of Justice. Civil Rights Section—Cases. 7. Complaint letters—United States.   I. Title.   II. Series: Chicago series in law and society.
    KF4749.L68 2012
    323.01'4—dc23

                                                                    2012003669

♾ This paper meets the requirements of ANSI/NISO z39.48-1992 (Permanence of Paper).

FOR CARRIE

Contents

Preface

Americans quite often use talk about rights, law, and constitutional history as they engage in everyday conversations and interactions related to political and social life. Observers have noted that peculiar attachment to law and rights since at least the early nineteenth century, and legalized discourses around rights and constitutional history remain quite visible in America's public political discourse. Today, as the United States confronts a complicated set of twenty-first-century problems, many people spend time discussing iconic political figures of the late eighteenth century and symbolic events like the Boston Tea Party.

This book explores the imprint that the tendency to talk in language of rights, law, and constitutionalism leaves on American politics and American society. It addresses important questions about the meaning and significance of popular attachments to law and legal discourses: How does the tendency to talk in legalized discourses affect democratic politics? How does the central place of legalized discourses influence the way people perceive and respond to injustice?

These are old questions that scholars have been exploring for a long time. My account is different from earlier studies because I reach very different conclusions about the nature of popular rights discourses and their place in American politics. I reach those conclusions after looking for answers in a very different place and developing data that shed new light on how popular legal discourses enter into everyday political encounters.

My conclusions differ from earlier accounts in that I provide a relatively optimistic account of the contribution that legal framings can sometimes make to American politics. Most scholars of legalized discourses have been quite critical of the American tendency to deploy languages of law and rights. Scholars worry that the habit of using rights discourses is damaging and constraining and that legal discourses reinforce an inaccurate and ideologically charged picture of legal processes and governance. One manifestation of these concerns is the way law expresses its own legitimacy through absolute promises that are not always fulfilled in practice. The Constitution's expressed guarantee of "equal protection of the laws," for example, has not always guaranteed that people are all equally protected by law. Yet despite law's shortcomings, legal authorities, especially judges, continue to express law in its idealized form as they try to justify their decisions. Such legalized pronouncements try to provide reassurance that government decisions are legitimate, fair, and just, but their legal form seems to distort how law actually works.

Scholars' concerns about the power of law to distort perceptions of legitimacy only grow when official legal discourses metastasize into popular political discourse. Because law is technical and obscure, the understanding of law expressed in popular legal discourses will inevitably be flawed and incomplete. Moreover, the reassurances provided by law's claim to legitimacy threaten to narrow citizens' judgments and create tolerance of injustice. People who believe that Americans have freedoms that are a unique gift of "Founding Fathers" and thus the envy of the world might not fully confront the fact that the United States incarcerates people at a rate that shocks most other developed countries. People with faith in law might believe that passage of antidiscrimination laws has eliminated racism as a problem in society. These examples suggest that faith in law and attachments to legalized discourses can also make people prone to manipulation. Law's power to legitimate outcomes makes it less likely that unjust outcomes will be contested. Assertions that something is legal or required by law will make the status quo appear natural and inevitable. Over time, alternative ways of doing things become unimaginable.

In this book, I present findings that challenge these sorts of critical claims about popular legal discourses around rights and constitutionalism. I find that legal discourses are more malleable than such claims suggest and thus less likely to limit people's imagination and understanding. I show how ordinary people appropriate the language of law not to mimic or honor official law but to frame expansive demands for new entitlements that go well beyond what authorities announce as legitimate or required by law. I also find that people can make idealized claims about rights and law while maintaining a realistic underlying understanding of law's limitations. As a result, the tendency of people to invoke legal ideals like rights when interacting with certain audiences need not indicate a belief in those ideals or a susceptibility to manipulation. People deploy legal discourses not to succumb to the legal order expressed as formal law but to express aspirations for a better legal order. Such findings challenge the widespread view that legal discourses inevitably distort politics, mask injustice, and lead to compliance or acquiescence.

I am led to these less pessimistic conclusions after searching for answers in a very different way. The chapters that follow examine a large group of complaint letters that people wrote to the federal government regarding law or rights, together with the responses made by government officials. Most of the people who wrote the letters were complaining about particular incidents involving perceived violations of rights or other legal entitlements. The letters were primarily sent to the Justice Department or the White House.

The letters that I use are particularly illuminating because they were written from 1939 to 1941, at the start of a second decade of very difficult economic conditions and shortly before US entry into World War II. The letters thus provide an opportunity to look at the way people deployed legal and constitutional discourses in a legal, economic, and social context that is very different from today's. The people who wrote letters expressed a very wide range of grievances and asserted quite a variety of rights entitlements. S. D. Brewton complained that seasonal lettuce pickers were forced to license their vehicles in California, Milton Kennedy complained that his ex-wife had stolen some movie scripts that were later sold by social workers to a Hollywood studio, and Hattie Mae Smith asserted that a zoning decision by a village board violated her family's constitutional "right to earn our own living selling just good food, ice cream, and pop."

Letters from the earlier time period are particularly illuminating because they provide a useful corrective to the common perception that the United States has an unbroken tradition of rights protection that goes back to the founding era. Letter writers complained most frequently about rights violations perpetrated by, or with the complicity of, state and local officials. The letters tell many stories of African American citizens being brutalized and murdered by corrupt law enforcement officials, of people encountering hostility and violence from "relief" agencies when traveling in desperate search of work, and of people being detained, imprisoned, or committed to mental institutions without basic protections for due process. People wrote to the federal government because state governments were not providing mechanisms to check such abuses. However, at that time, the federal government had almost no institutional capacity to provide any redress for such problems. As a result, innumerable instances of egregious rights violations went without remedy during those years.

My focus on the way legal discourses were used in letters to and from government officials provides a stronger empirical foundation than the accounts of more critical scholars. Some scholars have made claims about the effects of legal discourses on ordinary people without providing any evidence at all about how people use and respond to assertions of law. Other scholars have observed how people actually talk about law in their everyday lives, but their studies have not been designed to focus on instances where individuals use legal discourses to contest official law. The tendency to study the place of law in less contentious contexts has preserved the alleged links between popular legal discourses and legitimation, deference, and acquiescence to law. In contrast, this study shows how people used idealized legal discourses not to express of faith in law but because those discourses could also accommodate and help to communicate resistance and contestation. The letters record many exchanges where people used language of law, rights, and constitutionalism to make novel demands or contest official legal outcomes. People also used legal discourses to assert dignity, challenge the integrity of legal authorities, and express constitutional bases for alternative systems of justice. Many writers did these things as they expressed resistance in the face of towering injustice and shocking official indifference. Such findings make it seem less likely that attachments to legal discourses are the reason for the apparent acquiescence found by other scholars.

My findings do not mean that popular invocation of law, rights, and the Constitution is always effective or always constructive. I also find numerous instances where people articulated claims of "rights" in connection with relatively trivial matters. At a time when complaints about police officers who brutally murdered citizens went largely unheeded, some people wrote impassioned pleas suggesting that the constitutional republic would crumble if a city widened its sidewalks or forced dog owners to license their pets. A few of the letter writers also deployed the language of rights and the Constitution to support calls for repression of rights.

Nevertheless, recognizing people's capacity to engage the law and to deflect law's claims of legitimacy leads to a less pessimistic account of popular rights claims and a relatively optimistic account of Americans' capacity to act as engaged constitutional citizens. More important, my findings allow attention to shift from legal ideologies to other features of the political system that make it difficult for popular aspirations for justice to prevail. The letters show that it is a mistake to dismiss the transformative political possibilities of popular constitutional and rights discourses. The language of law, rights, and the Constitution may sometimes be the way Americans express selfish, distorted, confused, or partisan demands. But popular expressions of legal discourse nevertheless deserve to be listened to carefully. Such language is also the vehicle through which Americans express their noblest aspirations for a better society.

Acknowledgments

When I began work on this book, I envisioned a very different final product. I conceived a straightforward institutional study of the Justice Department's experimental civil rights prosecutions in the 1940s. I anticipated using that institutional case study to explore the kinds of theoretical puzzles about legal institutions, political accountability, and separation of powers that had occupied me in prior research. Over the course of what has turned out to be sixteen years (sigh), I have been led in a very different direction by a variety of unexpected events. The most important was the discovery of the letters when I began doing research in primary sources. Although I was immediately drawn to the letters, I resisted what felt like a siren song. I knew the easiest path to fame and fortune (or, at least, to tenure) was to plan a historical study of institutional processes that matched my prior training. Over time, the letters gradually assumed a more central role, but the project foundered and was sometimes abandoned for long stretches as I struggled to understand and articulate what the letters were teaching me. To learn from the letters, I had to become a different type of scholar. I was able to complete that transformative journey only because I had the interest, support, and encouragement of a large number of very helpful colleagues and friends.

The most important step in the journey was joining the intellectual community of the Political Science Department and program in Law, Societies, and Justice at the University of Washington. While I name some individual contributions below, the broader community of faculty colleagues, graduate students, and undergraduates deserves separate acknowledgement for providing a supportive and stimulating environment to develop and test ideas.

Many people read or heard earlier versions of the argument and responded with conversation, advice, encouragement, admonishment, or help with sources. I wish to thank Taunya Lovell Banks, Scott Barclay, Gad Barzilai, Larry Becker, Katherine Beckett, Anne Bloom, Pam Brandwein, Amy Bridges, Susan Burgess, Tom Burke, Nitsan Chorev, Rachel Cichowski, Larry Cushnie, Christine Distefano, Lynda Dodd, Jeff Dudas, David Engel, Paul Frymer, Angelina Godoy, Mark Graber, Seth Greenfest, Trevor Griffey, Brad Hays, Steve Herbert, Beth Hoffman, Peter Hovde, Lynn Jones, Ken Kersch, John Kingdon, Anna Kirkland, Bert Kritzer, Erik Larson, Scott Lemieux, Margaret Levi, Sandra Levitsky, Mike Lovell, Anna Marshall, Kevin McMahon, Sally Merry, Naomi Murakawa, Julie Novkov, Arzoo Osanloo, Chris Parker, Mitch Pickerill, Patrick Rivers, Mark Sawyer, Andrea Simpson, Mark Smith, Becca Thorpe, Chip Turner, Stephen Wasby, Josh Wilson, Jennifer Woodward, Mariah Zeisberg, Rebecca Zeitlow, and several anonymous reviewers. Keith Bybee and an anonymous reader read the entire manuscript and provided valuable suggestions. Hanes Walton Jr. first drew my attention to the CRS and was a font of information on the national and regional politics of civil rights. Risa Goluboff provided important advice about the Justice Department materials at the National Archives. I also obtained valuable help from audiences at Loyola of Los Angeles School of Law, College of Saint Rose, Indiana University Law School, the Georgetown/University of Maryland Constitutional Law Discussion Group, the University of Texas–Dallas, and the University of Washington Law School.

John Tryneski of the University of Chicago Press continued to offer helpful advice for several years after I first told him I would have a finished manuscript in less than a year. He asked important questions that no one else was asking and helped me to work through issues of framing and presentation. He later provided more specific advice while shepherding the manuscript through the review and revisions process. Thanks also to series editors Lynn Mather and John Conley for their support and suggestions.

I received financial support through the Royalty Research Fund Grant at the University of Washington and a Faculty Summer Research Grant at the College of William and Mary. Two department chairs, Steve Majeski and Peter May, remained patient and supportive when the oft-promised book made its annual nonarrival. My colleagues at the College of William and Mary and friends at the University of Michigan provided a stimulating environment during the earliest stages of the project. Devin Joshi, Chris Roberts, and Michelle Webster provided research assistance.

Earlier versions of material included in this book have appeared as "Justice Excused: The Deployment of Law in Everyday Political Encounters," *Law and Society Review* 40 (2006): 283–324; and "Imagined Rights without Remedies: The Politics of Novel Legal Claims," *Loyola of Los Angeles Law Review* 44 (2010): 91–119.

A few people deserve very special thanks. Kim Scheppele, my long-standing advocate, provided guidance on innumerable things big and small. Jamie Mayerfeld was forever willing to read things or provide thoughtful answers to complicated questions on short notice. Jeannine Bell has been a treasured friend through the entire journey—an inexhaustible source of advice, sharp critical engagement, encouragement, humor, and good food. Rose Ernst, who worked on the project as a graduate student research assistant, provided thoughtful input on the coding scheme and conceptual design at an early stage. She has since developed into a colleague and my key source of "gut-check" advice on the book. On paper, I was one of Rose's mentors, but whenever we discussed this project, it felt the other way around. Stuart Scheingold engaged this project in very thoughtful ways. At one early stage, he provided a devastating critique that I needed to hear, together with the ultimately very helpful advice that I had to find my own way out of the thorny problems that he identified. Michael McCann played several essential roles. He invited me to become a part of the intellectual community that developed and flourished under his leadership and provided much institutional support. He provided general guidance as well as very specific and sharp comments on multiple versions of every part of the book. Although Michael was not always able to hide his bewilderment at what I was doing and why it was taking so long, he always communicated his faith that I would eventually come up with something of value.

I must also express my appreciation to the people who wrote the letters that are so central to this book. Only in retrospect can I see how much I struggled to resist what they were eventually able to teach me. I searched in vain for a path to the story I expected to tell when I began working with the letters: a pessimistic account of the futility of rights claiming and the limits of popular rights discourses. A more pessimistic account would have been a better match for my generally gloomy outlook on things. The courage and initiative of the letter writers allowed me to break through the barriers created by my inclinations and gave me the exhilarating and much too rare experience of actually learning something in the research process.

Finally, I thank the circle of parents, family, and friends that supports me and makes life meaningful. Most important, I thank my life partner and best friend, Carrie S. Cihak. Her companionship and patient sustenance has been the most essential help of all.

Post Office, Belle Glade Florida, 1939

This Is Not Civil Rights

CHAPTER ONE

Voices from Peoria

On February 9, 1939, four women from Peoria, Illinois, wrote to US Attorney General Frank Murphy in Washington, DC. Margaret Brophy, Henrietta Jeffries, Matilda Hammel, and Elsa Hotze began by indicating that they were writing to Murphy after reading in the *Chicago Tribune* that Murphy had recently created a Civil Liberties Unit in the Department of Justice. The letter then explained how all four women had lost their jobs at the local post office. The women were laid off in 1933 as a result of Depression-related emergency legislation. Congress later passed legislation restoring many eliminated post office jobs but had not made provision to reinstate employees who had been laid off. As a result, the women were left "at the mercy of a newly appointed Postmaster" who had declined to rehire them. All four women had between thirteen and eighteen years of service when they were laid off. The women explained that they had been too young to qualify for retirement annuities but noted that annuities had been given to many older laid-off workers who had fewer years of service. They asked the attorney general for a "fair and just ruling, either reinstatement or an annuity retroactive from date of dismissal" (Brophy et al. to Murphy, February 9, 1939).[1]

The letter was one of the first of many thousands of letters claiming rights or other legal entitlements that the Justice Department processed over the next decade. The department processed civil rights correspondence through Murphy's new Civil Liberties Unit, which later changed its name to the more familiar Civil Rights Section (CRS), the name I use in the rest of this book. In this case, the unit's staff seemed surprised that the women from Peoria saw a connection between their loss of a retirement annuity and the attorney general's reported interest in civil liberties and civil rights. Henry A. Schweinhaut, the first director of the unit, apparently wanted nothing to do with the women's complaint. He wrote in longhand on the routing slip that led the letter to his desk: "This is not civil rights." He later dictated a short reply letter that claimed that legal limits on the Justice Department's jurisdiction made it impossible to provide any assistance. The reply claimed: "I am sorry to advise you that this is not a matter over which the Department of Justice has jurisdiction" (March 7, 1939). The department took no further action on the case.

The department's response to the letter from Peoria shows that the officials responsible for responding to civil rights complaints had ideas about what counted as "civil rights" that were quite different from the ideas of the women who had written from Peoria. The reasons for such different understandings are not easy to determine. The women's reference to the newspaper story makes it clear that they saw some association between their predicament and Frank Murphy's expressed interest in civil rights, but the four women did not say directly why they thought their complaint was a civil rights complaint. The women did not point toward a particular constitutional provision or other legal source of a relevant legal "right." They instead made a variety of more general claims that expressed their underlying conceptions of justice.

Specifically, the women made claims about procedural fairness, reciprocity, and personal responsibility. The women wrote: "We are out of the service through absolutely no fault of ours" and "This to us seems unfair and has destroyed the merit in Civil Service." The women noted that "the same amount was deducted and withheld from our salaries" as had been withheld from the older employees who had received annuities. Thus, the women suggested that it was "obvious" that they were entitled to a "pro-rated" annuity for their service. The women also adopted Franklin Roosevelt's own political rhetoric to link their problems to policies championed by the president. They wrote: "Not only have our positions been taken from us but also our security. . . . Our government is stressing Social Security. . . . Those of us compelled to bear the burden of the economy program are so few in number it would not be much of a financial strain on the pension fund, to provide for us." The women then returned to the theme of fairness and reciprocity, adding: "We have given the best years of our life to the service of our Government."

The women's broader claims about justice and reciprocity did not seem to register with the staff at the CRS. The reply letter sent by the CRS begins with a brief summary of the complaint. The summary characterizes the letter only as a personal request for reinstatement and a retirement annuity and ignored the women's broader suggestion that issues of rights and justice were at stake.

The Civil Rights Section and Citizen Complaint Letters

The exchange between the women from Peoria and the attorneys at the CRS reveals a gap between citizens' expansive ideas about rights and the narrower understandings of responding government officials. That gap appears with stunning regularity in the records of the early CRS. This book is based on an analysis of 879 cases of people who wrote letters to the federal government making rights-related claims. The letters in my sample were all processed by the CRS, but they are otherwise a very diverse group. Many were sent to President Roosevelt, Eleanor Roosevelt, or some other federal office and then forwarded to the CRS for a response after the recipients determined that they raised issues related to civil rights or liberties. The letters were written during the first few years after the CRS was created. In nearly every case, people who wrote letters did not receive any material help from the government. Almost all the people who wrote letters received only a short reply letter stating that the Justice Department could not help because the federal government lacked legal jurisdiction over the complaint.

Looking broadly at the letters processed by the early CRS reveals that people were endlessly creative in adapting familiar elements of popular rights discourses and other legalized language to communicate a wide range of concerns and problems, some catastrophic and some rather trivial. Most writers engaged government legal officials by making both legal and nonlegal arguments to support their claims. The writers' ingenuity produced some broad patterns in the letters that might be surprising when compared to the kinds of claims one might expect a civil rights office to receive today. Most strikingly, the letters were not primarily about problems related to race. Only 8 percent of the letters in my sample made any mention at all of race, and only twelve letters (less than 2 percent) mentioned concerns about segregation.[2] Less than 1 percent made claims about sex discrimination, and there are no letters in the sample claiming rights of persons with disabilities. Meanwhile, many more writers made claims of rights or entitlement that fall outside current understandings of "civil rights" and "civil liberties," including claims about rights to work, to welfare, and to equal economic opportunity. Writers asserted a wide variety of offbeat and sometimes quite specific rights. Henry Kost claimed a right to paint signs for a living and draw cartoons as part of his constitutional protection for the right to "pursue happiness" (November 30, 1941). Richard Terry claimed that Americans had "the right to do your bit of work, to keep from being a burden, a chisler, a liar upon self and other neighbors" (May 20, 1940).

At first glance, such examples may suggest that the people who wrote were bumbling and ill informed. More generally, the fact that so many people wrote letters without getting help suggests that writers had exaggerated ideas about what rights were protected by law and about what government officials would be willing to do to protect rights. However, the exchanges recorded in the CRS correspondence reveal something different and, perhaps to some readers, more surprising. Many of the letter writers showed considerable facility when communicating the demands and concerns that they connected to rights. Many letters were carefully constructed, and the pleas in the letters are often quite moving. Writers also showed a considerable capacity to deploy legalized discourses as a resource for expressing or strengthening their claims for attention from the government. Even when they were articulating novel entitlements that were not recognized by law, writers still quite often attempted to apply legal rhetoric to communicate requests and complaints to government officials. Most writers made at least some claims about rights, law, or justice, and quite a few added detailed legal arguments. Many writers without formal training in law cited specific constitutional provisions, text from statutes, or relevant case law as they built coherent legal arguments supporting their claims.

Given the time period, the tendency of letter writers to express grievances by making claims about rights or other legal entitlements is particularly striking. It is not obvious what would inspire so many writers to articulate such a broad range of grievances by using language of rights and other legal entitlements. Clearly, the inspiration was not coming directly from official law or judicial rulings. Other than the understaffed and largely unhelpful CRS, the federal government did not have any institutional capacity to protect rights. The letters were written a decade and a half before *Brown v. Board of Education* (347 US 483 [1954]) and related cases signaled a transformation in the institutional processes for protecting rights. The letters were also written long before the judiciary started being widely perceived as the branch of government responsible for protecting the rights of racial minorities or other subaltern groups.

The broad patterns in the letters thus raise some important questions about the relationship between official law and the ideas of ordinary people regarding legal entitlements like rights. If the "rights" claimed by letter writers were not recognized by law, where were writers' expansive ideas about rights coming from? Since the claims were addressed to elected officials and their representatives and not to judges, why did people so often formulate demands using legal rhetoric about rights and the Constitution? Did writers actually believe that their expansive claims expressed established legal entitlements and that the law would somehow compel executive branch officials to honor their demands? Or were they simply drawing on legal discourses as a familiar and thus potentially effective way to communicate political demands? More generally, what effect does a propensity to talk and formulate demands in a legalized discourse of rights have on political and social life in the United States? Does the drive to formulate novel entitlement claims as rights violations constrain what people ask for and what kinds of responses they get from government officials? Does the tendency of writers to articulate idealized claims about rights and other legal entitlements indicate that people had broad faith in law? Consideration of the letters processed by the CRS, along with the reply letters that the CRS sent, provides some illuminating insights that help to address these questions.

What Is in the Letters?

I catalog and discuss the substance of the claims in the letters in greater detail in chapter 3 and provide additional information about how writers used both legal discourse and other nonlegal claims in chapters 4 and 5. For this introduction, I provide only a few preliminary observations.

The people who wrote letters spanned a broad range of the socioeconomic spectrum. Writers include owners of large companies who complained that their workers were joining unions. Letters also came from destitute people traveling around the country in desperate search for work who complained about being treated poorly by state welfare officials. Some letters were typed on formal letterhead and written with considerable precision. Most, however, were handwritten and less formal. Letters often contained spelling errors and problems with grammar and diction; some are difficult to read because of illegible handwriting or the writer's difficulty with written expression. The letters came

overwhelmingly from individuals rather than from organizations or interest groups.[3]

My sample includes 879 encounters between letter writers and the
CRS, counting multiple letters from the same person on the same incident as a single case. Most of the encounters (710) consisted of reports
or complaints about individual incidents where rights were allegedly
violated, the rights of either the letter writer or some family member
or close friend. There is tremendous variation in the seriousness of the
incidents that generated complaints. Some writers told heartbreaking
stories about having their children forcibly taken away by corrupt state
welfare officials. Other writers complained that their rights were violated
by dog-licensing ordinances or by being asked to work on the Fourth of
July.

In the other 169 cases in my sample, writers expressed more general
opinions rather than reporting specific incidents. Many letters in this
group commented on some administration initiative or urged President
Roosevelt to veto proposed laws related to rights and liberties, particularly the anti-alien Smith Act. I include these letters in the study because
many of them articulate general claims about law or contain illuminating
and forceful expressions that reveal how writers thought about law and
rights. However, because these letters do not report on particular incidents, it does not always make sense to include them when I report on the
percentage of letters that do or say a particular thing. (I indicate whether
a reported percentage is a percentage of all 879 letters or a percentage of
the 710 "incident" letters.)

Why Did People Write Letters?

The answer to the question of why people wrote is not as straightforward
as it might seem. To be sure, there were some people who asked for very
specific things in their letters, and many other writers asked more generally for help with particular problems. Nevertheless, it would be a mistake
to assume automatically that a person's only reason for writing was the
expectation that federal officials would respond by solving their problems.
Many writers who demanded specific assistance also added things to make
it clear that they did not expect the government to help. There were also
many writers who, sometimes quite pointedly, did not ask for or seem to
expect anything from the government officials addressed in their letters.

Thus it seems fair to say that writers took the trouble to write for more complicated reasons than the simple expectation that their letters would lead to some material form of patronage. Among other important things, writing letters provided opportunities to give voice to complaints, to register protest, to provide information to government officials, and to create a record of an injustice.

Whatever the reasons for writing, it is important to observe that writing was not costless. In addition to the cost of postage and paper (which was not a negligible factor for some writers), writers put time, energy, and thought into writing. Even letters from persons of very modest means are often carefully typed or meticulously handwritten. Many writers did at least some research to try to build arguments to support their petitions or claims. A few writers also reported more serious costs. One example is Douglas Dorner of New York City, who wrote to complain about a dispute over wages with his Works Progress Administration (WPA) employer (March 9, 1939). Dorner later wrote back to report that he had been fired because the Justice Department had written a memo to the WPA informing them of Dorner's complaint (June 23, 1939). Other writers expressed concerns about the consequences of writing. When L. R. Pinckney wrote from Washington, DC, for help with a bigamy case, he included a self-addressed envelope. He explained that he wanted the department to send a reply in his envelope because he did not want a letter with a return address from the Justice Department to attract attention at his boardinghouse (March 29, 1939).

One important pattern in the letters is that very few writers specifically asked the government to prosecute perpetrators of rights violations. This pattern is striking because the CRS was part of the Criminal Division, and its mission was to conduct criminal prosecutions. Just 36 (5 percent) of the 710 letters on incidents requested that the federal government conduct a prosecution. Casting the net more broadly identifies more cases where people made requests that are at least indirectly related to prosecution. There were an additional 89 (13 percent) letters asking that the government conduct an investigation, while 122 (17 percent) asked for a federal official come to the scene to provide unspecified assistance. However, even that bigger net leaves nearly two-thirds of the letters that did not ask for either prosecution or any investigatory activity related to prosecuting crimes. Some writers specifically expressed a lack of interest in criminal prosecution. An example is H. W. Dail of Los Angeles, who complained about antiunion violence targeting a Teamsters local. Dail wrote, "We are more interested in protection than prosecution," and suggested that the mere presence of the FBI would likely be enough to deter some groups that were violating workers' civil liberties (April 7, 1939). Another writer who said he was looking for a largely symbolic response was Andrew Loewi, whose furniture store in Manhattan had been targeted by anti-Semitic picketers. Loewi said that he understood that the First Amendment made it difficult to go after picketers but asked that the president make a symbolic "statement" in response to growing anti-Semitism in the United States (April 21, 1939).

Many people wrote to the federal government for help because they had nowhere else to turn. Letter writers often reported unsuccessful attempts to get help from local and state officials or from private attorneys. In some instances, writers did not seem to know enough about government and law to know what to request. Others writers had knowledge and confidence to ask for quite specific remedies that only the federal government could provide. One interesting case is Dorothy Rogers, of Wilmington, Delaware, who wrote to her local US attorney to complain that local school officials were ignoring a recently passed federal law by compelling Jehovah's Witnesses to pledge allegiance to the American flag (October 20, 1942). The new law codified some rules regarding displaying and saluting the American flag. Rogers focused on the provision regarding the Pledge of Allegiance, quoting a clause that seemed to excuse people who objected to reciting the pledge ("civilians will always show full respect to the flag when the pledge is given by merely standing at attention").[4] Rogers reported that she had met with local officials and given them information about the new law, but they had rebuffed her claim that the federal law made compulsory recitation of the pledge unlawful. Rogers asked the US attorney to intervene because she expected the local officials to pay more attention if Justice Department officials would provide exactly the same legal information that she had already provided. She wrote: "Will you please do anything in your power to help the local school officials to realize that they have a responsibility to recognize the federal law." Clearly, Rogers was confident that her lay understanding of the law was superior to the legal views expressed by the local authorities who had turned away her claim that they were acting unlawfully. She also had a keen understanding that new legal protections for rights were not helpful in cases where government officials chose not to follow them. Not law itself but only law backed by the implicit threat of sanction by the Justice Department could change behavior.[5]

Some writers made quite unusual requests. One example is Mary Deming, who wrote from Mt. Pleasant, Michigan, to complain that her son was unjustly in prison. Deming asked Attorney General Robert Jackson to visit her son in jail (June 15, 1940). M. F. Compart of Waukegan, Illinois, complained that he had been overcharged by a lawyer and asked the department to provide a partial refund (September 9, 1939). Mrs. E. B. McMullen wrote from Everglades, Florida, to ask for the department's help in obtaining a legal document to confirm that she had been released from a mental hospital. McMullen specified that she had a "right" to a "legal document corresponding to the marriage certificate, death certificate, teachers certificate, etc. which I have and which would restore my civil rights. And I *know* I have a right to expect that to be given me without going to court or employing a lawyer. That is what I am asking you to do or have done for me" (January 13, 1940). Other writers made more ornate requests. Anna Mae Brown, who claimed to have been poisoned and then framed for a crime by local law enforcement officials in Lansing, Michigan, wrote: "This is to ask for more than an investigation. It is to ask that my rights be restored to me along with my father's property, my lost innocence, my job, my reputation, my family, my friends, My Happiness" (March 29, 1939).

While some writers made broad requests, others did not ask for anything at all and seemed motivated primarily by a desire to register protest or give voice to frustration rather than by an expectation that they would obtain help. For example, a letter from Rev. B. Sumner complained that officials in Lakeland, Florida, had interfered with his efforts to host a gospel tent revival. Sumner's letter consisted of a series of loaded rhetorical questions about what did or did not count as a rights violation, but he did not ever ask the department to do anything or provide any help (April 3, 1939).

Measuring the Political Impact of Popular Legal Discourses

The rest of this book examines the way people used legalized discourses of rights and constitutionalism in everyday political encounters. The letters used in this study provide a valuable resource for addressing some important general questions about how the habit of using such discourses matters in American politics and society. Those general questions have been asked by a variety of scholars interested in rights and law in the United

States. Since the time of Tocqueville, many observers have asserted that Americans have a unique tendency to frame and express political and social conflicts in terms of law and rights.[6] For the most part, those who have observed that tendency have been very critical of legal claims and "rights talk" in America's public political discourse and quite concerned that an American obsession with law and rights has a destructive impact on American politics and society.

The content of the letters processed by the CRS challenges such views and makes it possible to construct a more balanced account. My alternative account emerges through the two core findings that emerge in the letters. First, ordinary people have the capacity to use rights and other legal discourses expansively to frame demands for entitlements that go well beyond what legal authorities establish as official law. Second, the tendency of people to invoke legal ideals in certain kinds of interactions does not indicate their belief in the literal truth of those ideals or their belief in the legitimacy of authoritative expressions of law. People may have deployed legal discourses that portrayed law as universal and objective, but they understood that the actual operations of law were contingent and depended upon discretionary choices by government officials. Taken together, these two findings challenge much existing scholarship that portrays legal discourse as a legitimating ideology that distorts politics, masks injustice, and leads to acquiescence. My findings also raise some important questions about the methods scholars have used to develop their conclusions.

The findings here challenge several different types of critical accounts that have been made from a variety of political and methodological perspectives. Most famously, Mary Ann Glendon (1991) has claimed that the pathological and extravagant "rights talk" that dominates American political discourse makes it more difficult to find policy compromises and to build meaningful communal life. These problems occur, according to Glendon, because rights formulated as absolute and unqualified entitlements mask an underlying reality where competing rights claims must be balanced against one another and against other important considerations related to governance. Moreover, "rights talk" tends to focus on entitlements allegedly owed to isolated individuals and thus to ignore the way individuals are situated in broader communities that create mutual obligations. Other critics of rights discourse have focused on concerns about law as a carrier of ideological messages of legitimacy and worries that the habit of framing demands as "rights" will narrow the range of experiences that people or activists will perceive as grievable injustices (see, e.g., Tushnet 1984; Gabel and Kennedy 1984).

While the critics of rights rhetoric have provided powerful theoretical frameworks for understanding the limitations of rights formulations, they have been less successful in developing empirical evidence to support their claims about the impact of rights rhetoric on ordinary people. Legal academics in particular have tended to focus on the *production* of legal ideology in the written opinions of appellate court judges, without offering much evidence to support assertions about the *reception* of such claims among ordinary people. Glendon, for example, focuses her account on appellate court opinions and debates over policy in Congress. She provides anecdotes of silly "rights talk" by interest group leaders who appear on television (e.g., 1991, 8) but very little evidence about how ordinary people actually talk about rights in their everyday lives. My findings in this study reveal that the official legal sources that Glendon uses are not a reliable way of identifying how most people think about and respond to rights claims and legal discourses. They also challenge some of Glendon's central claims. For example, Glendon claims that Americans only developed their pathological attachment to "extravagant" rights claims in the aftermath of the civil rights movement. She blames the Supreme Court rulings favoring civil rights in the 1950s and 1960s (5–8) and the jurisprudence of some of the justices who supported those rulings (42) for today's "anemic" discourse of rights. Glendon supports such claims by looking to differences in opinions written by the Supreme Court before and after that period. However, the letters in my sample show that people adopted language of rights to a wide variety of novel entitlements long before the changes on the Supreme Court that she identifies.

My study of the letters is valuable because it allows me to observe the production of legal claims by government authorities (both judges and Justice Department attorneys) alongside the claims and responses that were made by individual citizens. In contrast to Glendon, I find that people who asserted rights claims in absolute form were quite cognizant that realization of rights depended on finding effective compromises between asserted rights and other legal and practical concerns. Moreover, the letter writers' assertions of individual rights did not blind them to concerns of community. Letter writers quite often emphasized shared values and responsibilities, as well as concerns about broader community, as they tried to persuade responding officials to honor their claims. In contrast to scholars who have focused on law as a constraining or legitimating ideology,

I find that people appropriated the language of rights to articulate quite a broad range of novel demands that were not recognized in official law and that they quite often challenged the claims of legitimacy expressed by official legal actors. While law's obscurity made it difficult for people to get all of the details right, people without legal training were nevertheless able to formulate coherent legal arguments to support normative claims that they consciously distinguished from official law.

My findings about the way people used legal claims instead provide support for the arguments about legal discourses that have been made by scholars of critical race theory. In particular, my effort to challenge critics of legal discourses parallels Crenshaw's landmark analysis of antidiscrimination law and its critics (1988). Crenshaw's analysis challenged some leading critiques of antidiscrimination law and other claims of "rights" by racial minorities. Like Crenshaw, I argue that those critics' assessments of law, legal discourses, and related ideology are based on insufficient attention to the contexts in which people deploy legal discourses. In particular, Crenshaw argued that critics underestimated the importance of violent and coercive conditions that cut off other avenues of resistance to racial injustice. As a result, the critics underestimated the potential of rights and other legal remedies to become, at least occasionally, a valuable weapon (see also Matsuda 1989; and Williams 1991). My study of the CRS letters helps to extend Crenshaw's argument by revealing how legal discourses were deployed in practical political contexts where people voiced a very wide range of novel demands or protests to government officials. Many of the stories told in letters from my time period provide vivid illustrations of the kinds of coercive conditions that gave people few practical alternatives to seeking legal remedies from government.

This study of letters to the CRS is also an empirical study of everyday interactions around law and rights. It is thus also closely aligned with two bodies of empirical work by socio-legal scholars: studies of rights-based legal mobilization and studies of legal consciousness of ordinary people. Many socio-legal scholars have looked beyond official legal discourses to observe how ordinary people actually talk about law. Most often, they have used open-ended interviews or participant observation to explore how people outside of government understand, use, produce, and respond to rights talk or other elements of legal discourse. Legal mobilization studies have sometimes examined the rights consciousness of participants in organized campaigns that use litigation processes to advance political goals (e.g., McCann 1994; Silverstein 1996; Luker 1994). Legal-consciousness studies, in contrast, have focused largely on people who are not part of organized movements. They have looked at how consciousness built around law has affected individuals who bring legal claims to courts (e.g., Merry 1990; Yngvesson 1993), negotiate everyday interactions in communities and workplaces (e.g., Ewick and Silbey 1998; Neilson 2003; Marshall 2003, 2005; Hoffman 2003, 2005; Kirkland 2008), and respond to legal enactments and legal barriers (Sarat 1990; Engel and Munger 2003; Hull 2003).[7]

Many of these socio-legal scholars have drawn conclusions that resonate with some of my findings in this study. For example, McCann's study of litigation campaigns for pay equity found that participants maintained heightened rights consciousness and expressed rights entitlements even after appellate courts ultimately rejected the movement's legal arguments. My findings also resonate with some of the findings in legal-consciousness studies. Those studies have confirmed the importance and pervasiveness of legal discourses. Scholars have found that ideas and categories appropriated from law are a core element of how people talk about and make sense of everyday life. Given these findings, it is not surprising that legal discourses figure so prominently in the letters people wrote to the CRS.

While I draw on many of the insights emerging from these studies, this book differs from studies of legal consciousness because I focus more narrowly on some political dimensions of popular legal discourses rather than on collective legal consciousness or the role of law in everyday life. Letters like the ones processed by the CRS are particularly useful when trying to evaluate the impact of rights talk and legal rhetoric on ordinary political processes. Because they reveal the way people use legal discourses to describe experiences of injustice and make demands to political officials, the letters also present an opportunity to frame and explore some important new questions regarding connections among legal discourses, judicial institutions, and ordinary politics.

Three additional points can help to highlight some of the ways my study of the encounters between the CRS and letter writers provide a useful supplement to more familiar ways of looking at the political imprint of popular legal discourses.

   1. This study locates talk of rights and other legal discourses within a political process where individual citizens directly confront elected officials and their representatives.

The letters to and from the CRS yield new insights into the political impact of rights and other legalized discourses because they take study of
the politics of rights discourse away from courts and the world of litigation. More typically, scholars associate rights claiming with litigation or
judicial processes and tend to think of judges as the government officials
who decide whether and when to recognize rights. Even scholars who have
looked beyond activity in courtrooms to examine the role of law in people's everyday lives tend to orient discussion of law around legal remedies
pursued (or not pursued) in court. Scholars have paid less attention to the
way people use rights claims when engaging in political action directed at
officials in other branches of government. (One exception is Ernst 2007.)

This study shows that claims about law, rights, justice, and the Constitution are very much a part of the give and take of everyday political activity,
including protests directed at elected officials and individual requests for
patronage. The letters to the CRS make it clear that legal discourses, and
especially talk of rights, are ubiquitous in a wide range of political encounters, not just when people formulate claims in courts of law.

The letters also call attention to two important but overlooked areas
of popular political contestation that are very much a part of the politics
of rights. These two areas call attention to the way the line between legal
processes and electoral politics are quite often blurred in practice. First,
many letter writers wrote to challenge the accessibility and adequacy of
the institutional system for obtaining redress for rights violations, particularly the civil justice system. Writers demanded that political actors
provide additional legal protections when those judicial processes failed,
either because of barriers to access or because of structural biases in the
court system. Second, letter writers contested federal policies that called
for a restrained response to civil rights violations and demanded that
the federal government devote more resources to providing redress for
rights violations. Writers who engaged government officials on these two
issues recognized that rights protections depended not just on decisions
by judges but also on choices made by elected officials about whether to
devote resources to rights protection.

Of course, the CRS records also show, quite powerfully, that letters
from isolated individual citizens to government officials are not an effective means of obtaining assistance or provoking policy change.[8] Nevertheless, such individual petitions to government officials are an important
component of popular participation and politics and deserve attention
from scholars interested in the political impact of legal discourses. Indi-

vidual petitions, however ineffective, are a basic and essential form of political participation.

By looking beyond judges and courts, this study also introduces some important considerations that complicate efforts to capture the impact of rights talk and other legal discourses. For example, the letters make it clear that judges are not the only government officials who produce ideologically charged pronouncements about law. When CRS officials wrote back to tell letter writers that the Justice Department could not provide help, the CRS's reply letters routinely explained the government's refusal to provide help by making *legal* claims about the Justice Department's jurisdiction. Nevertheless, the letters also make it clear that authoritative renderings of law, whether they come from judges or from executive branch officials, do not automatically trickle down to become part of popular political discourses or legal consciousness. Letter writers quite frequently challenged both judicial and administrative assertions of law.

More generally, the letters reveal that most letter writers did not link rights claiming to judges and courtrooms in the same way that most scholars do today. It is not difficult to imagine why. Writers of that era had no reason to think of judges as the primary protectors of rights. During the decade preceding the creation of the CRS, judges were most famous for acting as reactionary obstructionists of legislative efforts to protect people from economic turmoil. People certainly did not think of judges as champions of broad entitlements to government relief. The source of inspiration for the novel rights claims lay elsewhere. In many instances, writers' claims of novel rights seemed inspired by the recent dramatic growth of federal government responsibilities under the New Deal, particularly the growth of federal programs for social welfare provision. Writers sometimes revealed that inspiration directly by invoking elements of New Deal rhetoric, as when the women from Peoria referred to the administration's interest in "social security." However, writers' claims were by no means limited to policies that were already enacted. People often made very expansive claims of economic or other entitlements that went well beyond the New Deal. Such claims sometimes reflect the dynamic popular political culture of that era, which gave more prominent place to oppositional voices advocating for economic populism than our political culture does today.[9] Nevertheless, the era's politics also does not explain all the claims: many writers expressed ideas that had no trace in the public politics of that era.

Recognition that popular rights discourses have to be observed directly, across a range of political activities, brings with it some significant methodological challenges. One reason scholars gravitate toward judicial opinions in appellate court cases is that they are so readily accessible. More generally, scholars often use legal records because courts, more than other political institutions, routinely preserve detailed records of even routine cases and thus provide a valuable window into the past.[10] In contrast, it is difficult to find accessible archival collections that capture large numbers of routine interactions between the public and government officials over issues of law and rights. Letters from the public to government agencies are not as routinely preserved, and many everyday political interactions may never take written form. Nevertheless, this study shows written records can be quite valuable when they are available.

My focus on legal discourses outside of judicial processes also seems to capture accurately the character of the legal discourses actually deployed by the people who wrote letters to the CRS. Many letter writers quite consciously resisted the idea that judges had a monopoly on defining rights or determining the meaning of the Constitution and seemed to believe instead that both elected officials and the people themselves had a legitimate role in deciding questions about the meaning of law and rights. More important, writers did not indicate that they thought judicial doctrines were authoritative or even relevant to their claims about rights. Writers were far more likely to express faith in the text of the Constitution, or in broader constitutional values and moral ideals, than to express respect for appellate court doctrines. To borrow Sanford Levinson's analogy between concepts of Christianity and concepts of constitutionalism, the letter writers were like Protestants rather than Catholics with regard to who has ultimate authority to interpret the Constitution. Just as Protestants reject the authority of the pope, most letter writers seemed to reject the view that the Supreme Court was the ultimate dispenser of constitutional meaning. They instead insisted on the legitimacy of ordinary individuals' interpretations of sacred texts.[11]

I also follow the lead of the many letter writers when I use terms like *law, rights,* or *the Constitution.* Unlike most scholars, I do not limit the use of such terms to conceptions established by authoritative decision makers like judges. I treat the Supreme Court's voice as just one among many when I make claims about the meaning of constitutional text. More generally, I do not use *law* to refer only to officially recognized law or to identify something distinct from plural law, unofficial law, or "legality." I instead use *law* as the general term and distinguish authoritative law by using qualifiers like *official* or *formal.* Thus, when I say that people are "claiming rights," I do not mean to say that they are articulating claims that a judge of their era would have recognized as legitimate legal entitlements. I mean, more simply, that they are expressing some entitlement or expectation using the legal language like "rights" or closely related words like "liberty." The letters have convinced me that this way of using legal language is closer to the way legal discourses actually work in society. My usage also reflects a desire to avoid privileging authoritative renderings of law over popular conceptions. Popular conceptions are quite often more accurate and attractive than authoritative conceptions, even when evaluated using the standards expressed through official law. I develop this last point in more detail in my concluding chapter.

2. This study uncovers the legal discourses used by people who were not part of organized movements but who nevertheless engaged actively in resistance or political protest.

This feature allows me to fill a significant gap that has emerged between two dominant strands of socio-legal scholarship on legal discourses and the politics of rights. The first strand focuses on legal mobilization and rights-based litigation. These include studies of organizations that sponsor litigation (e.g., Kluger 1975; Tushnet 1987; Anderson 2004; Mezey 2007; Teles 2008), of lawyers involved in public interest litigation (Sarat and Scheingold 2006), and of people who get drawn into movements as participants (Luker 1984; McCann 1994; Silverstein 1996; Polletta 2000; Hull 2006). Scholars in the last group have often spoken directly to questions about rights consciousness and its effect on political actions. The study of people involved in such campaigns is obviously important, given the important role of litigation-oriented movements and political action through the courts. In contrast, the more recent body of legal-consciousness scholarship has trended in a different direction by focusing on more isolated individuals who are not involved in organized movements. The turn away from movement participants is motivated by an interest in answering general questions about how law affects people in their everyday lives. Legal-consciousness scholars have thus tried to document legal consciousness by observing a broader range of ordinary people, not just movement participants and activists.

These efforts to focus on more isolated individuals have come at a cost, however. Many of the studies of legal consciousness have focused on samples of people who do not seem very interested in pursuing legal remedies or in mounting challenges to government processes (e.g., Engel and Munger 2003; Marshall 2005; Bumiller 1988). Other studies have found that respondents express some resistance to law or to outcomes allowed by law. However, socio-legal scholars have also found that the reported resistance was invariably limited to minor acts of subterfuge that were largely hidden from view and did not directly challenge or disrupt outcomes mandated by legal authority. The acts of resistance that were observed were isolated deviations from the respondents' more general compliance with law (see, e.g., Ewick and Silbey 1998, chapter 6; Gilliom 2001, chapter 4; Nielsen 2004, chapter 6).

The failure to document much direct and active resistance has meant that many scholars of legal consciousness have remained preoccupied with questions about law as a hegemonic or ideological construct that can contribute to acquiescence. Studies of legal consciousness almost always find that people contest legal ideals and express only contingent commitments to law. However, they also find that people nevertheless report that they almost always defer to legal authority in practical situations. Scholars have tended to resolve this observed tension between contestation and quiescence by calling attention to the power of law as an ideological or hegemonic force. The problem, however, is that it is difficult to establish the empirical claim that legal consciousness or legal ideologies contribute to deference, compliance, or hegemony without encountering more variation in people's responses to law and injustice. The advantage of my study is that even though it focuses primarily on people who acted as individuals outside of organized movements, it nevertheless finds people who used legal and other claims to contest legal outcomes, to protest directly to government officials, or to resist authoritative pronouncements of law. The letters capture the way individuals created, received, and responded to various pieces of legal discourse while engaging in everyday political encounters. They often capture active and consequential forms of resistance and contestation that are absent from many studies of legal consciousness. Resistance was not hidden or expressed through minor acts of subterfuge that went unnoticed by legal authority. People who wrote letters quite often expressed challenges openly and in writing. They directed their protests to named government officials and sometimes made personal attacks on those officials. The letters also provide many examples of people directly challenging claims about law made by government officials. Understanding how legal ideology worked (or did not work) in such interactions is essential for rounding out understandings of the political impact of popular legal discourses.

3. This study is able to probe and reveal the underlying beliefs and commitments of people who make idealized claims about law and rights.

To understand the political impact of popular legal discourses and, more generally, the way law works as ideology, it is important to understand the nature of people's underlying commitments to legal ideals. Scholars need to know not just what people say in interviews or letters about law. They also need to know what the things people say reveal about their underlying faith in law and their understanding of the relationship between law and other sources of normative ordering. The nature of such faith and understanding will determine how well law works as a legitimating ideology. More specifically, understanding the political impact of popular legal discourses requires that scholars make distinctions between expressed familiarity with legal myths and an actual commitment to legal ideals. Scholars also need to distinguish between a willingness to recite familiar legal ideals and an underlying belief that such ideals capture the way official law works on the ground. The encounters between letter writers and the CRS provide numerous opportunities to observe those distinctions and a compelling demonstration of the importance of maintaining them.

The letters are revealing because they capture moments when people faced very practical problems that led them to speak out by attempting to persuade government officials to give attention to their concerns. That practical context led many writers to give voice to legal ideals that they expected to be familiar, and thus perhaps also persuasive, to government officials. Equally important, the practical context also led many of the same people to say things that revealed some limits to their faith in the legal ideals they recited. Analyzing a large number of these encounters thus provides an illuminating picture of people's complicated ideas about politics, power, and the legitimacy of law.

I find that the practical context of the letters quite often brought to the surface a disjuncture between writers' underlying commitments to law and the idealized form in which they expressed legal claims to government officials. Writers often used legal discourses that portrayed things like rights as universally recognized and inviolable and portrayed law as permanent and objective. Writers sometimes worded their assertions of rights in a way that suggests, in isolation, that they believed that they could secure redress by merely calling violations to the attention of government authorities. Such idealized claims about rights and other legal entitlements seem at first like an indicator of a widespread commitment to legal ideals of objectivity and universality, and faith in what Stuart Scheingold famously called the "myth of rights" (2004).

Tellingly, however, writers who made such idealized claims about law almost never relied exclusively on legal claims. They instead supplemented such claims with other persuasive claims that had nothing to do with law. When their idealized claims about law are interpreted in light of those extralegal arguments, it becomes clear that writers did not expect the legal claims, by themselves, to control the government authorities who responded. Thus the use of legal claims does not mean that writers blindly accepted the legitimating ideological messages of objectivity and universality that were often embedded in those claims. Writers did not mistake legal ideals for reality. The letter writers were often powerless, and in some cases inarticulate, but they were not fools.[12]

This interpretation raises an important question: if writers did not blindly believe in myths about law and rights, why did they make so many mythical claims about law? Individual letters do not provide direct answers to that question. Nevertheless, it is not hard to imagine reasons writers would deploy such legal language in these encounters, reasons that are consistent with the available evidence and that make sense given the overall context. For one thing, the language of law is an important and widely shared cultural resource for communicating political ideals and aspirations, for sharing grievances, or for asserting status and dignity. Rights are, as Jeremy Waldron writes, the "normal currency" for political discussion (1996, 88). The letters to the CRS show that the familiarity and versatility of legal discourses make them attractive vehicles for voicing protests and demands. Writers used assertions about rights both to express claims for novel entitlements and to dramatize the injustice of a society's failure to live up to the promises expressed through legal ideals. People recognized the power of such rhetoric and the importance and value of demonstrating some familiarity with it.

The capacity of legal discourses to accommodate aspirational demands means that the articulation of such ideas, whether in protest letters or in interviews, does not necessarily indicate an unrealistic understanding of law or a failure to see law's shortcomings. It is also particularly important to take into account writers' expectations about the audience for their claims. Most often, writers were addressing government officials at the White

House or Justice Department. Writers had reason to believe that such officials, although not fully controlled by law, would be broadly committed to
legal ordering and familiar with the legal ideals voiced in the letters. The
exchanges in the letters confirm that government officials had such commitments. The CRS officials who read and responded to the letters displayed their own expectations regarding the power and familiarity of legal
discourses when they relied upon legal claims to justify their decisions.

It is also important to point out that the choice by many writers to deploy elements of legal rhetoric as a normative basis for their demands on
government officials did not mean that official law became an exclusive or
even primary source of moral authority. When pronouncements of official
law failed to match letter writers' underlying beliefs about entitlements,
writers did not abandon those beliefs. They instead translated their perceived entitlements into legal languages, often while openly rejecting rival
pronouncements about official law from government authorities. Law's
claim to legitimacy did not crowd out other types of normative resources.
Writers creatively wove legal language together with nonlegal normative
resources as they developed claims for novel entitlements. Among other
things, writers combined appeals to law with appeals to religious beliefs,
general ideas about justice, and commonsense morality. Some writers also
drew upon the popular political rhetoric of the period, transposing elements of legislative and presidential rhetoric to express expansive claims
of individual legal entitlement.[13]

To be clear: my emphasis on the way writers freely mixed extralegal
normative resources with legalized claims does not mean that official law
had no influence on popular rights consciousness and popular aspirations
for entitlements. Law was important, just not all-important. For example, the women who wrote from Peoria about their jobs at the post office appear to have been influenced by the *absence* of now-familiar legal
protections when they made choices about how to frame their complaint.
In particular, their letter hinted at a problem that would today be considered actionable sex discrimination. The women noted in passing that
the postal service's layoff policy had resulted in many men being hired
to replace laid-off women workers. The women noted: "At the time of
our appointments, white men would not consider a clerical position in
the Post Office as the industrial plants offered larger salaries." The letter
also mentioned that "there were two ladies in the service of the Peoria
Post Office who have since married two employees of this office and these
married couples have retained their respective positions." These claims

about the unfair treatment of women workers seem, under today's official law, a much stronger basis for a claim of *legal* entitlement than the various claims about fairness and economic justice that the women made in the letter. Tellingly, however, the women did not place much emphasis on their claims about the treatment of women workers, burying them near the end of the letter. The women also did not try in the letter to connect their claims about the treatment of women workers to their more central claims about fairness and justice or to their interest in "civil liberties." The women's decision to emphasize other elements of their story may reflect their expectation that Justice Department officials would not be moved to act by concerns about workplace sex discrimination. There were, after all, no statutory protections against workplace sex discrimination at that time, and no Roosevelt administration officials were indicating that they had concerns about workplace sex equality that would make them receptive to such claims.

The failure of the women from Peoria to emphasize or even fully articulate a sex discrimination claim is part of a more general pattern that emerges in the letters. Only 6 of the 879 letters contain any hint, however oblique, that writers saw sex discrimination as part of their claim for government assistance. This is true despite the fact that about one-third of the letters from individuals were written by women.[14] It seems likely that the lack of such claims has more to do with the lack of legal protections against sex discrimination at that time than with a shortage of incidents of sex discrimination.

Protest Letters as Method

Of course, one reason for my finding that many writers deployed rights talk and other legal discourses to express opposition and resistance is that the sample of people that I observe in this study is not representative of the general population. The letter writers may in some respects be "ordinary citizens," but they were extraordinary in one very important and consequential way: they all wrote letters to the government. Moreover, the sample is skewed in a way that is likely to bias the outcome toward my findings about assertiveness regarding entitlements and about resistance to law. People who wrote letters were all people who responded to injustice by attempting to speak directly to persons in government rather than by ignoring grievances or seeking help elsewhere.[15] This potential source of bias creates some important concerns. Nevertheless, a strong case can still be made for using letters as a source of data, even while acknowledging the limitations of the sample.

Note first that there are no research methods that provide representative national samples that can be used to develop empirical evidence to address my central questions. Methods that can produce broader samples, such as telephone opinion polling, are able to register expressed approval for legal institutions or support for particular rulings or policies. But survey methods cannot reveal how people actually talk about law, rights, and politics in everyday interactions or how expressed attitudes relate to underlying commitments to legal ideals.[16] The limitations of traditional surveys are the reason that most socio-legal studies of legal or rights consciousness have used a relatively small number of intensive, open-ended, face-to-face interviews rather than more quantifiable data developed using more rigid survey instruments. The intensive interviewing techniques used in such studies have made it impossible to use representative national samples. Only one study of legal consciousness has been based on a broadly representative sample from a general population, and that study was limited to a single state (Ewick and Silbey 1998). Scholars have more typically focused on subpopulations of particular interest. Some early landmarks in the study of legal consciousness focused on unaffiliated individuals who pursued legal remedies by approaching courts (Merry 1990; Yngvesson 1993, 1994). Other studies have focused on people who are the intended beneficiaries of rights-protecting laws (e.g., Marshall 2003; Engel and Munger 2003; and Bumiller 1988) or on people confronting particular problems that they are likely to associate with specific rights or legal remedies (e.g., Nielson 2004; Engel and Engel 2010).

While no sample is perfectly representative, the problems of sampling bias might seem particularly problematic for my study. My most important and original conclusions are about resistance to official law's constraining categories and resistance to law's claims of legitimacy. Yet I have a sample that includes only people who actively participated in political processes by writing letters. Such people seem likely to be particularly inclined to express opposition and resistance. Thus the problem is not simply that my sample is unrepresentative but that it may be biased toward my key general conclusions. Unfortunately, there is no available way to broaden the sample to find out how other people of that era (i.e., those who did not write letters) were talking about law, expressing political ideals, or formulating grievances. Thus there is no way to measure precisely how much bias this sampling problem creates and no way to solve the problem by cooking the data. There are, however, at least some reasons for thinking that the problem is not enormous. It is, after all, not all that extraordinary to write a letter, particularly in an era before electronic communication and near universal phone ownership. In their study, Ewick and Silbey found that almost all of their 430 interviewees reported writing letters of complaint or inquiry. They describe letter writing as "nearly universal" and a "routine tactic" (1998, 101). Moreover, as noted above, my study fills a gap in the existing literature precisely because the letters reveal how legal discourses are used in the context of open contestation and resistance. Nevertheless, the imperfections of my sample and data source mean that I can draw only modest conclusions about how my findings might apply to other populations. In particular, I make claims about the *capacity* of ordinary people to contest legal ideology but not claims about the frequency with which such contestation occurs. The letters show that ordinary people have the capacity to resist law's claims of legitimacy but do not reveal how many people have the inclination to act on that capacity.

Given these limitations, it is worth drawing attention to some advantages to using letters that make them valuable as a source of data. Since open-ended interviews are the typical source of data for socio-legal scholars interested in legal discourses and legal consciousness, it is helpful to compare some of the strengths and limits of interviews and letters as methods for studying the political impact of popular legal discourses.

The most important advantage of letters is that they allow direct observation of actual law-related encounters between members of the public and government officials. In contrast, interviews can document only the narrative stories that people tell about such interactions. The letters reveal precisely what claims were made to government officials and precisely how those claims were articulated, framed, and supported. Looking at the letters thus allows direct observation of the way rights talk and other forms of legal talk affect everyday political encounters. This feature makes the letters particularly useful for illuminating political dimensions of law and legal discourses. I have access not only to the precise legal claims made by letter writers but also to the writers' nonlegal persuasive claims and the legal arguments made by responding government officials. Using the letters means that I do not need to rely on people's subjective or retrospective reports of their encounters with law or their attitudes and beliefs about law. That advantage may be significant. The content of the letters suggests reasons why interviews might underestimate active resistance to law. The practical dilemmas that led people to write also produced some letters that were very emotional, angry, or combative. If they had been interviewed much later in a less heated moment, it seems possible that many people who wrote such letters would have provided a selective account that downplayed the degree to which their letters had been emotional or resistant.

A second reason letters are a valuable source of data is that voluntary, written communication allows people to express their considered judgments. People who wrote had control over how they presented themselves and what information they included. This makes letters very different from interviews, where people can make more spontaneous but perhaps less thoughtful and genuine responses. Of course, this characteristic of the letters also creates some frustrating limitations. With interviews, it is relatively easy to obtain basic demographic data from respondents as part of an interview protocol. Research based on letters, in contrast, has to rely largely on information that writers themselves choose to provide. Interviewers can also ask follow-up questions that probe, clarify, and sometimes verify claims made by respondents. Some scholars have even allowed respondents to comment later on their write-ups of interviews (Engel and Munger 2003). However, the price of the spontaneity and flexibility allowed by interviews is concern that respondents' expectations and perhaps anxieties regarding the interviewing process will influence what they say. While well-designed interview protocols can help to minimize distortions, nothing can eliminate concerns about whether people can always accurately report subjective impressions. Of course, letter writers' expectations about what government officials might want to hear undoubtedly affect their choices about what to put in the letters. However, in the case of letters, those expectations are an essential part of what is being studied, not an artifact of method. Analysis of what writers chose to emphasize and what they omitted often provides important clues about writers' expectations regarding what kinds of claims were most likely to be persuasive to government officials and about their understanding of how government officials made decisions about when to execute the law.

A third advantage of using letters rather than interviews is that letters provide access to information about popular legal discourses in the past. Interviews cannot be conducted retroactively to study people who are now dead. There is often no better alternative to letters for uncovering the voices and opinions of ordinary people. That is why historians routinely use letters as evidence, even when letters are not representative of any broader population. Political scientists have also found that letters to government officials, in particular, are a valuable way to gauge evolving public opinion when they lack modern polling data (e.g., Lee 2002).[17]

This book is not primarily a historical study that seeks to draw conclusions about some period in the past or to make claims about changes over time. I am more interested in making general claims about the impact of popular legal discourse and people's capacity to draw on and resist law's power as ideology. Nevertheless, focusing on a now remote time period is quite useful in that endeavor. Because the legal and political terrain was so different in 1939, the letters introduce associations and categorizations that help to uncover and dislodge assumptions about rights that might otherwise be invisible to a researcher. Legal claims from the past also shine light on alternative developmental trajectories that now seem difficult to imagine, in part because those possibilities have been cut off by accumulations of narrowing choices that have produced the current state of law. As Risa Goluboff (2007) has shown in her study of civil rights law of the same period, scholars can learn a great deal about such alternative trajectories by working backward. Instead of using current law as a starting point and looking for the roots of that law in earlier strategizing or activity, Goluboff starts with the legal claims and strategies that were pursued in the past and uncovers strategies and alternative pathways that have now become invisible because they were later abandoned or rejected. Her study focused on some litigation strategies developed by two groups of attorneys, one working in government and one working through the NAACP and related organizations. My study, in contrast, looks more broadly at the legal possibilities imagined by nonspecialist complainants who hoped that claims about law might help to solve their problems. The possibilities they envisioned illuminate some important ways in which official law obscures legal and constitutional openings to alternative forms of rights protection.

While the study of popular consciousness in any past period can be illuminating, the period covered by my letters is particularly important and particularly likely to yield insight into the flexibility of popular rights discourses. The letters were written during a crucial moment in the development of societal concerns about civil rights and civil rights law, at the end of a period of prolonged economic turmoil, expansion of federal power, and constitutional crisis. They were also written just before a period of considerable transformation in attitudes toward civil rights and the political possibilities for advancing rights. Many historians have identified the

1940s as a crucial transitional period in civil rights consciousness among key elite actors (e.g., Kellogg 1979; Dalfiume 1968; Edgerton 1994).[18] The most important factor was World War II, which both changed attitudes and expectations and led to massive regional migration and related social transformations that changed the politics of civil rights for decades (Gregory 2005). Because the letters were written on the eve of the war, yet after a long period of neglect of rights, they capture popular expressions of rights at a crucial moment.

The letters were also written at a time of considerable uncertainty about the status of law. When the CRS was founded, there were almost no federal civil rights laws and almost no institutional capacity at either the state or federal level for protecting rights. However, the CRS strategy was based on the CRS's recognition that changes in public and elite attitudes regarding rights had made existing legal doctrines unstable and ripe for change. The background circumstances make this set of letters particularly fascinating and revealing. One reason is the background economic conditions that led many people write. Another is that the bureaucratic process through which the letters were routed collected a group of letters that contains many different types of claims. The CRS was given responsibility for tracking and responding to all civil rights complaints sent to the federal government. As a result, the sample includes not just letters written to the Justice Department but also many letters that were forwarded to the department after writers sent them to the White House or other federal agencies. While all the letters were processed by the same agency, they were intended for different audiences and thus range broadly. Some letters are specific requests for patronage or assistance, while others voice protests or express approval.[19]

Letters to the CRS and My Sample of Letters

The letters that I use for this study come from the general correspondence files of the Justice Department that are housed at the National Archives in College Park, Maryland. I provide more information about the sources of the letters and the Justice Department's records in the appendix. For this introduction, I make only a few general observations that help to explain my choices about how to analyze and present the letters.

When letters were received at the Justice Department, officials there classified and filed the letters using categories corresponding to the legal issues raised in the letters. The letters in my sample are from a general file designation for civil rights (144). As is always the case with archives, there is missing material. Some general correspondence ended up in separate files organized by state, but many of those state files are missing entirely and many others have significant gaps in chronology. Most of the archived files contain general letters from the public only up to early 1941.[20] The missing material makes it difficult to address some fairly basic questions about the letters, particularly questions about regional variation in the content of the letters or about changes in content over time. In the appendix, I explain how I selected a sample of the available letters for this study. My strategy was to capture as much regional variation as practicable. My sample includes more than half the letters to the CRS that were available in the National Archives when I gathered the letters in 2000 and 2001. The 879 cases consist of more than 1,000 letters that came from thirty-six of the forty-eight states.[21]

I coded the letters for various characteristics, such as where they came from, what writers asked for (if anything), what writers complained about, any rights the writers claimed, and what kind of reply the CRS made. In the chapters that follow, I provide some basic quantitative information based on the coding whenever numbers help me to provide a reliable and interesting observation about the letters. However, most of what is interesting about the letters cannot be captured with numbers based on general codes. I thus try, as much as possible, to allow letter writers to speak in their own words rather than relying on quantitative claims to summarize the letters. I preserve spelling and grammatical mistakes (without the constant use of the pejorative "*sic*") and preserve textual features that writers used for emphasis, such as underlining and capitalization. I also report allegations in the letters as though I take them at face value. This is not because I always believe what writers say but to avoid the constant use of distracting phrases like *alleged* and *allegedly*.

My account of the letters tries to answer the following questions: What concerns did writers express? What rights did they claim? What arguments or other means of persuasion did people include in the letters asking for help? What do the writers' choices about using legal rhetoric and other persuasive claims tell us about writers' commitments to law? What do those commitments tell us about the relationships between law, rights claiming, and other forms of political action and political expression? The diverse group of letters does not yield any simple or unqualified answers to these questions. I try in the chapters that follow to make empirically grounded analytic claims about the place of legal discourses in the letters while remaining true to the actual content of the letters and respectful of the people who created them.

A Note Regarding Agency and Social Knowledge

In much of what follows, I describe letter writers as individual agents making choices about what to include in letters. I also use information about the writers' choices to develop some claims about the goals that led them to write and about their understandings and expectations regarding law, rights, and related bureaucratic processes. Such an agent-centered account is sure to strike some socio-legal scholars as decidedly old fashioned, particularly in comparison to work by the important scholars of legal consciousness that I sometimes speak to in what follows. An interest in culture and social structure has led many scholars of legal consciousness away from individual-agent accounts. They have instead developed theoretical frameworks that emphasize the ways in which interests, desires, and aspirations develop through consciousness that is constructed collectively through social interactions. Such studies have eschewed explanations based on goal-oriented analysis of choices by individual actors and have tried instead to identify the shared schemas, repertoires, and stories that people *collectively* draw upon and help to construct as they make sense of and participate in social life (see, especially, Ewick and Silbey 1998, 2003).

The difference between my approach to agency and the approach taken by legal-consciousness scholars deserves a short explanation. My goal in this study is not to advance one position in scholarly debates over agency. I certainly do not mean to suggest that the people who wrote letters were completely isolated in their desires or that their agency was unconstrained by social conventions and expectations. My tendency to talk in terms of individuals with goals is dictated by my overriding interest in learning from a valuable and very interesting source of data that illuminates the way legal discourses shape everyday political encounters. The letters are, by their nature, chock-full of expressions of willfulness and individual agency. I do not know of a way to describe or, ultimately, to say anything at all about the letters without talking about the writers as motivated individuals. I found that if I focused exclusively on trying to identify some limited set of shared schemas or types that emerge across the letters, I would have produced an account of the letters that obscured the full range of their interesting content.

Nevertheless, I do find that the letters provide ample and interesting confirmation of the insights of scholars who have eschewed individual-agent-based accounts, and I thus draw on those insights in my analysis. My large sample of letters reveals some shared understandings and socially constructed conventions that shaped the way writers engaged government officials in their letters and offered support for their claims. While the writers were not all following the same script, many seem to have been trying to follow the established conventions of familiar genres. Still, those conventions and genres left writers with considerable room to experiment in novel ways while still communicating the substance of their concerns. I also find instances where writers tried to distinguish their cases by deliberately defying social conventions and expectations. I end up with an account that pays attention to the role of social conventions when they become visible but that does not aim primarily to identify the social structures that determined the content of the recorded exchanges.

The Plan of the Book

The remaining chapters present my analysis of the political encounters recorded in the public correspondence processed the CRS. Chapter 2 reviews the early history of the CRS and looks at how the CRS responded to the letters. I explain the CRS's responses by considering the legal, political, and institutional constraints that limited what the CRS could do. The core finding is that the letters from individuals did not result in helpful responses from the government. Most writers simply received a short, boilerplate reply letter that briefly summarized the complaint and then claimed that legal limitations made it impossible for the Justice Department to help. With only a handful of exceptions, writers did not receive any direct assistance from the federal government.

The CRS's very limited response becomes more understandable once I uncover the broader legal, political, and institutional context. Other than a few scattered provisions of Reconstruction-era statutes, there were no federal civil rights laws for the CRS to enforce. The CRS, despite being the only federal office dedicated to protecting rights, was a very small unit within the Criminal Division, staffed by seven or fewer attorneys during its first decade. To make matters worse, Supreme Court precedents appeared to limit the power of the federal government to intervene in most cases where rights were violated, leaving the power to provide redress to state governments. Unfortunately, most state governments were uninterested in pursuing civil rights cases, in part because state and local officials were the most frequently reported perpetrators of rights violations. The inability of the CRS to do more also reflected some significant political constraints. The Roosevelt administration was unwilling to take bold action on civil rights issues because Roosevelt needed support from white supremacist southern Democrats who wielded crucial power in Congress. Chapter 2 also explains the way CRS attorneys used legal claims about jurisdiction in written replies to letter writers.

Chapter 3 looks at the subject matter of the legal claims in the letters, organized by the type of right or other entitlement claims. Most frequently, writers complained about lack of fairness or "due process" in some government procedure. There are also numerous letters regarding violations of enumerated constitutional rights like free speech, free exercise of religion, and the right to property. Writers also expressed a wide range of entitlements to positive government assistance, including rights to relief from unemployment, rights to travel in search of work, and rights to run business enterprises without government regulation or excessive taxation. The key finding is that writers quite frequently, and often self-consciously, appropriated legal discourses to make claims for novel entitlements that were not recognized in official law. Another interesting finding is that writers often linked their demands for rights protections to claims about "democracy." Writers did not seem to recognize any tension between protecting rights and democratic governance and did not see demands for "rights" as an alternative to ordinary democratic participation. In this respect, the writers were quite different from many legal theorists who conceptualize rights protections in constitutional law as being in tension with majoritarian democracy.

Chapters 4 and 5 consider the persuasive claims that writers used to attract attention and give credibility to their requests or complaints. Although the strategies writers used did not secure government assistance, the persuasive claims warrant extended exploration because they often reveal writers' underlying ideas and expectations regarding rights and law. Chapter 4 looks at writers' legal arguments, while chapter 5 looks at writers' extralegal claims. The two types of persuasive claims are considered separately for analytic purposes. Almost all the writers made both types of claims.

Chapter 4 shows that writers were comfortable, endlessly inventive, and often quite adept when it came to constructing novel rights claims. With few exceptions, writers could not claim to be trained experts in law. Yet many writers were able to marshal at least some basic legal materials to support their pleas. Some writers would scour the Constitution's text in search of helpful provisions, resulting in some creative readings of open-ended constitutional text. Writers also made more general appeals to American ideals of fairness and justice by invoking symbols like the Statue of Liberty or the Liberty Bell or historic figures like Thomas Jefferson or Crispus Attucks.

While there is a tremendous variation in the capacity of writers to formulate coherent and grounded legal arguments, the letters do not suggest that writers were intimidated by the need to engage government officials with legal claims. There is also little to suggest that writers' sense of entitlement was dampened by their engagement with law. To the contrary, writers more often seemed *emboldened* by the choice of a legalized rhetoric of rights. Moreover, writers' enthusiasm for their positions did not waver when government attorneys told them that their legal claims lacked merit. A substantial number of writers (12 percent) wrote back directly to government attorneys to insist that their own legal position was the correct one. Another particularly interesting finding is that there was a significant social dimension to rights claiming in the letters. Writers making aspirational rights claims in the CRS letters did not typically rely on their individual status as rights bearers when trying to establish that they deserved help or that they were worthy claimants. Writers were far more likely to buttress their claim for help by emphasizing that there were many other similarly situated people who would also be helped if government officials chose to provide assistance.

Chapter 5 focuses on questions about writers' underlying understandings of law and legal processes. I look at several categories of extralegal persuasive claims that appear regularly in the letters. Writers most often made claims about their own character, asserting, among other things, that they were law-abiding, responsible, sober, native born, patriotic, or good providers. I also review things said by the numerous writers who spoke directly about their support for or faith in law. By considering the extralegal claims that appear side by side with the legal claims, I show that writers who made idealized claims about absolute and inviolable rights did not necessarily believe naively that rights were absolute and inviolable. Writers instead understood that, contrary to idealized formulations, the realization of rights entitlements was always contingent on discretionary choices made by government officials.

I conclude in chapter 6 by arguing that these findings call into question the power of legal discourses and the "myth of rights" to distort or constrain American politics. Socio-legal scholars have long puzzled over how public allegiance to law is maintained given law's frequent failure to live up to it's own expressed ideals of equality and fairness. The findings in this book suggest that scholars' long-standing quest to explain persistent faith in law may be misguided. Law and legal discourses certainly shape, and may sometimes distort, the public's perceptions of what is just and what alternatives are possible. However, the CRS letters show that the legitimating and constraining power of law is limited, even among people who are prone to making idealized and exaggerated claims about rights or other imagined legal entitlements. People who deployed legal discourses of rights and the Constitution were not deluded about law's inability to fulfill its broad, legitimating promises of equal treatment and reliable protection of core rights. People instead used idealized legal claims to connect personal circumstances to a more general sense of justice. Because they expected government law enforcement authorities to have their own commitments to legal ideals, writers also used legal claims to provoke those officials and challenge the sincerity of their commitments. Thus, rights discourses are not just familiar and established elements of political culture but also a powerful medium for communicating grievances and aspirations, for asserting personal dignity, and for asserting refusals to defer to legal authority. Chapter 6 also considers whether letters to government officials can be conceptualized as resistance to legal authority and legal legitimacy.

I also conclude that the choice to deploy legal rhetoric did not trap writers into accepting the claims of legitimacy that government officials express through official statements of law. CRS officials and other legal authorities who appear in the writers' stories quite often made *attempts* to use law to legitimate the status quo and destroy alternative assertions of legal meaning.[22] Writers, however, were clearly able and willing to resist such attempts at destruction. They quite often self-consciously articulated distinctions between what they saw as the right or just outcomes that would occur in a truly legitimate system of law and what government officials had identified as *the law*.

In theory, myths about law and rights might induce acquiescence that contributes to and reinforces powerlessness. The letters suggest that such faith is not as widespread as scholars have believed. It is true, of course, that most of the people who made rights claims in these encounters were quite powerless. They almost invariably failed to obtain a helpful response from government officials. However, the causes of that powerlessness were not constraints imposed by legal discourses, writers' unqualified commitments to law, or their belief in myths about rights.

CHAPTER TWO

The CRS's Legal and Political Strategies for Improving Civil Rights Protections

In December 1939, the Justice Department received two letters from Charlie Thompson. The handwritten letters, which arrived a few days apart, explained that Thompson had recently moved with his wife and eight-year-old son from Plainsboro, New Jersey, to Belle Glade, Florida. In preparation for the move, Thompson withdrew his life savings of $120 from an account at the Plainsboro post office. Upon arrival, Thompson had deposited eighty dollars of the remaining money into a new account in the Belle Glade post office. Thompson's first letter, dated November 30, 1939, explains what happened next:

> That same night the chief of police an the 2 night men came to the house and asked me where I got the money I told them the truth we worked for it and told them we had it put up so they went away that Wednesday the same men came back to the house and took me out of town 6 miles pulled of all of my clothes and Beat me and kept asking me where I got the money I did not no what to say I was telling the truth so they said for me to say I found $82.00 they said if I did not say so they would kill me. so I had to say so. Then they took me and put me in jail. They told me to tell my wife to bring the postal stubs up to the jail the next day when my wife come they put her in jail took me around to the post office and made me sign the stubs one $50 one 20 and 10 then he told me to go home and keep my mouth shut if I told any one they would take me out and kill me so we left town the same day.

I noted in chapter 1 that most people whose letters were processed by the CRS did not get help. Thompson was one of the few exceptions. Instead of having staff send Thompson the usual reply letter indicating that the department lacked the legal power to help, Assistant Attorney General O. John Rogge instead wrote to the Post Office Department and asked that it look into the complaint. Rogge's letter said that Thompson was "forcibly and fraudulently" deprived of his money, and it included a copy of the "affidavit" that Thompson had sent to the department (December 12, 1939). Rogge also wrote to US Attorney Herbert S. Phillips in Tampa asking that he also look into the case (December 12, 1939).

An investigation was conducted, although not by the Justice Department but by the office of the regional postal inspector in Miami. A postal inspector traveled to Belle Glade to interview police and post office officials and also communicated with postal officials in New Jersey. The investigator was able to confirm many of the details in Thompson's story. In his report on the case (February 6, 1940) the inspector stated that Thompson had withdrawn the money in Plainsboro and later deposited it in Florida. The inspector also confirmed that Thompson had later returned to the post office in Florida with local Chief of Police Lloyd to withdraw the funds.

The postal inspector interviewed Chief Lloyd, the Belle Glade postmaster, and a witness named J. D. McEady. The three men gave the inspector an elaborate cover story. According to their initial accounts, McEady had lost eighty-two dollars in cash on the same day that Thompson arrived in town. McEady had allegedly reported that he had lost four twenty-dollar bills and stated that he would be able to recognize his bills because he always folded money in a distinctive way. The Belle Glade postmaster claimed that Charlie Thompson had appeared in town that same day and presented four $20 bills folded in precisely the manner McEady described. The postmaster immediately told the police chief, who then questioned Thompson. Thompson claimed that he had withdrawn the money in Plainsboro, but the postmaster there told his Florida counterpart that Charlie Thompson had no account in Plainsboro. (This was an apparent miscommunication. According to the report, the Plainsboro postmaster had reported only that Thompson did not *currently* have an account in New Jersey, thus ensuring his eligibility to open a new account at a Florida post office).

The chief of police also told the postal inspector that Thompson decided to "return" the money McEady had purportedly lost. The chief admitted that he had detained Thompson but did not detail his treatment of Thompson. The chief also claimed that he had considered "rewarding Thompson for turning over the money by giving him a position on some Government project" but that "the negro left town before he was employed." The chief reported that he remained certain that Thompson had found the money that McEady had lost.

After being told this elaborately concocted cover story, the postal inspector decided that the police chief and his corroborating witnesses were lying. The inspector found that some of the participants backed down quickly when confronted with facts from the investigation. The inspector reported, for example, that Mr. McEady abandoned his belief in Thompson's culpability once the inspector told him that Thompson had withdrawn the funds in Plainsboro. The inspector also reported that McEady "immediately tendered $80.00" to return to Thompson.

The postal inspector's efforts made Thompson's case one of the few in my study where an individual claimant received the requested material redress for a rights violation. On the same day that the inspector filed his report, the US attorney in Tampa received a telegram from Thompson, who had fled to Huntersville, North Carolina. Thompson's telegram said that he had received his money (February 6, 1940). Of course, Thompson was forced to abandon his plan to move his family to Florida, and the local officials who conspired to rob and beat him never faced legal sanction for their actions. But the fact that Thompson got his money back meant that his case had a more satisfactory outcome than the others processed by the CRS.

What explains the relatively positive outcome of Thompson's effort to get help from the CRS? If the case is looked at in isolation, a number of striking factors stand out as possible reasons federal officials would help Thompson. Perhaps the most striking element of his story is the egregiousness of the conduct that he reported. Thompson claimed that a local police chief had conspired with a federal postmaster to rob him of his life's savings. Both Thompson and his wife had been unlawfully detained and threatened by law enforcement officials, and Thompson had been severely beaten. There are some additional factors, beyond the seriousness of the charges that might at first seem to explain why Thompson got help. Thompson was able to communicate both the substance of his grievance and the urgency of his need for help. His letters, though handwritten and unencumbered by punctuation, were articulate, moving, and expressed his position with clarity. More generally, Thompson's letters reveal that he was a sophisticated and resourceful person. He had saved a considerable sum of money and was able to twice relocate his family, once in flight from a gang of brutally corrupt government officials. He was able to build relationships with postal officials and employers in Plainsboro who helped to corroborate his story. He had also consulted a private attorney, who had helpfully suggested that he write to the attorney general in Washington.

Thompson also displayed a basic understanding of the underlying legal issues. He framed his complaint to the Justice Department in a way that emphasized links between what happened and his constitutional rights. He specified, for example, that he had been denied bail and access to a lawyer, and not just that he had been stripped, beaten, and robbed by the police. The mention of two privileges enumerated in the Bill of Rights suggests that Thompson was familiar with the Constitution's text. Thompson attempted in several other way to mimic legal language or legal form. His first letter concludes with the statement "this is the truth nothing but the truth so help me God. Thanks." He also accompanied one letter with a separately titled "affidavit" where he repeated the key facts in the case and attested to their truth in a more formal manner.

Thompson also worked hard to persuade government officials to pay attention to his case and respond favorably. Thompson reported that his wife and young son were hungry and desperate due to a lack of food. He emphasized that he would have nowhere else to turn for redress if the Justice Department declined to provide help. ("I been to every Body so please help me please.") In his second letter, Thompson wrote that "we are begging you to investigate," and "if you will help us it would Be easy to get our money Back we are Broke and hungry and need it." Thompson's letter also included claims about being a hardworking and dependable employee. He noted: "I had never Been in jail Before they put us in jail without charge against us we had done nothing wrong." Thompson's deployment of persuasive claims about his character and the hardship he faced may have helped to generate sympathy and thus favorable attention from government officials.

Factors like the egregiousness of the offense and Thompson's ability to articulate his case persuasively seem like plausible explanations for the helpful response from federal officials if the case is looked at in isolation. However, in the broader context of the CRS's numerous responses to civil rights complainants, those factors no longer seem to provide a sufficient explanation. Quite a few other people who wrote equally moving and persuasive accounts of egregious injustices did not receive any help from the federal government.

Consider, as a contrasting example, another incident that came to the attention of the CRS. On February 1, 1942, Private Thomas Broadus, an African American soldier on leave from nearby Fort Meade, was killed by a Baltimore police officer named Edward Bender. Broadus and three companions had attempted to get into an unlicensed taxi after being refused by several white cabdrivers. Officer Bender intervened, demanding that Broadus call for a licensed taxi. Broadus and the officer ended up in an argument in which Broadus was heard to say, "I'll spend my money wherever I like." At that point, the officer grabbed Broadus and began striking him in the head with his billy club. The two men tussled on the street for several moments, the officer beating the soldier with his club until Broadus managed temporarily to regain his footing. At the urging of the crowd, Broadus tried to run away from the officer. Witnesses reported that the officer rose, drew his pistol, and took careful aim at the hobbling and weakened Broadus. The officer shot the soldier in the back. As Private Broadus fell to the ground and tried to crawl under a parked car, the officer walked toward him and shot a second time. The officer then began kicking Broadus, who remained motionless beneath the car. The officer threatened a gathering crowd with his revolver. A man who approached Officer Bender to offer to transport Broadus to the hospital was threatened and later arrested for interfering with an officer. Private Broadus died that evening from two gunshot wounds in his back.[1]

The CRS addressed the murder of Private Broadus after Baltimore attorney W. A. C. Hughes Jr. wrote to CRS head Victor Rotnem about the shooting in December 1943. Hughes reminded Rotnem that he had expressed some interest when they had discussed the case at a conference the previous week. The letter included the names and addresses of fourteen eyewitnesses to the attack who were willing to cooperate in any investigation. Hughes also explained that he sought help from the federal government because the State of Maryland had made only halting efforts to respond to the murder. A grand jury initially indicated approval of an indictment of Officer Bender for unlawful homicide, but the indictment was withdrawn two days later, and the initial investigation ended. The state's attorney refused numerous requests to reopen the case. In response to the Broadus case and several other instances of murder and brutality by the Baltimore police, a group of two thousand staged a protest march on Annapolis, the state capital. The governor responded by forming a Commission on Problems Affecting Colored People.[2] A committee from that commission later conducted its own investigation of the Broadus case. The committee, chaired by a federal circuit court judge, recommended that the case be reopened and that charges be filed against Bender. State prosecutors refused that recommendation. Bender, who had shot and killed another African American named Charles Parker in a similar incident a year earlier, remained armed and dangerous on the streets of Baltimore.

The Broadus case was at the intersection of two alarmingly common problems that the CRS wanted to be able to address: police brutality targeting African Americans and violent attacks on returning African American servicemen. While a large number of such cases were brought to the attention of the CRS, CRS attorneys most often decided not to become involved. In the Broadus case, Tom Clark, then the head of the Criminal Division, wrote an inquiry to the assistant US attorney in Baltimore (December 10, 1943). The letter indicated that Rotnem believed that the US attorney had looked into the case. However, an assistant US attorney wrote back to report that Rotnem was mistaken. The only investigations had been the one conducted by the local prosecutor and grand jury and the one by the governor's commission (December 16, 1943). The US attorney in Baltimore, Bernard Flynn, also wrote to Clark, stating defensively, "No complaint has ever been filed in this office" and noting that the commission's report was never forwarded to his office. These claims may have been meant to indicate that Flynn did not know of the case when it happened. However, that seems quite unlikely. The killing generated immediate newspaper coverage and had led to a protest march on the state capitol. Flynn's letter to Clark made it clear that he was not interested in pursuing the case, explaining, "I do not believe successful prosecution could be obtained at this late date" (December 16, 1943). Clark wrote back to say he agreed (December 21, 1943). He then wrote back a letter to Hughes thanking him for bringing the case to the department's attention and stating that the Justice Department was unable to pursue the case (December 22, 1943).

While the Broadus case is shocking, the records of early CRS activities reveal many other instances where Justice Department attorneys claimed that they were unable to act, even when there were credible claims of egregious rights violations perpetrated by state officials. The CRS could not provide help more often because the unit faced enormous legal and practical constraints. The CRS was a small office within the Criminal Division and did not have resources to investigate every credible allegation of a rights violation. During the two years in which most of the letters in my sample were written, the Justice Department conducted only five civil rights prosecutions.[3] The office gradually became more active through the 1940s under Attorneys General Francis Biddle and Tom Clark. However, the unit remained quite small and inadequate to the task of protecting civil rights. After reviewing the CRS program in 1948, President Truman's Committee on Civil Rights concluded that the program was insufficient and recommended that the federal government devote considerably more resources to protecting rights. One stark indicator of the CRS's inadequate size is the finding that the CRS received between 1,500 and 2,000 complaints of relevant rights violations per year during its first eight years but prosecuted just 178 cases over that period (President's Committee on Civil Rights 1948, 120).

Because the CRS pursued so few cases during the early years covered by my sample, there are no simple formulas that can explain why each of the cases that the department did pursue were chosen for more favorable treatment. Cases that got attention happened to be at the confluence of some idiosyncratic set of favorable factors. Charlie Thompson got his money back because the CRS could draw on the resources of the postal inspector's office and because the investigator assigned to the case happened to be thorough, conscientious, and open minded enough to believe an African American man and report that white government officials were liars. (There was no guarantee that such a locally based federal official would be so sympathetic to Thompson. The US attorney in Tampa had initially expressed skepticism about Thompson's story and had no interest in investigating the case.)[4] In addition, as explained below, the CRS consciously sought unusual case profiles so that it could sidestep some of the more volatile political issues related to segregation and racism in the South. For example, the CRS tried to find a test case for a lynching prosecution where the victim was white or where the incident occurred in the North (Carr 1947, 172).

While the CRS did pursue a handful of strategically chosen cases between 1939 and 1941, resource constraints meant that the overwhelming majority of complaints from the public would go unheeded, no matter what. The cases to which the CRS did devote significant resources came to the CRS's attention through press coverage or through the FBI, not through letters from individuals.[5] Because there is so little variation in the responses that the CRS made to letter writers, my goal in this book is not to explain why the CRS investigated some cases and not others. As explained in chapter 1, I am instead interested in how both complainants and CRS officials used legal discourses in these everyday encounters.

I present my analysis of letter writers' use of legal discourses in chapters 3, 4, and 5. This chapter provides important background information about the CRS. I look first at the legal obstacles faced by the CRS and then turn to explaining the constraints created by the political context. In the concluding section of this chapter, I provide an overview of the responses that the CRS made to the letter writers and an analysis of the way the CRS used legal discourses in their written responses to the letters.

The Legal Context

One of the first letters processed by the CRS led to an exchange that hints at some of the legal constraints that made it difficult for the CRS to pursue rights violations. The letter came from Manila and was written by Antonio Bautista, the president of the Civil Liberties Union of the Philippines. Bautista began his letter by noting with enthusiasm that newspapers in the Philippines had reported that Frank Murphy was working to preserve civil liberties in the United States. Bautista asked that Murphy provide information about what led him to create the new Civil Liberties Unit, what civil liberties problems existed in the United States, and what "method and procedure" the attorney general planned to use to combat those problems. Bautista expressed his belief that problems in the United States had counterparts in the Philippines and said he hoped to learn from the "wisdom of your method and solution" (February 18, 1939).[6]

A reply letter, drafted by Henry Schweinhaut, the first chief of the Civil Liberties Unit, and Brien McMahon, the head of the Criminal Division, was sent over Murphy's signature on April 6, 1939. The reply "noted with interest the distinguished list of members and the statement of objectives" that Bautista had sent and stated that the members of his civil liberties organization were "to be congratulated on your awareness of this problem so important in the functioning of a democracy." The reply letter also listed two criminal and two civil provisions of the federal code related to civil liberties. Tellingly, however, the reply also tried to correct Bautista's assumption that the "wisdom" of the United States' "method and solution" could be a model for the Philippines or any other country. Regarding the list of code provisions, the reply stated, "You will note that all of these statutes are very old. They are not suggested as models if you are contemplating a legislative program" (April 6, 1939).

The Department of Justice had to reject the suggestion from the Philippines that the United States could be a model because there were almost no effective civil rights law in 1939. While casual observers of today's constitutional law sometimes imagine that robust legal protections for constitutional rights have always been there since they were promised as a permanent gift of the Founding Fathers, the reality is quite different. As a practical matter, there was almost no institutional capacity to provide meaningful protection for many rights until the second half of the twentieth century. When the tiny CRS was formed in 1939, it was the only federal office devoted to protection of civil rights and liberties. Congress had not passed a civil rights statute in decades, and the filibuster power wielded by southern Democrats made it impossible to pass meaningful civil rights statutes until 1964. Even bills that had broad public support, like proposals for a federal antilynching law, were blocked by such obstruction (Zangrando 1980).

The few scattered civil rights provisions in the federal code in 1939 were rarely enforced and largely forgotten. The lack of more effective federal civil rights laws in 1939 reflects the tragic history of race and rights in the aftermath of the Civil War. The period of Reconstruction that followed the war produced three transformative amendments to the Constitution. Each of those amendments gave Congress and the federal government new powers to protect rights. Congress began to use those powers during Reconstruction, passing a variety of civil rights laws and taking steps (such as impeaching President Johnson) to try to ensure that those laws would be enforced. However, after the election of 1876, the political faction that supported expanded federal civil rights protection fell out of power. The result was a long period of retrenchment. Between the end of Reconstruction and the beginning of the twentieth century, decisions by Congress and the Supreme Court whittled away almost all the provisions of the federal civil rights laws passed after the Civil War. The court also established new doctrines that limited the reach of Congress's new constitutional powers to protect rights. Most notoriously, in 1896 the Supreme Court ignored the constitution's text and its own precedents as it allowed states to establish a legal system of apartheid (*Plessy v. Ferguson,* 163 US 537 [1896]).[7]

When the CRS was created in 1939, some things were beginning to change. Political support for civil rights and civil liberties was growing. The Supreme Court indicated some new interest in protecting rights by reading some of the protections of the Bill of Rights into the Fourteenth Amendment. That gradual process of incorporation expanded federal protections against rights violations by state governments. The court had also shown at least some willingness to protect the rights of disfavored racial minorities (e.g., *Powell v. Alabama*, 287 US 45 [1932]).[8] Nevertheless, these shifts were only beginning to take hold in 1939. The fundamental problem of inadequate federal civil rights statutes remained.

Given this legal background, the goals of the CRS program were modest. Shortly after the CRS was formed, Frank Murphy explained those goals in a revealing summary of his expectations for the CRS. Murphy outlined the goals in a letter to Senator Edward Burke, a Nebraska Democrat who had written a friendly inquiry about the CRS program (April 24, 1939). Murphy wrote that he had ordered the attorneys assigned to the new Civil Liberties Unit to begin by conducting legal research so that "the law of the subject can be reasonably ascertained" and to produce an "up-to-date treatise for United States Attorneys." He also wrote that the existing laws were "old" and that he expected them to be inadequate. He said that the law had to be "modernized and made to more appropriately apply to present social and economic conditions." The reality of the South's stranglehold on the Senate meant that Murphy did not have any clear plan for getting such legislation passed. He noted that the department might recommend new legislation to Congress but added, "We are proceeding very slowly and cautiously with respect to the preparation of new legislation" (May 4, 1939).

The legal research that Murphy's staff conducted eventually identified three provisions in the federal code that could potentially be used to prosecute crimes involving rights violations. All three provisions were originally passed during Reconstruction and had lain mostly dormant since that time. Each provision had gaps or technical flaws that limited its potential reach. The CRS researchers also found that important legal and constitutional issues regarding these statutes were quite unsettled. The provisions had not been used often and had not generated much case law. It was not clear how judges would construe the provisions or what kinds of novel prosecutions judges would tolerate if the CRS did try to revive the laws.[9]

The most promising of the three provisions was a federal antipeonage statute (18 USC 444, now 42 USC [1994]). That provision was on relatively firm constitutional footing because the Thirteenth Amendment clearly enumerated the power of the federal government to combat involuntary servitude. However, the statute's application was also relatively narrow: it could be used only in peonage cases.[10] In contrast, the other two extant civil rights provisions used more general language and thus appeared to cover a broader range of rights. Section 51 (now 241) of title 18 provided protection for "any right or privilege secured . . . by the Constitution or laws of the United States." Section 52 (now 242) covered violations of "any rights, privileges, or immunities secured . . . by the Constitution and laws of the United States." Unfortunately, however, these broader provisions had other limitations that created potential problems for the CRS.

Section 51 applied only to *conspiracies* and thus could not be used to go after solo perpetrators. Section 52 did not require a conspiracy but did specify that the perpetrator had to have acted "under color of law" to "willfully" violate rights. (The word "willfully" was added to the provision in 1909.) The federal courts had never established a definitive gloss on those two qualifying phrases, and CRS attorneys were not certain how judges would interpret them. A related, and more general, problem was that neither section 51 or 52 had been used in the types of cases that interested the CRS. Section 51 had only been used in cases involving violations of a few narrow rights, such as the right to inform federal officials of a crime or the right to hold land under the homestead laws (President's Committee on Civil Rights 1948, 115–16). Section 52 had had almost no use, and its constitutionality had never been established. Given these issues, the CRS researchers concluded that there was real uncertainty about whether existing statutes could be used in the types of cases that most interested the CRS, such as police brutality and lynchings.[11]

The CRS attorneys expected that the uncertainties would be resolved as defendants raised constitutional objections to any attempts to bring prosecutions using the three provisions. They were also far from certain that judges would side with the Justice Department in such cases. One potential problem was that the expansive language expressing which rights section 51 and 52 protected was a double-edged sword. On the upside, the CRS attorneys hoped that open-ended language about "any right or privilege secured . . . by the Constitution or laws of the United States" would allow them to use the statute in a broad range of novel cases. Among other things, the language might be used in cases involving rights that had only recently been incorporated by the Supreme Court into the protections of the Fourteenth Amendment and cases involving violations of newly created statutory rights, such as the right to strike in the Wagner Act of 1935. The downside, however, was that the expanding scope of federal rights could also create constitutional problems for prosecutors using section 51 or 52. Defendants might argue to judges that prosecutions using section

51 or 52 were unconstitutional because the due-process clause prohibits criminal statutes that define forbidden conduct in vague or ambiguous language.

The statutes would also run up against the Supreme Court's restrictive state action doctrine. As that doctrine was understood in 1939, federal power to protect rights under the Fourteenth Amendment was limited to rights violations perpetrated by state governments or state officials acting in their official capacities. The doctrine was significant because it meant that federal prosecutors could not prosecute private actors who violated rights unless those actors conspired with state officials. People who were not state officials would remain reachable by state governments, but the systematic failure of states to address widespread problems of civil rights violations was one of the main reasons for the administration's interest in expanding federal capacities.

The state action doctrine created a shield that allowed many rights violators to avoid prosecution.[12] Some perpetrators deliberately conducted themselves in ways that made it difficult to establish federal jurisdiction. For example, in lynching cases, state officials like jailers and police officers deliberately positioned themselves as "bystanders" rather than as direct participants. In some of the CRS's police brutality cases, local law enforcement officers removed their badges or used their private automobiles while they engaged in rights violations, in an apparent effort to dissociate themselves from their official roles (e.g., *Screws v. United States,* 325 US 91 [1944]).

During the time period covered in my sample of letters (1939–42) CRS attorneys were uncertain whether judges would allow federal power to reach into new areas. While there were some obvious reasons to be concerned about potential judicial obstruction, there was also reason to hope that the justices on the Supreme Court would be inclined to relax the doctrines restricting federal power. The court had established the relevant doctrines more than a half century earlier, in a very different political climate. Moreover, the CRS was founded just as the new "Roosevelt Court" was becoming established. The court had recently backed down from a constitutional confrontation and had begun supporting newly expansive interpretations of federal powers, at least with regard to the federal power to regulate the economy. Moreover, the court had a growing number of civil libertarians, in part because of a conscious FDR administration strategy of using the Supreme Court as a vehicle for advancing civil rights. As Kevin McMahon (2003) has shown, key political leaders in the administration enabled such appointments because they wanted the court to take a lead role on civil rights issues. Those leaders felt that they could better manage difficult fissures around race within the Roosevelt coalition if the court would sometimes take the lead role. These evolving conditions made the state of civil rights doctrines uncertain at the time of the CRS founding. Because the Supreme Court does not give advisory opinions, there was no way to resolve the uncertainty besides bringing test cases. Such test cases could give the new justices an opportunity to revisit constitutional issues around federal power, civil rights, and state action. Because Congress was not able to pass any new statutes, the Justice Department had to bring any test cases under the flawed laws that were already on the books.

The CRS responded to these background conditions with an incremental strategy. The department would at first pursue only a small number of carefully selected test cases. If the courts supported an expansive view of federal power, such tests would open up new legal and political possibilities that could be helpful to future efforts to expand federal capacities to protect rights. Although prosecutions would ordinarily be conducted by locally based US attorneys, the CRS worked to control what kind of cases were brought. CRS staff developed the policy circulars that instructed US attorneys on the legal issues regarding the civil rights statutes, and CRS attorneys in Washington were routinely consulted by locally based federal prosecutors in civil rights matters. In the policy circulars, the CRS advanced interpretations of civil rights statutes that allowed them to be applied to police brutality and lynching cases. The CRS suggested, for example, that the phrase "under color of law" meant that section 52 could be applied to state officials whose actions were facilitated by their position or title, even if they were acting outside their official capacities. More creatively, the CRS attorneys publicly advanced their theory that deliberate *inaction* of state officials to prevent lynchings was a form of state action. CRS officials published a set of law review articles defending this view of state inaction as a form of state action in the early 1940s, arguing in favor of a federal right "not to be lynched" (Rotnem 1942, 1944; Coleman 1944).[13]

Uncertainty about how judges would respond to novel statutory and constitutional arguments led CRS attorneys to be very selective. The CRS knew that even sympathetic judges would not be eager to enter into the political thicket of racial politics. A strategy of avoiding race issues is evident in the first CRS test case to reach the Supreme Court, *United States v. Classic* (313 US 209 [1941]). The Supreme Court in that case upheld a federal prosecution for rights violations that occurred in connection with a state primary election. The court overturned an earlier case that had declared that state primary elections were beyond the reach of federal power. *Classic* is an important case because it marked a significant step toward the landmark Supreme Court rulings that helped to dismantle the white primary system in the South. That system prevented large numbers of African Americans from casting meaningful votes in elections. *Classic* was an attractive test case because it was a case about a primary election where the alleged offenses did not involve racial exclusion from voting. The case was instead about a rigged vote count that had disenfranchised white voters. The victory in *Classic* did not embolden the CRS to go after the white primary directly, however. When the court ruled on that issue a few years later, the case that reached the court was a civil action sponsored by the NAACP rather than a CRS prosecution (*Smith v. Allwright*, 321 US 649 [1944]). Tellingly, the Justice Department did not file an amicus brief in that more racially charged case. *Classic* did provide NAACP attorneys with a helpful precedent, however.

The need to convince appellate judges to accept novel legal arguments also created more general reasons for keeping the federal civil rights program quite small. Nervous judges might balk if they felt that the federal government was circumventing Congress and spreading aggressively into areas traditionally belonging to state governments. The CRS's modest program made it easier to reassure judges that the Justice Department's civil rights program was not going too far too fast. CRS briefs in test cases included information regarding the very small number of cases pursued by the CRS, as well as information about CRS policies that demonstrated the CRS's commitment to try to work with state governments and convince state governments to conduct their own prosecutions.[14] The policies the Justice Department cited in its briefs created significant restrictions for federal prosecutors. One policy required that the CRS drop cases if states were conducting their own investigations. States like Maryland could thus shield themselves from federal attention by stringing out their own inadequate investigations, as happened with the murder of Private Broadus.

The reaction of appellate courts to the CRS's early test cases demonstrates that the CRS officials were right to expect judges that might not take their side. Some judges supported the CRS by upholding indictments and convictions, but even when the CRS won favorable rulings in appellate courts, judges displayed considerable reluctance to make broad rulings. Judges frustrated efforts to clarify the law by refusing to give definitive rulings on key constitutional questions regarding federal power. In the cases that reached the Supreme Court, the CRS was frustrated by the divisions on the court and the justices' inability to stake out clear and consistent positions that could guide future prosecutions. The courts also overturned some successful CRS prosecutions, most importantly in *Screws v. United States* (1944). In that case, federal prosecutors had (miraculously) convinced an all-white Georgia jury to convict Sheriff Claude Screws and two codefendants. Screws had led a drunken posse that had clubbed to death an African American man named Robert Hall as they "arrested" him on a phony warrant. Screws targeted Hall because he had challenged the sheriff before a grand jury and had been active in a local organization called the Negro Betterment Society. (The Supreme Court avoided mention of these facts even though they were established in the record of the lower court.)[15]

Seven justices on the Supreme Court decided that the conviction should be overturned because the prosecution violated Sheriff Screws's rights. However, the majority was badly divided into two groups and could not produce an opinion of the court. In a remarkable move, one justice (Rutledge) wrote a separate opinion explaining that he believed the court should uphold the conviction but that he was voting with one of the groups favoring reversal in order to allow the court to dispose of the case. Thus a plurality opinion that focused on trumped-up grounds of a supposed flaw in the jury instructions prevailed. (The alleged flaw that the opinion focused on was one that the defendants had never even mentioned at any point in the case.) Rutledge voted the way he did to avoid the outcome favored in another opinion, jointly authored by Roberts, Frankfurter, and Jackson. Those three justices wrote together to excoriate the Justice Department for "relieving" the state of responsibility by prosecuting the sheriff for his allegedly "local crime." That opinion also claimed, remarkably, that the Fourteenth Amendment "does not create rights and obligations actively enforceable by federal law" and dismissed all the existing federal civil rights statutes on grounds that Reconstruction was "envenomed" with a "vengeful spirit" (140).

Rulings like *Screws* were no doubt devastating to prosecutors at the CRS. Sheriff Screws was retried, but a second jury acquitted. As was obvious from the record that reached the Supreme Court, Georgia had no willingness to conduct any investigation or prosecution. Screws was never punished for murdering Hall, and he went on to serve in the Georgia state legislature. Frustrated by such failures, the CRS gradually abandoned the project of using existing federal laws as a tool for expanding rights protections by the end of the decade (Elliff 1967, chapter 4). It would be a mistake, however, to see that outcome as a foregone conclusion. As already noted, initially there were a lot of good reasons for the CRS attorneys to hope that judges would move the law in a positive direction. The uncertain state of the law is underscored by the fact that even individual justices took shifting positions in CRS test cases. An astonishing five justices switched sides between pro-CRS and anti-CRS positions from *Classic* to *Screws.* Expected friends on the Supreme Court did not turn out to be reliable allies. The most striking example is Justice Frank Murphy, who had created the CRS while attorney general and who had a lifelong record of support for civil rights before being elevated to the court. Murphy joined a dissenting opinion in *Classic* that suggested that the entire CRS prosecution program was unconstitutional. Murphy switched sides, again, however, in the *Screws* case, writing a blistering dissenting opinion that argued for a strong federal role and broad interpretation of section 52. Meanwhile, Robert Jackson, who had succeeded Murphy as attorney general overseeing the CRS, coauthored an opinion in *Screws* that, like the dissent in *Classic,* seemed to reject the entire CRS program.

As Risa Goluboff (2007) has recently demonstrated, the uncertain status of the law created not just barriers but also fertile ground for creative lawyering. Goluboff looks at the development of civil rights law from the perspective of appellate advocacy by both government and interest-group attorneys and reveals a number of possible trajectories of law that were open at that time but that seem closed off today. The fact that the law subsequently moved in one specific direction should not obscure the fact that alternative paths seemed open to many experts in 1939. It is also instructive that some contemporaneous observers felt that the CRS program was far too cautious. President Truman's Committee on Civil Rights reviewed the CRS program in 1947 and concluded that the CRS should have been more aggressive and pursued more cases in efforts to get favorable appellate court rulings (120).

It is impossible to know in retrospect whether the CRS would have been more successful if it had pursued a more aggressive strategy. It is clear, however, that the direct impact of the CRS's actual activities on civil rights problems was small. The early CRS did have some significant success using peonage prosecutions to combat some of the worst labor practices in the South. The CRS also won a handful of convictions using sections 51 and 52. In addition to the landmark victory in *United States v.*

Classic, the CRS won a notable circuit court ruling upholding the prosecution of West Virginia officials who participated in a horrendous vigilante attack on a group of Jehovah's Witnesses (*Catlette v. United States,* 132 F. 2d 902 [1943]). Unfortunately, there were also cases where the CRS's prosecutions failed despite strong efforts by Justice Department officials, including cases where juries refused to convict even though CRS attorneys felt they had presented very strong cases (Carr 1947, 136–42).

The Political Context

While the legal and constitutional limitations on federal power were an important factor shaping the modest program of prosecution pursued by the Justice Department, they are only part of the story. The bigger issue is that the CRS lacked the resources to pursue a more aggressive or comprehensive program for protecting rights. The lack of resources was in turn a reflection of political constraints on the CRS.

In thinking about the "politics" of the CRS program, it is important to recognize that the CRS program was imbricated with the civil rights politics of its era in two very different ways. First, the complicated racial politics of the period were an external factor that constrained what the CRS could accomplish. The political conditions that made it impossible to pass new federal civil rights statutes also made it quite difficult for the CRS to secure resources and obtain logistical support from other government agencies or offices. Second, officials at the CRS were themselves engaging in politics through their work: Justice Department officials sometimes acted to build both elite and mass support for their goal of expanding rights protections. They made efforts to publicize their interest in civil rights and encouraged the public to bring concerns about rights violations to the Justice Department.[16] In addition, the CRS test prosecutions were designed, in part, to open up new political possibilities for federal action on civil rights. There was also, I show below, an important political dimension to the replies that the CRS routinely sent to people who wrote letters about rights violations.

Politics as an External Constraint

The key to understanding the complicated civil rights politics of the period is the fact that President Roosevelt's ruling coalition included two

fundamentally opposed constituencies: African Americans (and sympathetic white liberals) in northern swing districts and the white supremacist
southern wing of the Democratic Party. Maintaining that coalition was a
difficult balancing act. While many liberals in the administration and in
Congress supported civil rights, the southern wing of the party was determined to preserve the apartheid system in the South and thus vehemently
opposed to any effort to expand federal capacities to protect rights. Because southerners occupied key leadership positions in Congress, they
could obstruct any effort to pass new civil rights legislation. They could
also use oversight powers and budget control to thwart efforts to revive
and enforce existing civil rights laws.[17]

The need to maintain support from two opposed groups led the administration to take complicated positions on issues of civil rights and race.
Sometimes administration officials were able to make modest gestures in
support of racial justice. Frank Murphy's decision to create the CRS is an
example.[18] However, the administration had to accompany any gestures in
favor of civil rights with credible reassurances to southern Democrats that
the scope of any action was modest and that the administration would not
go so far as to dismantle the racial caste system in the South. Of course,
not all the cases that the CRS pursued were about race, and most of the
complaint letters in my sample did not make race-related claims. Nevertheless, southern Democrats were sensitive to the fact that race was inevitably in the background of any actions that expanded federal powers to
protect rights.

The tensions within the Roosevelt coalition shaped the day-to-day activities of the CRS in significant ways. Most fundamentally, the Roosevelt
administration proved unwilling to devote significant resources to the CRS
effort. The office was staffed with no more than seven attorneys during its
first decade. CRS staff was based in Washington, DC, and thus dependent
on the FBI or local US attorneys to obtain information or conduct investigations about events in remote areas. Such locally based federal officials
were often reluctant to cooperate with the CRS. US attorneys and FBI
agents had close professional and personal ties with local law enforcement
officials and were reluctant to cooperate with investigations that might
implicate those officials in crimes.[19]

Some examples can help to illustrate the problems related to the institutional constraints, particularly the need to rely on locally based federal
officials. One case involved the 1939 lynching of W. C. Williams in Ruston,
Louisiana. After receiving a complaint about the lynching from Gordon

McIntire of the Louisiana Farmer's Union, the CRS asked the local US attorney to look into the case. The US attorney later forwarded to Justice a letter from the local sheriff, J. B. Thigpen, providing his account of the case. The sheriff claimed that Williams had twice attacked couples at a lovers' lane near his home. He claimed that Williams had murdered one man and repeatedly raped a woman in the second attack. In response to credible claims that Williams had nothing to do with any such attacks, Thigpen reported that Williams had confessed to the crimes. The sheriff also acknowledged that the confession had been obtained only after a red-hot screwdriver had been inserted into Williams's rectum. The sheriff defended his interrogation technique, however, by claiming that the screwdriver had proven Williams guilt by prompting Williams to reveal (unspecified) information that only the perpetrator could have possessed. The sheriff also claimed that he tried valiantly to prevent the lynching by negotiating at length with the mob. However, Thigpen also reported that he concluded his valiant negotiation by inexplicably leaving the scene before the mob dispersed. He claimed that he later tried to return to the jail but was intercepted by the mob. After receiving this remarkable report, the CRS lost interest in the case. It reported back to the Louisiana Famer's Union that it could not prosecute because the local law enforcement officials had done what they could to prevent the lynching.[20]

Another case that reveals how organizational tensions within the federal government hindered investigations is that of Charles Bishop. Bishop, an African American ex-convict, wrote to Eleanor Roosevelt from St. Louis reporting that he had been framed for a robbery (August 1, 1940). After being blamed for the crime by a group of men he knew from prison, Bishop was arrested by the St. Louis police and then beaten and tortured until he "confessed." Bishop, who wrote from a hospital because of the injuries inflicted by the police, begged Mrs. Roosevelt to help him avoid a likely life sentence in prison. The letter was forwarded to O. John Rogge, the head of the Criminal Division, who quickly wrote to Harry Blanton, the US attorney in St. Louis. Rogge's letter pointedly requested that Blanton "conduct a confidential and preliminary investigation" into the allegations. Rogge stated that if Blanton so advised, "an investigation will be immediately requested" (August 14, 1940).

Blanton either ignored or misunderstood the point of Rogge's instruction to conduct a "confidential" investigation: Rogge wrote that line because he was hoping to keep the FBI away from the case. Blanton wrote back to Rogge two days later to report that he had asked a local FBI agent to conduct an investigation. Rogge also received a letter directly from J. Edgar Hoover that, like many of Hoover's letters in the CRS files, is a masterpiece of passive aggression. Hoover noted that the US attorney had requested an FBI investigation and was also careful to reveal that he knew that Rogge had asked the US attorney to conduct a "confidential" investigation. The perturbed Hoover included peripheral claims to make it clear that he understood that Rogge did not trust the FBI to investigate the case. Hoover also wrote, as he often did in cases involving civil rights, that "no investigation will be conducted by this bureau" until the Criminal Division gave him "specific instructions" to conduct one (August 22, 1940). The department almost always backed down when Hoover signaled such resistance. Rogge quickly wrote back to advise Hoover that no investigation was being requested. Rogge also wrote back to Blanton, this time stating more directly that he did not want the FBI involved in the case. He explained that the original letter "intended . . . that the inquiry into this matter be made by your office, without the aid of the Federal Bureau of Investigation." Rogge also asked Blanton to give the matter his "prompt attention" (August 27, 1940).

Blanton responded to the second, more pointed, request by digging in his heels. He wrote: "I am sorry that I have no way of making a personal investigation into the merit or lack of merit in this complaint." He sarcastically noted that if he were to interview Bishop in the hospital, the result would be "nothing more than a restatement" of his letter to Eleanor Roosevelt, while an interview with the police would "no doubt, result in a denial of the charges." He protested that only the FBI had "the necessary facilities for making these investigations" and that the "volume of work in our office makes it impossible" to give attention to "these matters" (September 10, 1940). He concluded by saying he would not conduct any investigation and would await "further suggestions." Faced with such resistance from their representatives on the local scene, and lacking resources to have anyone else give the case attention, Rogge and the CRS dropped the matter.[21]

Such problems did not always prevent the CRS from pursuing cases. For example, in 1940 the CRS prosecuted an Atlanta police officer who had tortured an African American man named Quintar South into confessing to a theft. In that case, the CRS won a helpful district court ruling upholding the indictment under a broad reading of the "color of law" language in the statute (*United States v. Sutherland*, 37 F. Supp. 344 [1940]). The case proceeded despite the fact that the attorneys at the CRS had difficulty obtaining cooperation from either the FBI or leaders in the Justice Department. The FBI resisted an early CRS request that it investigate the police force, fearing that such an investigation would damage its relations with the Atlanta police. CRS attorneys sought help from Assistant Attorney General Matthew McGuire, but McGuire refused to order the FBI to conduct a more comprehensive investigation. The prosecution went forward anyway but was not ultimately successful. After two mistrials, the CRS dropped its pursuit of the case.[22] Of course, FBI agents and US attorneys are, in theory, under the supervision of the Justice Department and attorney general. Stronger political support from the White House or political appointees in the Justice Department might have made it easier for staff attorneys at the CRS to secure FBI cooperation. However, the pattern of CRS activities makes it clear that higher-level political support was not typically available. Bureaucratic resistance was thus allowed to prevail.

Another case involving the US attorney in St. Louis reveals that obstruction also worked in the opposite direction (i.e., where the Justice Department rebuffed local officials who expressed concerns about civil rights violations and sought federal help). The US attorney's brother, David Blanton, was a local prosecutor in Scott County, Missouri. David Blanton wrote to Harry Blanton in St. Louis to warn him of a group of white vigilantes gathering in the town of Oran in 1939.[23] The letter reported that the vigilantes were using threats and beatings to prevent African Americans from moving into a settlement in the town. He asked formally for advice and help from the federal government. The US attorney forwarded the letter to the department in Washington and asked for instruction on how to respond.[24] Criminal Division head Rogge replied that the federal government should not get involved, stating: "It would seem that the acts complained of constitute merely a series of assaults and batteries that should be treated as a local law enforcement matter."[25] As this case shows, the logistical and political calculations within the Justice Department do not always fit into a single neat pattern. Noncooperation by locally based officials was not the only factor that made the Justice Department reluctant to become involved in cases involving racial violence.

CRS Activity as Part of Politics

Thus far I have looked at the effect of politics as an independent factor that influenced CRS capacities and activities. However, the CRS was not simply buffeted about by external political forces. The CRS program was also linked to efforts to build outside political support for expanded federal civil rights activities. CRS attorneys traveled to speak to local bar associations about their program and advocated their doctrinal arguments in law review articles. The CRS also made efforts to publicize the CRS program to the general public. Frank Murphy gave a nationally broadcast radio address announcing formation of the CRS, and CRS attorneys visited with regional attorneys' groups and asked members to bring civil rights problems to the attention of the Justice Department.[26] Such outreach efforts sometimes generated local newspaper coverage that reached broader audiences. Many who sent letters directly to the CRS stated that they were inspired to write by Murphy's speech or by newspaper stories on other CRS outreach activities (16 percent of the incident letters referred to media coverage of federal civil rights initiatives). More generally, the CRS processed a large volume of correspondence from the public and wrote replies to most of the letters.[27] In addition to mail sent to the Justice Department regarding rights, the CRS also corresponded with many people who had written to the president or to Eleanor Roosevelt. This happened because the CRS was also tasked with responding to rights-related mail sent to other executive branch offices and agencies. The CRS even processed a handful of letters that members of Congress forwarded for a reply.

The CRS's outreach and communications activities were in part efforts to gather information about rights violations. However, such efforts also have an obvious political dimension because they affected public understandings of federal power, public knowledge of administration policies, and thus public support for civil rights programs.

CRS officials clearly saw these public communication and outreach efforts as a very important part of their overall mission. When Murphy wrote to Senator Burke of Nebraska to explain the CRS program, his letter placed considerable emphasis on the outreach activities and the CRS's responses to complaints from the public. Murphy noted: "A system of cooperation between civil rights committees of the American Bar Association and State and local bar associations is being evolved so that there may be an exchange of information and so that the active aid of State and local lawyers may be enlisted for the protection of the people." Murphy also made some claims about CRS processing of civil rights complaints, including the very disputable claim that every report that indicated a basis for federal jurisdiction was referred to local US attorneys (May 4, 1939).

CRS Replies to Letter Writers

There is also a significant political dimension to the replies that the CRS routinely sent letter writers. While the CRS almost never intervened directly to provide assistance to complainants, the CRS almost always sent reply letters to people who wrote letters regarding particular incidents.[28] This was true even though the CRS was not under any legal obligation to reply. The messages in the CRS's reply letters, particularly the legal claims that the CRS made to explain the department's refusals to help, provide some clues about the unit's stance toward the public.

Almost all of the reply letters followed the same boilerplate structure. The replies began with a short paragraph acknowledging the letter and attempting to restate the subject of the complaint in one sentence. The replies then asserted that the law made it impossible to provide assistance. More specifically, the CRS claimed that the Justice Department could not help because the matter fell outside of federal law or outside of the department's jurisdiction.

The claim that the federal government lacked jurisdiction to help appears with numbing monotony in the department's reply letters. The department utilized several different formulations of that legal claim. A typical example is a reply sent to Pearl Squires Olsen, who wrote from Manistique, Michigan, to complain about corruption on a local school board. The CRS wrote in reply: "From the information contained in your letter, there is nothing that would indicate that the matters complained of are not purely local. In these circumstances, the Department of Justice would have no jurisdiction to intervene" (March 21, 1939). Another example is the reply sent to George Ruzicka, who wrote from Sayville, New York, to ask whether he could be forced to work against his will under an employment contract. The response read in part, "From the facts set forth in your letter, the remedy open to you for the protection of your rights lies in the courts of your state. There is nothing under these circumstances which would permit the federal government to intervene" (April 28, 1939). Some CRS dismissals have a slightly harsher tone. Dave Moore wrote to President Roosevelt from Postelle, Arkansas, to report that the police had worked with a local business owner to break into Moore's home and remove his "stuff" (July 11, 1940). The removal of Moore's property was connected to a dispute over a debt, but the letter suggested that the police had no legal basis to seize his property. Moore claimed he was unable to pay the business owner the amount he demanded to get his things returned. Moore also wrote: "We are poor people and we need help and asking you for help." The department's reply to Moore stated: "The matter of which you complain is one obviously within the sole jurisdiction of the law enforcement authorities of your state. The Federal government may concern itself only when it appears that the provisions of a specific Federal criminal statute have been violated. Inasmuch as there is no indication of such violation, the Federal Government is without authority to act pursuant to your request" (July 22, 1940). The untypical use of the word "obviously" may indicate that CRS staff was irritated and felt this was not a serious complaint.

While the CRS almost always included a claim indicating that legal limits made it impossible for the department to help, the replies never included the kind of information that complainants needed to understand, evaluate, or respond to the department's legal claims. The replies would indicate that the writer had not met some legal standard, but the standard itself went unstated. When the department claimed categorically that the it lacked jurisdiction over the reported case, it did not provide a general account of what *did* qualify for federal jurisdiction. Replies stating that there was "nothing" that the department could do under "these circumstances" provided little help to writers who would presumably want to understand why their government was so powerless and to understand what alternative circumstances might allow the government to help. Even when asked, the CRS declined to provide helpful information about legal standards. People who asked questions about the status of law or the basis for federal jurisdiction were told that the attorney general was only allowed to give legal opinions to the president and the heads of federal departments. People who asked for copies of laws or information about cases were told to go to a library.

The archived records do not provide information to reveal how the CRS staff evaluated particular letters before deciding how to respond. For most exchanges, the only documents in the files are the citizen's original letter and a carbon copy of the reply sent by the CRS. However, a few cases generated some additional records that provide some revealing clues about what CRS staff were thinking as they processed the letters. In some cases, there are signs that staff at the CRS appeared to get a chuckle out of the complaint letters. George Runyan, for example, wrote from Lansing, Michigan, to complain that that a local judge had slapped him with an injunction after he had criticized a local car dealership for selling

him a lemon (December 28, 1939). A staff member forwarded the letter to CRS head Henry Schweinhaut with a note saying: "Henry, I think
you'll enjoy this one."[29] More often, the records indicate some staff concern and regret. For example, there were sometimes small breaches of
routine where staff tempered the coldness of the department's boilerplate
refusals with an expression of regret. When Florence Brown wrote from
Baltimore to complain of her husband's wrongful criminal conviction, the
CRS replied: "This Department would like to be of service to you but
the matter you complain of appears to be within the exclusive jurisdiction of the State of Maryland" (January 10, 1941). After telling Alvina
Douglas of Ann Arbor, Michigan, that it could not help to reverse her
daughter's murder conviction, the department noted: "It is well understood that the cause for which you plead is a matter of deep concern to
you, and it is with regret that you cannot be favored with a more encouraging reply" (March 12, 1940). Such expressions of empathy were not
routine. Their appearance may indicate cases where the staff were particularly moved by the complaints and frustrated that they had to refuse to
help.

There are other instances where the bureaucratic monotony of processing correspondence produced replies that must have struck letter writers
as unusual or nonsensical. Quite often, the one-sentence restatement of
the complaint in the department's reply letters misstated the nature of
the actual complaint.[30] In other cases, there were claims made in boilerplate reply letters that fully attentive staff should have recognized as as-
tonishingly unhelpful. For example, the department sent numerous letters
telling destitute complainants that they had to get help by hiring private
counsel. In other cases, the CRS told complainants to take their problems
to a private attorney even though the complaint letter made it clear that
they had already consulted with an attorney.[31]

In other cases, crossed signals or bureaucratic mistakes resulted in replies that must have been particularly disappointing, or even distressing,
to letter writers. Emily Brunner wrote to Frank Murphy after hearing
Murphy give a radio address expressing his interest in civil rights cases.
The speech inspired Brunner to ask for federal help in connection with
the death of her dog (March 29, 1939). She explained that her dog had
contracted rabies from a botched vaccination and complained that her entire family had also been forced to undergo costly rabies treatments. The
department responded with a cheerful letter that thanked Brunner for her
appreciation of the speech but failed to even mention her story about her

dog. While misunderstandings were common, such obvious snafus were relatively rare.

It is important to acknowledge that there are also a few cases where CRS officials did try to help letter writers even though the department decided not investigate or prosecute the case. In addition to Charlie Thompson's case, there is the case of Frances McNutt. McNutt wrote to Eleanor Roosevelt explaining that her father had been denied the right to vote in California because he was illiterate (August 23, 1939). In response, the Justice Department decided not to follow its alleged policy of never giving legal advice to anyone except the president and department heads. The reply letter provided a lengthy quote from a relevant clause of the California state constitution. The reply (September 11, 1939) also suggested that McNutt take the quote (and, presumably, the supportive letter from the Justice Department) to the local registrar of voters.[32]

Other cases show Justice Department officials making considerable efforts to accommodate difficult letter writers. A man named James Allen wrote deranged letters to the president and attorney general (March 28, 1939; June 25 1941), and apparently wrote a much larger number of letters to the US attorney in Wilmington, Delaware.[33] Allen expressed a variety of unusual complaints and demands related to allegations of a government conspiracy. At one point, Allen was invited to come to Washington to meet with CRS head Henry Schweinhaut. Schweinhaut's memo on the meeting (May 24, 1941) reported that Schweinhaut had invited Allen to Washington "in an effort to finally dispose of him" because Allen "wore out the patience" of the US attorney in Wilmington. However, Schweinhaut concluded that "it is now apparent that it is impossible to do anything with him. He is obviously *non compos mentis*." Schweinhaut suggested that the department stop replying to his letters. A later "Memorandum for the Files" (September 24, 1941) reported that Allen nevertheless continued to get attention. He met twice with the second CRS head, Victor Rotnem, later that year. It is clear that these meetings were not easy. Rotnem's memo noted: "Allen is extremely deaf and uses a mechanical device to aid in his hearing." To accommodate Allen's demands, a stenographer was present at one two-hour meeting, producing a sixty-page transcript. The memo also reported that Allen alleged a "gigantic conspiracy" involving "several score persons" including state elected officials, police officers, "all grand jurors who have refused to indict the persons complained of by Allen, various attorneys who have refused to handle Allen's numerous attempted suits, and finally his wife, mother in law and certain of his children." The memo also noted that the Secret Service had recently filed a complaint with the US attorney in Wilmington because Allen had threatened the president in a letter.[34]

The amount of attention paid to Allen is very unusual. Most writers received only a reply letter, and most of the letters stopped after stating that the department could not help. The department did sometimes add a line with general information about another place the writer might look for help. Eleven percent of writers reporting incidents were told they should instead try to get help by hiring a private attorney. Eight percent were told that they could visit the local US attorney if they could provide additional information to demonstrate there was a basis for federal intervention. (Many of the referrals to the US attorney came only after a complainant wrote back to repeat a complaint or to question the CRS's refusal to help.) It is not possible to tell precisely how many people followed the CRS's suggestions about going to the US attorney. The cases where there is evidence about what happened when a writer visited a US attorney invariably reveal that writers did not get any help.[35]

Evidence also suggests that Justice Department referrals to other officials were intended not so much to help the complainant as to make the complainant go away. An example is the case of Eugene Causey, who wrote to Frank Murphy from Detroit claiming that he had lost his job after refusing to support the "communist" United Auto Workers local at the Hudson Motor Car Company. Causey's letter noted that his father had been a slave and that he was an "honorable citizen" who had been a reliable worker for more than fifty years (December 27, 1939). The department's initial reply came from Edward Kemp, assistant to the attorney general. It stated: "I regret to advise you that there is no action which the Department of Justice can take with reference to the matter of your employment" (January 12, 1940).

Causey wrote back to Kemp (January 18, 1940) asking a series of pointed questions that were clearly intended to express his disappointment in the reply. ("If a group of men prohibit anyone from working to make an honest living by honest means, has those men violated the Constitution of the United States or has they violated any law whatever.") Two weeks later, a response letter was prepared with help from the CRS and sent over Kemp's signature.[36] The second reply responded to Causey's rhetorical questions with the unhelpful but routine line: "The Attorney General is authorized by law to give opinions only to the President and heads of Executive Departments." The letter also suggested that Causey could contact the US attorney in Detroit (February 14, 1940). The determined Mr. Causey did later meet in Detroit with US Attorney John C. Lehr. However, the run-around continued. Lehr sent a letter to the CRS reporting that a "colored gentleman" had visited his office. Causey had again complained that the union had forced him out of his job and also reported that he could not take a new job at the Hudson plant because "he was in fear of great physical violence at the hands of the local CIO." Lehr expressed sympathy for Causey's position: "This case is certainly one that appeals to the sympathy of a decent American." Nevertheless, Lehr refused to offer any help. He instead gave advice that he admitted was unhelpful: "I have advised Mr. Causey that in my opinion the best procedure for him to follow is to refer this matter to the Prosecuting Attorney of Wayne County, although I doubt that he will obtain much help there" (February 14, 1940).

To be clear, if there is reason to be concerned about these kinds of responses, the reason is not simply that these Justice Department officials did not provide more help. As already noted, the CRS faced a variety of important constraints that limited how much it could do in civil rights cases. It will also become clear in later chapters that not every writer made credible claims about serious rights violations. Many writers took up the department's time with relatively trivial complaints. In many instances, the CRS might have quite justifiably decided that writers' claims were not credible enough or important enough to be worthy of its very limited resources. Remember also that the CRS was in the Criminal Division and tasked with conducting criminal prosecutions. Given that role, the appropriate standard for providing help was not whether the allegation contained any plausible basis for federal jurisdiction but whether the CRS could accomplish anything by conducting a criminal prosecution. The CRS could have reasonably determined that successful prosecution was very unlikely in the vast majority of rejected cases.

Nevertheless, even when the CRS's decisions to refuse to help were justifiable, there is still room to be concerned about the way the CRS tried justify its refusals by making broad legal claims in reply letters. In almost every case, the *only* reason the CRS gave for the refusal to help was that legal limits on jurisdiction made it *impossible* to help. The department never mentioned its need to make choices about where to direct scarce resources and never told complainants about the difficulty of getting cooperation from locally based officials or about the general political constraints that limited federal civil rights initiatives. Yet it is clear from the record that those sorts of factors, and not simply technical decisions about jurisdiction, were driving the CRS's choices about whether to provide help. It is also clear from the record that the department was evaluating complaints for credibility, gravity, and the likelihood of obtaining a successful prosecution. Those factors also fail to appear in the department's explanation for its choices. Thus, however justified the department's refusals may have been, the relevant justification in many cases was not the one actually expressed in the reply letters.

Moreover, it is often difficult to accept at face value the department's rote recitation of the claim that legal constraints made it impossible to provide any help. The bold claims about jurisdiction are expressed with a certainty that masks the fact that the law of federal jurisdiction was quite unsettled. As the CRS well understood, the reach of existing law had not been firmly established, and there was good reason to believe that judges were no longer committed to maintaining doctrines limiting federal power. The unsettled state of law also meant that the department's determinations about its jurisdiction were not simply technical legal judgments about applying clear standards but informed guesses about what kinds of novel federal interventions the judges in office at that time would tolerate.

Most important, there are quite a substantial number of complainants who reported incidents that appear to meet the basic thresholds for federal jurisdiction. Of course, the unsettled state of law meant that no one knew for certain what the operative legal standards were. It is thus impossible to give a precise number of incidents where the CRS claims about its jurisdiction were exaggerated or false. Nevertheless, it seems clear that the department made questionable claims about its jurisdiction in many cases. One striking indicator is that nearly half of the complaints about incidents in my sample were complaints about actions of state or federal government officials (348 of 710, or 49 percent). The state action doctrine, the primary constitutional limit on federal jurisdiction in rights cases, was simply not relevant to such complaints.

Beyond the broad patterns, there are a few cases that show clearly that the department's claims about jurisdiction were at least sometimes disingenuous. An example is the case of George Rogers, who wrote in March 1940 to complain that he and three other men had been arrested in Newport, Arkansas, for allegedly trespassing on railroad property. Rogers reported that he and several other men were forced at gunpoint to perform a day of labor for the city and suggested that the city and the railroad were running a "boodle system." The department initially showed interest in pursuing this complaint. The head of the Criminal Division wrote to Sam Rorex, the US attorney in Little Rock, noting that the case appeared to be a violation of both sections 444 and 52. However, instead of asking Rorex to investigate Rogers's case, the department asked the US attorney to find out "whether this practice is customary in that locality" (March 29, 1940). Presumably, the department wanted to know whether it was a widespread practice because they did not think it was wise to devote scarce resources to an isolated case.

Rorex wrote back and assured the department that the practice was not "customary," thus suggesting that the incident reported by Rogers was singular. The department then chose not to pursue the case. While that choice about how to use resources is certainly defensible, the reply that the department sent to George Rogers did not explain or even ac-knowledge the fact that the department was making any choice at all. The reply instead stated categorically that the department had "no authority to act" because an "investigation" had determined that there had been no violation of a federal statute (May 18, 1940). That claim is not truthful. The department's conclusion that the practice was not "customary" had no bearing on whether federal jurisdiction obtained in Rogers's case or whether a federal statute had been violated.

The broad patterns in routine CRS records, together with additional in-formation from a few cases that left records of the department's decision-making process, make it clear that the CRS was not always forthcoming in its replies. The reason for many of the CRS's refusals to help was not simply a lack of jurisdiction or legal authority.

So why did the CRS routinely use legal claims about jurisdiction with-out ever offering a broader explanation? The reason, I believe, is that legal claims about jurisdiction allowed the CRS to characterize its response as a technical determination rather than a discretionary judgment. Presum-ably, CRS officials preferred to defuse uncomfortable confrontations with distressed citizens. For such officials, claims about legal standards are an attractive strategy because such claims mask the department's evaluations of individual cases and resulting discretionary choices. By doing so, the claims about law depoliticize the encounters.

To understand that interpretation, it is first important to again note that the routine bureaucratic exchanges between the CRS and the letter writers have a significant political dimension. As I noted in chapter 1, indi-vidual petitions to government are an essential form of political participa-tion in a democratic society. People who wrote to federal officials for help likely did so because they believed that their problems were significant and that federal officials, particularly high-ranking ones like the president or attorney general, had the power to help them. Such people thus needed some explanation if they were to understand why the government was refusing to provide help. Such an explanation would have allowed letter writers to evaluate the decision to refuse assistance and decide how to respond as citizens of a constitutional democracy. At this basic level, the department's failure to provide a more forthcoming explanation meant that the department was missing the opportunity to engage letter writers in the political discussion and exchange initiated by the decision to petition government.

The claims about law and jurisdiction in the department's reply letters depoliticized the encounters in two specific ways. First, the department expressed jurisdictional limits as brute facts, without any hint of when those limits were established or who was responsible for creating them. Instead of presenting legal limits on jurisdiction as the contingent result of reversible choices by government officials, the department's letters expressed the jurisdictional limits as though they were timeless and beyond human agency. The replies thus hid the fact that limits on jurisdiction might themselves be subject to political contestation. The replies never hinted, for example, that many of the shortcomings of federal civil rights statutes could be fixed immediately if enough elected legislators were willing to pass new civil rights legislation. The replies also never mentioned that CRS attorneys were working at the same time to develop test cases that, they hoped, would lead to the relaxation of the jurisdictional limits.

The second way the legal claims about jurisdiction depoliticized the encounters was by allowing officials to avoid saying anything about the department's evaluation of the credibility or seriousness of the complaints. The reply letters almost never indicated that the department had doubts about the credibility of complaints, reservations regarding the seriousness of the offense, or concerns about whether allegations could be proven in court. They also, understandably, did not say whether the government attorneys had shared a chuckle over the complaint. The broad jurisdictional claim instead communicated that it was *impossible* for the federal government to help in cases like the complainant's, thus suggesting that evaluations of credibility or merit were not even relevant to the decision. Note also that from the letter writers' perspective, legal jurisdiction is not necessarily the relevant standard. Even if there was absolutely no legal basis for federal jurisdiction, it was not *impossible* for federal officials to provide any help. While the federal officials did not have the resources to help everyone who wrote, they were not powerless to provide help to any single complainant. The claims in reply letters about the Justice Department's jurisdiction must have been particularly puzzling to the many people who had written directly to the president. The White House has resources that give the president numerous ways to help individual people. Consider, for example, the recent case of Henrietta Hughes, a homeless woman who spoke to President Obama at a televised public forum and was quickly provided with a new home through the president's direct intervention.[37]

One way to dramatize the political dimension of the department's jurisdictional claims is to compare the CRS's actual responses to a hypothetical alternative strategy: brutal honesty. The CRS could have written reply letters stating that the federal government chose not to help after a lower-level worker made an instantaneous assessment that the complaint was not serious or credible enough to be worthy of the few symbolic resources that the Roosevelt administration was willing to devote to civil rights. A brutally honest reply might also have stated that there were people in the administration and president's party who wanted very much to change the law and do more to protect rights, but their efforts were routinely obstructed because the president needed support from southern Democrats to enact his preferred programs and assure his reelection. Such a reply would have drawn more direct attention to the fact that the Roosevelt administration was making discretionary and political choices about where to use resources and not mechanically following unchangeable dictates existing in some transcendent realm of law.

I am not prepared to argue that honesty is always the best policy. My point is not to blame the CRS for not writing more straightforward replies that acknowledged the CRS's limited discretion. I also do not want to suggest that the way the letters were handled is somehow peculiar to the CRS. Official efforts to use legal claims to deny or mask the exercise of discretion may be a standard operating procedure that influences a very broad range of citizen interactions with government officials.[38] Anyone who has routine encounters with public or private bureaucracy has probably been told, somewhat dubiously, that a preferred course of action is "impossible."

Moreover, a certain amount of the brutality in the honest response might not serve any purpose.[39] More direct efforts at political engagement may not have resulted in better overall outcomes. If the CRS had made more overt efforts to build the public's knowledge of and support for constitutional changes around rights, it might only have agitated or confused individual letter writers trapped in difficult circumstances. Brutal honesty might also have made it more likely that writers would continue to hold out false hope for a favorable outcome and continue to press their futile demands rather than moving on. It is also not clear that more direct engagement would have resulted in better political outcomes or strengthened the CRS's position in the administration. More political engagement with the public by the Justice Department might have provoked powerful southerners in Congress to use oversight and budgetary powers to stop the CRS from acting at all.

While the hypothetical brutally honest response is not a realistic or attractive alternative, it does help to highlight the ways in which the department's actual replies evaded political engagement. Note also that the reliance on legal claims to defuse the encounters also suggests that the CRS saw the encounters as adversarial. The adversarial nature of these exchanges is perhaps inevitable. People were asking for or demanding attention, and government officials were refusing to provide help. The desire of the CRS to defuse the encounters is thus understandable, as are the efforts to "dispose of" nuisance letter writers like James Allen.

Nevertheless, the CRS's choice to eschew politics and instead deploy legal claims seems particularly discomfiting because these encounters did not have to be experienced as entirely adversarial. Ironically, the exchanges quite often show that instead of being adversaries, the letter writers and the CRS shared important goals and constitutional values. People looked to the federal government to protect rights because they understood quite well that state governments were often incapable of providing meaningful protection. State governments were the most frequent violators of rights in the cases brought to the department's attention. Very similar beliefs and commitments seem to have been motivating much of the appellate work of the CRS attorneys. The common ground between the CRS and the letter writers was quite broad. Both letter writers and the CRS wanted the federal government to play a more active role in protecting citizens' rights. Many writers agreed with the attorneys handling the CRS's appellate advocacy that the Constitution's text and history provided a strong constitutional basis for expanding federal power to protect rights.[40] Yet despite these important areas of agreement, the CRS reply letters relied on legal language to avoid engaging citizens in the broader, long-term political processes that would eventually lead to the constitutional and institutional changes that both sides of the exchanges wanted. The replies not only failed to alert writers to the fact that elected officials could fix many of the statutory limitations on the department's power, they also failed to acknowledge or take credit for the CRS's active efforts to use test prosecutions to relax the doctrinal limits. Thus the legal claims not only hid the information that citizens needed to evaluate the department's decision, they also hid the broader political conflicts that were constraining federal responses to civil rights violations.

Even though CRS's routines are understandable, it is nevertheless disheartening to find that activist and well-intentioned government attorneys are led, perhaps inevitably, to avoid political engagement with supportive elements of the public. The road not taken of greater political engagement is particularly attractive in this case because many of the people who wrote to the CRS were admirably engaged constitutional citizens. The content of the letters generally reveals that complainants were not just naive supplicants who believed they were automatically entitled to some legal remedy. As I show in chapter 5, writers understood that government officials had to make discretionary decisions about when to devote scarce resources to the problems reported in letters. The inability of the CRS to engage this motivated public reveals that the CRS was committed to an insider strategy. Its program was about one set of government actors trying to convince another set of government officials to change their minds. Such strategies may be less capable of producing meaningful institutional and political changes than campaigns that ask the people themselves to take part in broader processes of constitutional change.

It is also striking that the CRS's test-case strategy was directly at odds with many of the claims about jurisdiction in the letters. The CRS attorneys were articulating different and seemingly contradictory accounts of law to different audiences. While the CRS replies made broad and absolute legal claims about the federal government's legal authority, the entire CRS program of test prosecutions was based on recognition that the law of federal jurisdiction over civil rights was unsettled and that it needed to evolve to meet changing conditions. The CRS told hundreds of people who had complained about rights violations by state actors that the federal government had no jurisdiction to intervene, but the attorneys responsible for those replies were at the same time telling appellate court judges, readers of law reviews, and various local bar groups that such jurisdiction did exist and that the existing law provided room to expand jurisdiction even further. The differences between the accounts given to different audiences raise questions about the legal commitments of CRS attorneys and illustrate how legal officials can simultaneously deploy conflicting versions of "law." The phenomenon of people adopting poses based on expectations about their audience is one that comes up repeatedly in these exchanges.

The department's efforts to use legal claims to depoliticize encounters also provide a palpable example of legal authorities attempting to take advantage of law's power as ideology. Claims about law, particularly when articulated by government officials, carry with them signals about the legitimacy of rules, processes, and outcomes. When such legal claims are expressed to people like the ones who wrote letters, they read as a demand for deference to government officials with the expertise and authority to make such legal pronouncements. Such signals are troublesome in a democratic society because law is often expressed in an obscure or technical form that is only fully accessible to trained experts. Authoritative claims about law may thus lead to deference that is unwarranted. People may defer to wrong or contestable claims about law because they do not understand what the claims mean or how to evaluate whether the claims are accurate.

The jurisdictional claims in the CRS reply letters thus provide fairly concrete examples of the attempted *production* of legal ideology by government officials. It is important to note, however, that such attempts to deploy law as ideology are not automatically successful. Whether such idealized claims successfully depoliticize encounters or legitimate outcomes depends on how the claims are received and reproduced by the targeted audience. In the chapters that follow, I show that the CRS's ideological deployment of legal rhetoric to defuse or depoliticize encounters quite often appears to have been spectacularly unsuccessful. I show in chapter 4 that a very substantial number of letter writers wrote back to contest, and often mock, the CRS's legal claims about jurisdiction. I show in chapter 5 that people who wrote letters making rights claims usually understood that the government's response was not, as the CRS's response letters indicated, fully controlled by law. People instead understood that the CRS's responses reflected discretionary choices by government officials. Meanwhile, I do not find evidence to suggest that the legal claims in the letters convinced any of the complainants that the failure to provide help was justified. There is thus nothing to show that writers accepted the CRS's legal claims at face value and decided that the resulting outcome was legitimate.

CHAPTER THREE

Dead Dogs, Bad Divorces, and Dope-Peddling Sheriffs

The Subject Matter of Civil Rights Complaint Letters

People who wrote the letters processed by the CRS used legalized language of rights, liberty, and constitutionalism to express a wide range of concerns and complaints. In some instances, writers made quite sweeping claims about their rights. Anna Mae Brown, of Lansing, Michigan, cataloged her constitutional entitlements by stating: "I have the right to vote as I please; to worship as I please; to express my opinions as I please; to do anything in self-defense if necessary" (March 29, 1939). Other writers made offbeat claims to very specific rights entitlements. Alex Gast sent a letter to the Justice Department claiming that he had an "inalienable right to earn my living as an employe in my own business even though it is temporarily in charge of the Government" (December 31, 1940). Henry Kost claimed a right to paint signs for a living and to draw cartoons as part of the Constitution's "right to 'pursue happiness'" (November 30, 1941). Richard Terry claimed that Americans had "the right to do your bit of work, to keep from being a burden, a chisler, a liar and others upon self and other neighbors" (May 20, 1940). A telegram from a group calling itself "Laundry Employees" complained that the Los Angeles Board of Supervisors canceled the Fourth of July holiday and thus violated their "right to celebrate that independence," a right they claimed came from the authors of the Constitution (June 24, 1940). A nurse named Eleanor Watjus claimed that her work supervisor had violated "my civil rights as a citizen by taking the liberty to publicly suspend and put me on probation for what Mrs. Messner should have been blamed for" (February 10, 1941).

The government lawyers who processed such claims clearly had different ideas about rights entitlements than the people who wrote them. Very few of the people who wrote letters obtained any remedy from the CRS or the Justice Department. The fact that the government almost universally rejected writers' requests makes the propensity of letter writers to articulate claims in such legalized language quite remarkable. Even though the federal government of that era was not able to do very much to protect rights, people still sent petitions to federal officials that expressed demands using imaginative and expansive claims about rights and related legal entitlements.

This chapter provides an overview of the subject matter of the complaint letters, organized by the type of rights claimed in the letters. I provide information about the prevalence of different claims as well as examples to illustrate the kinds of incidents that writers reported as rights violations. I begin with letters claiming core rights that are enumerated in the Constitution's text. I cover claims related to the First Amendment, claims related to guarantees of "due process" or criminal procedures, and then claims related to property rights. I next examine claims related to racism and racist violence. The discussion then turns to some of the more imaginative rights claims regarding economic opportunities and rights related to work. A final section discusses writers' claims related to voting and democracy.

In addition to making claims of various entitlements, almost all the writers who reported incidents provided a narrative account of the circumstances of alleged rights violations. In some cases, the stories were as short as a single sentence. Some letters went to ten or more pages. Taken together, the stories people told about the incidents that led them to write provide a vivid picture of conditions on the ground at that time. There are stories of vigilante violence against racial minorities, abusive policing practices, disrupted worship services, violence in labor disputes, corruption among local government officials, and displaced workers traveling long distances in search of work or fair treatment from relief agencies.

While the writers' stories bear the imprint of the tough economic times, the rights claims in the letters often seem influenced by the dynamic political climate that arose in response to the economic crisis. Writers' demands for new entitlements from the federal government were being made at the end of a decade that saw a dramatic expansion of the federal government's role in regulating the economy. Franklin Roosevelt, the dominant political actor of the era, connected language of "freedom" and "liberty" to entitlement programs that aimed at economic security. Letter writers sometimes adopted New Deal catchphrases like "social security" or other elements of Rooseveltian rhetoric in their letters. An example is a letter from Erman Lockhart and Letha Pelton of the Workers Alliance of America local in Porterville, California. They complained about a California law prohibiting persons on relief from paying dues to organizations or engaging in political activity and asked the attorney general to come to the aid of those who were "ill-fed, ill-clothed, and ill-housed." A more subtle reference came from J. B. Roarke, whose complaint that his business was ruined when he was subjected to involuntary "fever treatments" was typed on the letterhead of the "New Deal Tire Shop." Beyond Roosevelt, popular political culture was also influenced by opposing voices that articulated sharp, class-based attacks on elites and populist demands for redistribution of wealth or attacks on privilege (Brinkley 1982). Thus, while some of the claimed rights seem exaggerated or extravagant given the relatively narrow range of political discussion in American society today, writers around 1939 could expect some of their imaginative claims to have some familiarity and resonance with government officials.[1]

Writers responded to that dynamic political culture not by simply mimicking what they heard but by transposing elements of familiar rhetoric to make expansive and sometimes very creative claims for novel entitlements that law had not yet recognized. I use terms like *novel* or *expansive* to describe claims for entitlements that were not at that time recognized as entitlements in official law or by responding government officials. When I say that writers were being "creative," I do not mean that writers were being *entirely* original or expressing ideas that came out of nowhere. I find that writers drew upon a wide range of normative resources, some peculiar to their time period, some more universal. Their efforts were creative in that they picked from that broad range of resources to construct unique combinations of familiar persuasive claims and were able to relate those familiar and general elements to their unique predicaments. Writers often made some surprising and exaggerated analogies as they stretched familiar normative resources to cover novel claims. However, writers did not simply invent brand new rhetorical tropes. They could not have expected their claims to be persuasive if they were entirely alien or unfamiliar. Writers thus seem to have gravitated toward claims and metaphors that they expected their audience to be familiar with and thus perhaps also more likely to see as persuasive or worthy of attention.

I expect readers to have a variety of responses to the way the writers used claims about legal entitlements, particularly claims about "rights." While some writers provided shocking accounts of egregious violations of core rights, there are also a substantial number of letters that make more fanciful claims in response to relatively minor deprivations. Looking at these rights claims in isolation, skeptics might say that the primary lesson that emerges is that using rights rhetoric to express demands is futile and thus a waste of time. For skeptics, the many claims about broad but unprotected rights would confirm that America's obsession with rights gives people shockingly unrealistic understandings of how rights actually work. I will reject such conclusions in chapter 4 and chapter 5, arguing that the unrequited rights claims can be evaluated more favorably in light of other features of the letters. Taking a broader view will eventually reveal that writers who made imaginative rights claims had a sensible understanding of legal and political processes. While they understood that claims about "rights" have a certain rhetorical force in American political culture, they also understood the limitations of legal argumentation and legal processes.

First Amendment

Freedom of Speech

The centrality of freedom of expression today as a core element of American constitutionalism makes it easy to imagine that free-speech protections have always been there, as part of an unbroken tradition that stretches back to Jefferson or Madison. Reality is more complicated. The Supreme Court did not begin hearing free-speech cases until the first decade of the twentieth century. Before then, judicial protection for free speech was nearly unheard of, despite the fact that state and federal government sometimes engaged in efforts to suppress "speech" in ways quite shocking by today's standards.[2] The first wave of Supreme Court cases involved constitutional challenges to criminal prosecutions for radical political speech during and in the decade following World War I (e.g., *Schenck v. United States*, 249 US 47 [1919]; *Gitlow v. New York*, 268 US 652 [1925]; *Whitney v. California*, 274 US 357 [1927]). In that first wave of landmark cases, the court consistently sided with government, upholding long jail sentences for people who spoke in favor of unpopular political ideas. Before the 1930s, American courts also routinely used injunctions to limit the communication and protest activities of labor organizations (Forbath 1991;

Orren 1991). The court had begun to shift in the years leading up to 1939 and established some legal protections for free expression. For example, just before the CRS was founded, the court struck down a city ordinance that prevented Jehovah's Witnesses from distributing literature (*Lovell v. City of Griffin*, 303 US 404 [1938]). The court was also in the process of recognizing picket lines as a constitutionally protected form of communication (*Thornhill v. Alabama*, 310 US 88 [1940]; *Senn v. Tile Layers Union*, 301 US 468 [1937]). Nevertheless, free-speech protections still remained weak by today's standards. The Supreme Court continued to allow federal prosecution and incarceration of alleged subversives long after the formation of the CRS (*Dennis v. United States*, 341 US 494 [1951]) and did not fully repudiate the earlier line of decisions upholding state laws targeting radical speech until 1969 (*Brandenburg v. Ohio*, 395 US 444 [1969]).

While judicial protections for speech were limited and unreliable in 1939, the letters processed by the CRS reveal that many people saw free speech as a core, inviolable constitutional right that merited protection from federal officials. Despite the uneven history of rights protections, letter writers tended to portray perceived interference with free expression as a surprising aberration from a norm of broad respect and protection for free expression. Those writers who tried to explain the foundations of free-speech rights located the right in the broad formulation of the First Amendment's text, not in the more qualified pronouncements of the Supreme Court.

Eleven percent of the cases in my sample (95 of 879) include at least some reference to free speech or free expression. The claims about free-speech are diverse and scattered in subject matter. Writers complained that their rights to free speech were violated when they were unable to place Bibles in public spaces, to listen to Father Coughlin's anti-Semitic radio broadcasts, and to "sell liquor to Indians."[3] A writer named Dr. C. C. Probert wrote from Flint, Michigan, to complain about the Post Office Department's refusal to accept bulk copies of the *American Guardian*, a socialist newspaper that was critical of the New Deal (July 22, 1940). M. Mills of Ellicott City, Maryland, wrote to the attorney general to complain about a news story reporting that a man named Patrick R. Kiernan had been sentenced to three months in the New York State Workhouse for making an anti-Semitic speech (October 21, 1939). Some writers complained about local laws or legislative proposals that threatened freedom of speech, including complaints about a Cumberland, Maryland, law that banned pickets (Lee Pressman, March 20, 1939; C. E. Stutzman, December

31, 1940); a Fall River, Massachusetts, law that banned all leaflets that were not preapproved by the mayor (William Ross, April 26, 1939); and a proposed law in Cambridge, Massachusetts, banning all writings by Marx and Lenin (Maphtaly Levy, December 28, 1939).

Writers also reported instances where local government officials cooperated with private actors to limit free expression. One example is George Runyan of Lansing, Michigan, who wrote to the department to complain that a state judge had issued an injunction to prevent him from criticizing a Chrysler dealership. The dealership had sold him a car that burned oil, had "rotten retreads," and a clutch that had been "doctored with tin" (December 28, 1939). After the dealership refused to honor its verbal warranty, Runyan began putting signs in his parked car that were critical of the Chrysler Corporation and the dealership. One read:

Happy George is sad and glum
Bought a used Chrysler
His Guarantee
Wasn't worth a dum.

Failing to appreciate Runyan's poetry, the dealer was able to get a local judge to issue an ex parte restraining order forbidding Runyan to post any signs critical of the auto company. Runyan wrote that the judge who issued the order on behalf of the dealership had threatened to take his property if he failed to comply with the order. Runyan also complained that the dealership tried to get him fired from a construction job.

Runyan expressed surprise and outrage that his right to free speech could be curtailed so easily and with the aid of state actors: "Now it has been my belief that as long as a citizen obeyed the laws of the land . . . he was entitled to protection of his constitutional right of free speech and free press." The judge, Runyan claimed, was "prosecuting a person for what he says and he is trespassing on a persons civil liberties when he enjoins anyone from warning the public that a lying swindler is preying on the used car buyers of Lansing." It is striking here that legal language not directly relevant to his case ("prosecuting," "trespass") grows on Runyan's letter like mushrooms on a damp log.

While most writers supported and seemed to expect free-speech protections, some writers complained instead that there was too much speech rather than too little. Tyson Pearson wrote to request that all foreign-language publications (and radio addresses) be banned in order to protect against "our enemies both with and without our boarders." He also suggested that it should be made "treasonable to possess a letter press without appropriate license or to possess printed matter in a foreign language unless approved by the proper authority" (October 12, 1940).

One of the strongest patterns that emerges among the free-speech letters is a connection between free speech and labor organizations. Approximately one-third of the letters that mention free speech (31 of 95) also made claims about the rights of workers or about labor organizations. The work-related complaints focused on both government and employer efforts to prevent workers from speaking out. For example, C. C. McGee, a railroad trainman from Missouri, complained that his rights were violated when he was fired for speaking out about safety issues (April 7, 1939). Efforts by state and local governments to control the political and organizing activities of schoolteachers also led to some interesting complaints connecting free speech and labor. For example, W. Daniel Boyd complained that the City of Jacksonville, Florida, violated the right of schoolteachers to speak out by firing a group of teachers who had attended an American Federation of Teachers meeting (October 25, 1939). Boyd claimed that officials were "denying to the teachers the rights of assembly, and denying to them the right to speak freely on political topics." Boyd also made a constitutional argument for a federal interest in protecting the teachers, claiming that school officials had violated the "spirit" of the Constitution. The CRS was particularly hostile toward Boyd's claim. In an unusually detailed response, the CRS rejected outright the claim of a rights violation, stating that "it appears that you have freely exercised these rights" because the teachers were able to attend the meeting. The department's reassurance rings hollow given that Boyd had reported that forty teachers had been fired.

The frequent connections between worker rights and free speech is consistent with historical scholarship showing important links between labor organizations and the expansion of civil rights protection in the first half of the twentieth century. David Rabban (1997, chapter 2) has documented the crucial role of organized labor in the constitutional fights over free-speech rights earlier in the twentieth century. More directly on point, many of the lawyers who staffed the early CRS had participated in some early cases involving interference with labor rights. The Justice Department first became interested in reviving Reconstruction-era civil rights laws in some cases involving intimidation against unions that were brought just before the formation of the CRS (Carr 1947, 27–29; Elliff

1967, 73–86). The connections between labor and the creation of the CRS have also been explored with great insight by Risa Goluboff (2007), who traces important associations between labor and the development of civil rights from the 1930s to the 1950s. By looking at the legal strategies pursued by both government attorneys and the NAACP, Goluboff's account illuminates an alternative road not taken of a system of civil rights closely tied to labor. If those alternative pathways had continued to develop, the resulting system of free-speech protections might have resulted in a very different politics of freedom of expression today. After all, ordinary people are today more likely to have their ability to speak freely limited by sanctions from their employers than by sanctions from the government. Yet only government interference with speech is typically reachable under current judicial conceptions of the Constitution's general guarantee of "the freedom of speech."

It must also be noted that not everyone who associated free speech with labor was writing to support worker rights or labor organizations. Several letters instead complained that worker organizations were interfering with First Amendment rights. One writer complained that the Congress of Industrial Organizations (CIO) used claims of civil rights as a "cover" for terrorism and violence. That letter, which was signed only "A. Citizen," also expressed general doubts about the value of government protection of the right to free speech: "The quiet, real citizens, at home, are not out milling in mobs. They are not complaining about Civil Rights. It is always the agitators, the destroyers, the trouble-makers" (March 27, 1939). Another, over-the-top, letter came from Fred Hall (June 3, 1941), who urged that labor organizers be deported to Central America to work on the "Nicaragua canal" and that communists be sent to concentration camps. Such letters provide a reminder that efforts to unleash rights as tools of empowerment can easily provoke a backlash (Dudas 2008). Significantly, all of the letters that complained about too much free-speech protection included complaints about worker organizations. That backlash was likely inspired by the important advances in the legal rights of workers that Congress created during the 1930s.

Religious Freedom

Forty-three (5 percent) of the letters raised concerns about freedom of religion. The largest subcategory within this group (14 of 43) consists of letters about the Jehovah's Witnesses, who were subjected to a substantial number of violent attacks during the period covered here (Goldstein 1990, 45–47; Carr 1947, 15–17, 184–85, 196–97). As noted in chapter 2, CRS prosecutors brought some successful prosecutions against government officials who participated in these attacks. The nature of the attacks is captured in a letter from W. E. Bullard to Attorney General Francis Biddle (September 22, 1941). Bullard reported receiving a severe beating while canvassing in Fairview, Oklahoma, and described his unsuccessful effort to obtain help from local authorities. Bullard reported that the local prosecutor had told him that "he had no doubt as to the truth of both my, and my witnesses statements" regarding the attacks. However, the prosecutor had nevertheless told him that he would not bring charges because "public sentiment is so strong against your religion that I will not be able to get a jury that will convict."

Some of the writers who complained about violence toward Jehovah's Witnesses embraced American constitutional values in their letters. For example, Alice Townhill, who complained about an attack in Joliet, Illinois, wrote: "I have been one of Jehovah's Witnesses for ten years. While I don't salute the American or any other flag I have the greatest love for our flag and country and will not do any-thing contrary or against our country. But I notice the greatest flag-saluters are taking away our liberties which we cherished so much liberty of speech, of worship of Almighty God" (September 11, 1941). Curiously, Townhill also openly expressed her own form of religious intolerance even as she defended religious liberty. She complained that she had been accosted by a "Catholic Policeman" and asked pointedly: "Can the Romans do things in America that we Americans (100%) have no right to do? Please investigate before we Americans are sold to Rome."

There were also letters complaining that government officials were targeting other religious groups. Writers claimed that local officials were shutting down worship services or preventing people from preaching in public. A letter from Rev. B. Sumner in Lakeland, Florida, for example, posed a series of rhetorical questions related to efforts to shut down his gospel tent. Sumner's letter suggested that a local "ministerial association" was keeping his gospel tent from getting a permit because they were opposed to his "methods of worship." Sumner asked: "From constitutional rights is there any restrictions on preaching the gospel in any city without permits from city officials? . . . If the city will not give a permit, and I erect a tent in city, on property on which I have permission to erect my tent, am I subject to arrest, and imprisonment etc." (April 3, 1939). Another letter from Rev. M. D. Willet complained that the police had shut down a worship service in Little Rock, Arkansas, for allegedly disturbing the peace (October 27, 1940). Although Willet did not directly address the motives of the local officials, he did mention that the service had been attended by large numbers of both black and white citizens and that his sermon had focused on the need for black and white farmers to recognize their common interests in economic struggles. It is unlikely that Arkansas law enforcement officials were thrilled that Willet was spreading such messages.

Some letters alleged that local officials who targeted religious gatherings were in league with particular religious groups. For example, J. H. Tidwell and several other churchgoers from St. Louis signed a letter complaining that local police and judges had targeted them because they were Protestants in a city ward that was dominated by Catholics (July 15, 1940). Other worship groups were targeted for conducting services in private homes or apartments. A letter from Hattie Cochrane complained that police had arrested a man whose home was used for a worship service, "the charges being loud piano playing and singing" (August 28, 1939). Cochrane reported: "We have no church building in which to hold our meetings and cannot afford to build one as most of our people are on direct relief." Cochrane quoted the First Amendment's guarantees of the right to free expression and assembly as well as the privileges and immunities clause of the Fourteenth Amendment to support her claim that the arrest was not "lawful."

Government Procedures and Due Process

In my sample, complaints about the fairness or lawfulness of government processes are more common than any other broad category of rights claim. Twenty percent (146/710) of the writers reporting on incidents either invoked the phrase "due process" or made claims about "rights" that were connected to a government's failure to provide an appropriate or fair process for some decision of consequence. Many of the letters expressing concerns about process referred to specific procedural protections in the Constitution, such as the confrontation clause or the requirement for reasonable bail. Other writers complained quite generally about unfair or corrupt actions by government officials without tying their concerns to a particular constitutional or statutory provision.

Criminal Justice and Detention

Some of the most striking letters complaining about process were letters from or about persons who were in government custody. There are forty-eight letters from or on behalf of people in detention, including sixteen people in state psychiatric facilities and thirty-one in state jails or prisons. Writers complained about being framed by police and about convictions based on tainted evidence or forced confessions. Writers also complained about not being allowed to call supportive witnesses, about not being able to adequately defend themselves at trial, and in some cases about a failure of authorities to hold any trial proceedings at all.

The stories told by people in detention are often poignant. C. C. Harris wrote from Folsom Prison in California to report that he was wrongly sentenced to life in prison because he had been unable to afford a lawyer. He reported: "I must remain in prison, the victim of promises, concessions and illegal conviction simply because those higher up have elected to use every trick within their grasp to see that the right of due process of law is frustrated" (June 1, 1941). Mrs. Harry Hudspedth wrote from Chicago on behalf of her husband in prison. She claimed that his conviction was based on "circumstantial evidence" and rested more on "poverty than on facts." More specifically, she claimed that her husband could not afford to transport witnesses who would have helped his case at trial and had also had a very inexperienced lawyer (August 11, 1940).

One sizable group of letters about people in detention concerned persons committed to psychiatric facilities. While I cannot evaluate the mental health of the people writing the letters, it is important to note that many of the letters in this category are thoughtful, lucid, and moving. Some writers in this group told sad stories about family members conspiring to commit unwanted relatives to mental institutions. Many complain that the processes for involuntary commitment did not provide an opportunity for people to defend their interests or demonstrate their sanity. In some cases, writers alleged more systematic corruption involving government officials. A writer named Katharina von Dombrowski claimed that government officials were extorting money from new immigrants who were being unjustly identified as insane and then detained at a US Marine hospital on Ellis Island (November 29, 1939). Another example is a letter from Joseph Langhorne Walker, a former officer in the navy who had spent time in the psychiatric ward of a military hospital. Walker reported that a single doctor at the hospital had been declaring a large number of officers to be "criminally insane." Walker claimed that the doctor was working under orders to transfer more patients to the psychiatric ward so that various members of Congress could be accommodated in the officers' ward (July 13, 1939).

Complaints about bad police officers were one of the most common threads in the letters regarding due process and detention. One repeated variation concerned people who were harassed, detained, or falsely charged with crimes by corrupt local police departments targeting out-of-town drivers. For example, William C. Smith, an embalmer from Chicago, complained that he had been picked up by police officers while driving through Hialeah, Florida, early one morning. According to Smith, the officers detained him at the station, beat him with a blackjack and fists, and falsely accused him of drunk driving. He was later "railroaded thru Kangaroo court" and fined fifty dollars. When he asked the judge if he would be allowed to present evidence at the trial, the judge immediately declared him guilty. Interestingly, Smith did express a willingness to tolerate at least some forms of local government corruption, which he saw as widespread throughout the country. However, he urged the Justice Department to recognize a difference between "instances of grafting" in places like Chicago and more severe practices that are a "matter of personal, physical injury" (January 16, 1940).

Another report regarding corrupt policing practices in Florida came from Harry Levien of the Bronx. Levien claimed he was stopped by police in Miami after a minor traffic accident and falsely charged with reckless driving. Levien claimed the police had targeted him because he had New York license plates and was Jewish (January 10, 1940). Another story of false arrest and detention for drunk driving came from Pat Mohr of Eloise, Michigan. Mohr claimed that he had been sent to a mental institution without access to any legal process after he had been falsely arrested for drunk driving (December 2, 1939).

Other writers told of being targeted because police officers had personal grudges or because powerful private interests were in league with the police. For example, Shelby Toombs of Anguilla, Mississippi, wrote to President Roosevelt to report being harassed by the police and falsely accused of robbing a store and beating a man (May 14, 1940). Toombs reported that the police knew that he did not commit the crime. He explained that he was targeted because "I am a negro of 25" and "they don't like me." Toombs was not ultimately charged or kept in prison, but he did end up losing his job as a result of the initial accusation. In his letter,

Toombs placed a great deal of emphasis on a particular constitutional violation, a warrantless search of his home: "I was at work that Friday May 10 they came to my house and searched it and didnt even have a search warrant My wife was about 75 feet from our house there in the white lady kitchen cooking when they came. they no where she was working. But they didn't ask her nothing they just Broke in the house and searched everything they went all through her private peaces had them laying all over the floor when we come home and I no that ain't write." Toombs's account of the search provides a good example of the type of arbitrary police harassment reported in the letters.

Other writers reported even harsher encounters with police. Frank Duggan provided a six-page narrative of an encounter with "thugs" working in collaboration with the police in Detroit. Duggan claimed he had lost an eye after being slipped a "mickey" and beaten in a tavern (October 26, 1940). A more unusual story was related by Frances McKoney, who claimed that a false arrest in Silver Spring, Maryland, had led to the death of three of her dogs. McKoney explained that she was moving her twelve dogs "with a truck I had hired and paid cash for" and was taking one sick dog to the hospital.

> All of a sudden two great big Policemen drew up beside me and demanded that I come with them. They did not have any Warrant or Summons. . . . They let the driver of the truck beat and kill three of my dogs and then three the others in the Pound. I am still locked up Will you help me. The dog I was taking to the Hospital had saved my life once and I came 1100 miles to save his. . . . [M]y ill dog died a miserable death in some persons back yard from hunger cold and being beaten to death. . . . I was not allowed to even telephone and try and get someone to care for my dogs while I was kidnapped. (December 26, 1940)

Winton Church, who claimed police in Pontiac, Michigan, targeted him for his union activity, reported that he had lost his job as a mail carrier after the police framed him for drunk driving (July 12, 1939). An attorney named Stuart Kroesch reported an even harsher form of retaliation. Kroesch claimed that his client had been falsely charged with rape of his stepdaughter and sentenced to one year to life in prison. The motive, according to Kroesch, was that his client, a former police officer, had angered corrupt officials by breaking up a bootlegging ring (July 7, 1941).

Some of the letters complaining of corrupt practices by local governments came from people or groups making broad complaints about bad practices rather than people who reported a single incident where they were personally victimized. For example, Racene McGraw, representing a group called the Descendants of the American Revolution, sent the department a copy of a resolution concerning violations of the Constitution by police in Washington, DC. The resolution claimed that "more than 40% of all arrests are made without warrant or legal charge in three precincts of the city investigated by the Bar Association of the District" (June 17, 1939). Other writers made even more sweeping claims about corruption. Lee Jones wrote from Arkansas to complain about "a little town across the river from Fort Smith that reeks with a bad odor." According to Jones: "Law abiding citizens are picked up and incarcerated in this little jail, people who pass thru in the day time are fined for speeding, and those that drop in at the night clubs, or near them spend at least four hours in this fair city's stone house, which is a sordid excuse for a jail" (September 22, 1940). Viola Kendt wrote to complain about the corrupt mayor of Chicago. She claimed he "represents the red devil" and was in line with the "red jews" (September 19, 1940). Tillie Hubbard wrote to President Roosevelt to complain that Rochester, New York, was turning into "a hell on earth" and a "screaming hellhole". She claimed that the city was overrun with vice that the police could not control because they were "on dope" (March 31, 1939). Pearl Squires Olsen, of Thompson Township, Michigan, explored a similar theme, alleging that a "dope peddling sheriff" was at the center of a broad pattern of local corruption (March 11, 1939). Virginia Lambert wrote a very long letter from Pineville, West Virginia, detailing a pattern of boozing, prostitution, and general corruption by a town government run by family clique (April 7, 1939). Not all the complaints about local corruption involved booze or drugs, however. James Minnis, who claimed that Michigan was "ruled by outlaws," placed all the blame on a bad legislative apportionment (September 15, 1939).

Some writers complained more narrowly about particular government processes. David Curtis wrote from Chicago to complain about a monopoly granted to the Checker Taxi Company. Curtis claimed that the mayor and an alderman were major stockholders in the company, which had been taken over by gangsters during prohibition and was controlled by the Teamsters. He also stated that several officials affiliated with the company were on trial for federal tax evasion. Curtis asked the federal government to intervene and ensure that workers at the company could control their representatives through democratic processes (June 22, 1939).

One allegation of local "grafting" that did at least temporarily attract the attention of the CRS came from Thurman Reed Rigdon, who was in jail in Rockville, Maryland. Rigdon included a catalog of claims about violations of prisoners' rights and made allegations of bribery among judges and prosecutors. He wrote that it was a "common thing for a man with money to get his case fixed" by paying a fee directly to the judge or by getting a recommendation from the "head of the democratic committee" (May 2, 1942). Only one of Rigdon's allegations interested the CRS: Rigdon claimed that inmates were being forced to work in crews on the homes of state government officials. The notes in the file indicate that CRS head Victor Rotnem asked a staff attorney to look into that claim, but after a conversation with a Maryland official, the CRS lost interest in the case.[4]

Civil Process

A substantial group of the due-process-related letters raised objections about civil rather than criminal processes (31 of the 146 due-process letters). Some of the letters in this group claimed entitlements to government assistance in finding redress for largely private disputes. For example, a letter from Harry Reynolds of Detroit claimed that the state violated his due-process rights by granting his wife a favorable divorce settlement after she left him for another man. He also complained that the city had refused to prosecute his wife for perjury (September 23, 1940). Another writer, John McVeigh of Ft. Worth, complained that Texas had violated his rights by waiting two years before releasing his wife's estate in a probate hearing (March 22, 1939). A writer named L. E. Carpenter wrote three times from Los Angeles to complain that he was having difficulty obtaining compensation for damages caused by a drunk driver. Carpenter claimed that he could not recover damages in a civil case because the city's sloppy criminal prosecution had led to an acquittal of the driver (November 29, 1939; December 16, 1939; December 28, 1939). The letters about civil disputes also include claims from people seeking help from the federal government in cases involving disputes with employers or labor unions. Ben Copean of Baltimore wrote to suggest that the due-process clause of the Constitution protected him from being fined by a union (March 8, 1941). Eleanor Watjus, a nurse from Joliet, Illinois, wrote to demand that President Roosevelt help her after the American Nursing Association declined to provide legal assistance in a dispute with her supervisor (February 10, 1941).

Right to a Jury Trial

Writers also referred to the Constitution's provisions regarding juries when complaining about government procedures. These writers demanded that juries be given responsibility for making decisions in a variety of legal and administrative processes. One example is a letter from A. E. Elmer (January 14, 1940) that complained about being involuntarily committed to the Elgin State Hospital in Illinois. Elmer complained that he was imprisoned based on the testimony of two doctors rather than on a conviction by a jury. Mr. Elmer may have overestimated the likelihood that a jury would have been more supportive than the two doctors. His letter admitted that he had been committed after engaging in fisticuffs with his mother. (He explained he was "in a scuffle to protect myself from a threatening club which my mother intended to use on me after I pushed her through a doorway which she blocked.") However, other writers had more reason to believe that a jury of their peers would empathize and provide a favorable ruling. For example, Mrs. O. P. McCoy's letter explained that she and many other people were losing farms in foreclosure proceedings resulting from the escalating price of water rights in Tonasket, Washington. McCoy felt that "justice" required that questions related to foreclosure proceedings be decided by "a jury of our peers" (March 31, 1939). It seems reasonable for McCoy to expect a more favorable ruling if a jury drawn from the Okanagan Valley farming communities near Tonasket made decisions about foreclosures and debt restructuring.

Property Rights

Property rights were the only category of enumerated constitutional rights with a long tradition of aggressive judicial protection at the time of the CRS founding (see, e.g., *Prigg v. Pennsylvania*, 41 US 539 [1842]; *Dred Scott v. Sanford*, 60 US 393 [1857]). In my sample, fifty-four letters (8 percent of the incident letters) made claims related to the loss of property or "property rights." The property-rights letters provide a particularly interesting illustration of the ingenuity and expansiveness of the rights discourses used in the letters. Property rights today stand out as exceptions among the most familiar categories of rights in the United States because they are associated with conservative political causes. Property rights also seem more likely than other rights to be invoked by persons in relatively privileged positions rather than by people who lack material resources or are members of disfavored minority groups. This is because American courts have only recognized as "property rights" claims that are about maintaining existing entitlements, not claims for new entitlements for people who lack property or claims for egalitarian allocation of property.

Given these expectations, the pattern that emerges among the CRS letters is somewhat surprising. There are certainly some letters that express concerns like the ones associated with conservative property-rights causes today. Roy Schwing, for example, wrote to the CRS to complain that emergency relief legislation had violated his property rights by reducing his short-term profits on a securities investment (March 5, 1939). There are also writers whose claims to property rights might today be dismissed as the grumblings of relatively privileged, "not-in-my-backyard" suburbanites. For example, Marie James wrote several letters complaining about efforts by her town to widen the street in front of her house in Florida (June 19, 1939); Julia Smith wrote from Long Island to complain about the construction of an airport runway (October 28, 1939); L. L. Wells of Jacksonville wrote to complain that contractors working on a federal project had installed a power line near his home (April 6, 1939); Carl Miller wrote from Winnetka, Illinois, to complain that a local zoning decision had hurt his business interests (March 28, 1939); and Charles Moussie wrote to complain that a judge had given his wife too much property in a divorce settlement (March 29, 1939). Counting letters like these, I find that a third of the property-rights letters (18 of 54) express concerns that indicate that the writer is in the relatively privileged position of trying to protect an existing property entitlement.

Surprisingly, however, there are an even larger number of the letters mentioning property rights that came from people who claimed a relatively deprived status (20 of 54).[5] Many of the letters in the group of relatively deprived writers express visions of "property rights" that might, if implemented, transform property rights from conventional tools of maintaining existing entitlements to radical tools of empowerment and redistribution. This group includes letters from people who claimed property rights after losing access to land that they had been farming under leases (Bob Zagonel, February 14, 1939; G. R. Fox, August 20, 1939) or as squatters (L. B. Hampton, December 24, 1939). Other writers complained more generally that the government's tattered social safety net and failure to provide adequate relief from economic depression was itself a violation of the Constitution's guarantees of "property rights." For example, George Trinckes mentioned property rights in a complaint about the failure of California to provide him with unemployment benefits (April 3, 1939). Other letters portrayed large accumulations of economic power as a threat to the property rights of ordinary people. George Hurley of Bakersfield, California, argued that large companies were able to influence government policies regarding development and thus threatened democratic institutions (January 15, 1941). Georgiana Wines of Los Gatos, California, complained that the Ford Motor Company had violated her rights by selling her a lemon. Wines urged the government to limit the power of large corporations to use deceptive practices to interfere with her property rights (April 18, 1939).

These letters suggest that the association of property rights with conservative political causes or with claims of privilege and protection of the status quo is not inevitable but rather an artifact of historical developments and the selective responsiveness of government officials.[6] The writers' efforts to use property-rights language to express novel entitlement claims also provides another reminder that public conceptions of rights are quite malleable. Once again, people who felt a need to deploy rights language in political encounters did not also feel they had to confine their claims to rights that judges were likely to recognize as part of official law.

Beatings, Bombings, and Special Examinations: Racial Discrimination and Racist Violence

As noted in the first chapter, only 8 percent of the letters in my sample make any mention of race. The small number of letters does not indicate that rights violations related to race and racism were occurring less frequently than violations in other categories discussed here. More likely the people who experienced rights problems related to racism were less likely to write letters to the federal government than people experiencing other types of rights violations. In addition, my sample does not include all of the letters related to racism that the Justice Department processed during these years. There are also some letters related to peonage cases that were given a different file designation because they fell under a different criminal statute. Risa Goluboff discusses several such letters, written between 1936 and 1943, in an article and recent book (1999; 2007, chapter 2). Goluboff also reviews numerous letters that African Americans of that period wrote to the NAACP, complaining about workplace discrimination and other problems related to employment (2007, chapter 3). More generally, Goluboff provides an account of working conditions during the period that makes it clear that serious rights-related problems were pervasive.

The letters in my sample that do talk about race are some of the most compelling and relate some of the most disturbing stories of egregious rights violations. Many of the letters addressing race speak movingly and passionately about conditions in African American communities and problems created by police brutality and other forms of organized violence. For example, a letter from Baltimore signed only "A Reader" made a powerful appeal on behalf of children who were being brutalized in the criminal justice system. The author wrote: "Gov Ohannon is not doing anything about the killing of two High school youth 16–17 years old. . . . We pay our taxis I guess to have our children shot down like dogs. . . . [O]ne of the officers stated that he ought to put another ball in him after he had kicked the poor boy which died in the gutter" (September 30, 1939). A writer named A. P. Smith wrote to Roosevelt to complain about a near lynching in Coffeeville, Alabama. Smith reported that a young man was taken from his home in the middle of the night by authorities, including the mayor, who proceeded to "Beat Him Mercyful Leaving Him in the Woods Speechless." Smith reported: "His people not knowing what He Had Done with Him Hunting Him and Found Him Friday morning About 11:30 not Dead But not able to walk." Smith made a fairly general request: "So Now Dear President you know the conditions of the Southern States and too you have the Authority to tell your Helpers what Shall Be Done." Smith's letter also included a variety of biblical allusions and religious claims. He asked the president generally to "[s]ee after the Future of the colored People of the South Stop Being Beat and mobed up with out a cause you know god is not Pleased with no Such Doings I am a Poor colored man of the South trusting the Lord" (July 16, 1939).

The CRS was certainly interested in finding ways to address problems related to racism and racially motivated violence. One of the animating goals of the CRS was to be able to provide some federal response to police brutality and lynchings. However, the Justice Department's strategies and efforts were not significantly shaped or inspired by letters from individual citizens to the CRS. The kinds of lynching and police brutality cases that the department was willing to pursue attracted enough outside attention to alert the department before the department received complaint letters from individual citizens. Individuals who did write letters about lynching cases usually presumed that the Justice Department was already aware of reported incidents and their letters read as efforts to register protest rather than attempts to inform the department that a rights violation had taken place.

While the letters from individuals regarding racism did not often prompt the CRS to take action, the letters quite frequently provide moving descriptions of the costs that racism imposed on both individual citizens and communities. The letters also reveal how unchecked racial violence breached citizens' underlying sense of the social compact. Some examples can be found in several letters and postcards that protested the bombing of the home of Edna Hollands in Washington, DC, in April 1940. Hollands, a black schoolteacher who had been active in a worker organization and had recently moved into a white neighborhood, escaped injury when a bomb went off on the porch of her home. Several people wrote to protest the bombing, labeling such intimidation as "un-American" and "undemocratic."[7] A resolution from the Central Northwest Citizens' Association in Washington, DC, invoked the Declaration of Independence, stating that every American "in the pursuit of his happiness may select a home in the country or in a city and if in the city, a street in which he can live, and when this has been done, that house and home in that street becomes his castle." The organization resolved: "Any attempt to molest or disturb him or his place of abode, except by due process of law, is un-American and not civil." The group asked: "If the monster of un-Americanism can raise its fangs and strike on Harvard Street in the Capital of the Nation, where can we go to speak or complain of crime, intolerance, and injustice?"[8]

The CRS files also include numerous complaints from African Americans who had troubling encounters with police officers or corrupt police departments. Roxanna Harris wrote from Baltimore to report: "I have never in my 80 years . . . seen an officer nor a sheriff arrest people nasty as they do here in Baltimore." Harris described numerous incidents of rough treatment that she had witnessed from her apartment. She wrote to the CRS because she had recently been arrested in the middle of the night after she had called from her second story window to ask a group of officers engaged in a beating to stop disturbing the peace (September 21, 1939). Harris was released the next day without being charged but remained quite upset that the police would not return a flashlight that they had taken from her during the arrest.

The letters also provide an example of a relatively privileged white man who confronted racist police officials. Royal Wilbur France, a college professor from Winter Park, Florida, sent Murphy a copy of a complaint that he had sent to the chief of police in Orlando, Florida (June 13, 1939). France's teenage son had been arrested after he and some friends had observed the police as they raided a nightclub in one of Orlando's African American neighborhoods. France noted that an officer had told his son, "[Y]ou ought to have the shit kicked out of you." He wrote to the chief: "Such talk and conduct on the part of an officer does not tend to create respect for the law or its enforcers in the minds of decent people." Near the end of his letter, France calmly but forcefully challenged the chief's racist worldview and its effect on the chief's approach to policing: "I do not subscribe to your theory that a white man is not safe in a Negro section. I believe that few if any Negroes would raise a hand against a white man anywhere in this country unless under extreme provocation. . . . I wonder whether a Chief of Police who speaks scornfully of 'niggers' and 'nigger-town' is in a position to get the best results in law enforcement among the colored section of our population." France's cover letter to Murphy explained that he was forwarding a copy of his letter only to provide information and did not indicate that he wanted or expected the CRS to help him. Nevertheless, the CRS wrote back with the ritualistic statement that the department lacked jurisdiction to help with purely local affairs.[9] France's willingness to directly confront the police chief for his racist behavior is admirable and courageous. It is notable, however, that unlike Roxanna Harris, his resistance did not cost him a night in jail.

While there were many complaints about police brutality and racial violence, very few writers complained about workplace discrimination, one of the primary targets of the federal civil rights legislation that was eventually passed in the 1960s. The cases where writers did complain about employment discrimination make it clear that the reason there were few letters was not that employment discrimination was not occurring. The stories told in the letters show that problems of workplace discrimination were ubiquitous. A particularly revealing letter came from a white business owner. Alford Baker of Baker's Barber and Beauty Shop in Corrigan, Texas, wrote to report that a young white man who worked in a neighboring drugstore was threatening his "Negro porter" and telling him to leave "this part of town" (March 30, 1939). Baker declared that the porter "was very humble, and attends to his own business." Tellingly, Baker's expressed concern was solely for his own rights, not the rights of his employee. He declared that his hiring of a porter was "in common with most other business establishments of this nature" and that his business was "being placed at a great disadvantage" by the threats from the drugstore employee. Baker said he could not solve the problem by firing the porter and replacing him. The person making the threat had told Baker that he would chase away any black man employed in Baker's shop. Baker also explained that "this kind of work is considered work for a negro." He added: "I do not like the idea of a smart aleck boy running my business, when I am a native born American citizen." In an unusual move, the CRS wrote back with the claim: "Your complaint appears to have real merit." However, CRS made a shift away from Baker's focus on his own interests. The reply, signed by Brien McMahon, noted that Baker's employee "has certain rights guaranteed by the Federal Constitution" (April 6, 1939). Nevertheless, the department declined to help and instead directed Baker to seek help from local authorities.

Another incident in a case file provides a telling glimpse of workplace discrimination and the inadequacy of existing remedies. The case was brought to the CRS's attention by Lawrence Cramer, the executive secretary of the president's Fair Employment Practices Commission (FEPC). Cramer wrote in January 1942 to report that Mr. J. G. Lemon had complained about racial discrimination at the FBI. Lemon had been submitting job applications to the FBI since 1935. He was finally given a job interview an in April 1941 and complained to the FEPC after he was not offered a job. J. Edgar Hoover responded to the department's inquiry about the complaint with a memo to the attorney general's office. Hoover explained that Lemon was given a "special examination and interview" by a former FBI agent and claimed that Lemon "failed in the examination." The former agent had reported that "from the standpoint of personal qualifications, [Lemon] was in no way qualified for appointment as a Special Agent in this Bureau." Hoover did not specify the qualifications the Lemon lacked. Although he had already acknowledged that Lemon was given a "special" examination, Hoover simply asserted: "Mr. Lemon's application was accorded the same treatment as in the case of all other persons who possess the requisite qualifications." Lemon, who was a graduate of Northwestern University Law School and had been practicing law for several years, had told the FEPC that he did not believe he had failed the interview. Nevertheless, the Justice Department apparently accepted Hoover's sweeping claim that "[t]his Bureau has never during my administration discriminated against any applicant because of race, creed, or color." The department quickly sent Cramer a letter declaring that Lemon's complaint "is not justified" and noting that "the Bureau has a definite policy" against discrimination. The mere existence of such a policy was apparently enough to credit Hoover's broad claim that discrimination had never occurred at his agency.[10]

Such responses provide some clue about why more people did not feel motivated to write to the federal government to complain about workplace discrimination. There are, however, some indications that people sometimes took steps to combat discrimination through collective action rather than through government assistance. For example, a writer named Eugene Davidson forwarded to the Justice Department a letter that his group, the New Negro Alliance, had written to a five-and-dime store in Washington, DC. The group was announcing a boycott of the store, which served the African American community but refused to hire any black employees (December 11, 1939).

There are even fewer writers who complained directly about segregation. Only twelve letters even mention segregation, and just one focuses entirely on a complaint about segregation. In that letter, Francois S. Leroseau III wrote to President Roosevelt to express his "amazement" that he had discovered segregated men's rooms in the Federal Reserve Building (May 9, 1940). Leroseau, a Washington resident, compared segregation to the activities of the Nazis in Germany. The White House referred the letter to the CRS, which then sent it to the Federal Reserve, but the file does not indicate that the Federal Reserve responded to either the CRS or Leroseau.

It seems quite unlikely that the paucity of complaints about segregation means that people were not experiencing problems or that people accepted the practice as just. There was, of course, little reason for writers to expect the president or Justice Department do anything to end segregation. However, such expectations cannot by themselves explain the lack of complaints about segregation. I show below that many writers made imaginative and expansive claims about rights entitlements related to work or to direct relief from difficult economic times, claims that were also unlikely to be honored by government officials. Segregation was different from such issues of economic justice in at least one significant way, however. Neither Roosevelt nor any other political figure of that era was speaking out against segregation or otherwise providing a rhetorical foundation on which writers could creatively build as they challenged the practice. The concessions Roosevelt made on issues of race, such as the creation of the FEPC and modest efforts to combat discrimination in federal hiring, did not challenge the network of laws that segregated education, transportation, recreation, and other public facilities in the South. In contrast,

Roosevelt did speak out about economic justice, the need for fair distribution of the burdens of the economic downturn, and the need to share and expand economic opportunities. Letter writers could appropriate and expand such rhetoric to advance novel claims of economic entitlement. Some letter writers who addressed racism also appropriated Roosevelt's language of economic justice as they challenged racist practices. I discuss several such examples, as well as efforts to appropriate Roosevelt's anti-Nazi rhetoric, in chapter 4. The desperate need for economic relief might also be part of the reason writers did not more often make legal segregation the focus of their complaints.

Welfare, Economic Justice, and Positive Rights

In addition to complaining about government officials actively interfering with rights, some writers complained that government was not doing enough to help people to survive the severe economic downturn that had begun a decade earlier. Many of the writers making such claims used the language of rights, often constitutional rights, to claim entitlements to positive government action or attention. Such positive-rights claims, which were sometimes quite expansive, seem to fall outside of the mainstream of rights talk today. The protections that American courts have afforded to rights have largely been protections for *negative* rights to be free from government interference. Claims for positive-rights entitlements, such as "welfare rights," are certainly articulated by some activists, but such claims are less likely to be broadly honored by government authorities, particularly by judges.[11]

As already noted, the broader climate of expanding government social programs makes it easier to understand the apparent ease with which writers in the late 1930s could make imaginative claims of entitlement to government assistance. The letters in my sample were written at the end of a decade of economic crisis. The Great Depression had led to a dramatic growth in the capacity of the federal government to assist citizens. Most of the letters using rights discourse to demand government assistance were primarily concerned with Depression-related welfare and relief agencies.

Roosevelt's concept of the "Four Freedoms," which was immortalized in a set of famous Norman Rockwell paintings in 1943, is one enduring marker of the connection between the era's expansions in government programs and popular ideas about rights and government obligations.

Two of the four freedoms, "freedom from fear" and "freedom from want," seem relatively easy to associate with positive forms of assistance from the government. The influence of the Four Freedoms on the letters was not direct. Roosevelt did not introduce the phrase until 1941, after most of the letters in my sample were written.[12] Nevertheless, related shifts in elite conceptions of government responsibility toward citizens in an industrialized economy had been evident in Roosevelt's rhetoric since the early 1930s. The ease with which Roosevelt (and Rockwell) could popularize a link between "freedom" and growing entitlement programs reflects a political climate that provided fertile ground for imaginative and motivated citizens to express novel rights claims.

The articulation of novel claims to broad entitlements, and the use of rights language to express those claims, are nevertheless remarkable given the underlying reality of a federal government that could do very little to prevent or provide redress for egregious violations of core rights, including the right not to be lynched or murdered by state law enforcement officials. Letter writers were very likely aware that egregious incidents occurred in the United States. There is thus a gap between a political culture that fueled claims for expansive entitlements and people's lived experiences. Actual experiences with government are not likely to have created strong expectations that government officials would respond favorably to expansive claims for "rights." Moreover, there was not at that time a strong foundation for believing that framing demands as legal "rights" was an effective political strategy. The claims considered here were made long before *Brown* and other landmark cases created a compelling and inspiring model for using constitutional rights claims in campaigns for social change.[13] Nevertheless, many people were moved to express aspirations in the era's soaring rhetoric of rights and freedom rather than accept their difficult experiences as permanent or natural.

Welfare Rights and Welfare Agencies

Many of the writers who demanded rights to government assistance complained about the adequacy or fairness of existing government programs for economic relief. George Trinckes of Stockton, California, for example, wrote to the Justice Department to complain that the state was violating the Fourteenth Amendment by denying him unemployment and veterans' benefits because he was a single man with no children (April 3, 1939). Snowden Haslup of Baltimore, used a dictionary to make a point about welfare entitlement: "There isn't a Lawyer in this country that knows the definition of *Welfare.* Webster's dictionary—'prosperity and happiness.' The only prosperity and happiness in the Department of Public Welfare, Balt. Md . . . is among the High Salaries executive and workers are getting more than they could earn in private business there." Haslup complained that a local "political gang" had left "millions and millions" of dollars in relief funds unused, and he urged the federal government to step in to ensure a "distribution of Jobs and Wages." The angry letter noted: "I am 100% physical and normal as to ability and want a job, not charity" (July 24, 1939).

Numerous other writers echoed Haslup's concern about the way relief agencies treated recipients of government benefits. In particular, some writers challenged laws that limited the activities of persons receiving relief by placing conditions on receipt of relief money. One example is a letter complaining about a California law prohibiting persons on state relief from owning more than one car, paying dues to any organization, or engaging in any political activity. The letter, from Ermon Lachart and Letha Pelton of the Workers Alliance local in Porterville, California, contended: "By what right and whose authority does the state legislature intimidate the rights of our citizens. . . . It seems plain that a club is held over the heads of the state relief clients, taking away the necessities of life from their families because of any political belief, or union activities. After all the Bill of Rights is still part of the constitution even if some of our lawmakers is not aware of the fact, that it applies to the unemployed as well as the more fortunate" (February 25, 1940). Another example is a letter from John S. Barbara of New Orleans complaining about laws that placed limits on the political activities of WPA workers. Barbara complained that "this is deprivation of our rights as an American citizen"(April 2, 1939).

Other letters told stories of people running into very serious troubles in connection with their interaction with relief agencies. For example, Mrs. William H. Smith reported that a friend, Earl J. Berry, was sentenced to six months in jail as a result of a miscommunication with a California relief agency. The agency had paid for some repairs to Berry's car in exchange for Berry's promise to leave California and return to his home in Pennsylvania. Shortly after making that agreement, however, Berry obtained a job in California. According to the letter, Berry quickly returned to the agency to report on his change of plans and "straighten up" the situation. Unfortunately, after a series of bureaucratic miscommunications, Berry was charged with larceny for taking the money without living up to his agreement to leave the state. In the end, Berry lost both his freedom and his long-sought-after job (February 19, 1940).

Another complaint about running into problems with relief officials came from William Bork, who had traveled from Pennsylvania to San Diego in search of work. Bork was frustrated in his efforts to obtain help from Pennsylvania welfare officials as he tried to stay in contact his wife back home. He claimed that the Pennsylvania officials had encouraged him to go to California to search for work and had promised to take care of his wife while he was gone (May 12, 1941). Bork complained that they had "bare faced lied to" him. After being told by the CRS that the matter was not within federal jurisdiction (July 19, 1941), Bork wrote back to express a broad entitlement to obtain justice from the federal government. Bork explained that he had already contacted numerous state and local officials and that he had been constantly "told to go from one to the other." Bork pleaded: "So being this to be a Dept. of Justice I am writing to you giving facts just as they are. . . . I don't know whether the commissioners are state or federal. Should this matter when it comes to an injustice?" (July 28, 1941).

Some of the most distressing claims about treatment from welfare officials are in letters about children being removed from families. These letters often asked the federal government to intervene because local officials were corrupt or untrustworthy. A letter from Mr. and Mrs. Leonard Griffin of Los Angeles claimed that the couple had been coerced into giving up two of their five children to state custody. State officials told the Griffins that the state would take away all five of their children if they did not volunteer to give up at least two. Their letter asks Roosevelt: "We would like to know what right Mrs. Richardson, a probation officer, has to do such without going to court. We would like for you to step in and help us get our children back" (August 16, 1940). The Griffins also claimed that they had the means to support all of their children and that officials like Richardson were breaking apart families simply to make work for themselves. That last claim was echoed by Anna Hopson of Chicago, who wrote that many children were taken away from good parents by state welfare officials for "trumped up" reasons (January 12, 1940). Lonnie Griffith of Klamath Falls, Oregon, reported that social workers had taken away his two sons because he had been unable to get off of relief (March 30, 1939).

There is also one poignant letter from a citizen who felt that welfare officials were asking for too much rather than providing too little. Horace Howard, an elevator operator from St. Louis, was arrested for failure to support his twelve-year-old daughter. Howard, who had been separated from his wife for six years, claimed that he had always provided support for his daughter from his salary each week. ("I have never refused my daughter at no time. I have helped her at all times.") Nevertheless, he was arrested and convicted of nonsupport. (Howard claimed that he had not been allowed to show his receipts for prior support at his trial.) Now on parole, Howard was ordered to pay five dollars a week from his wages in order to avoid additional jail time. However, Howard's salary was only thirteen dollars per week, and he maintained that he could not pay the full required amount while still paying for his own food and a place to live. Howard pled with President Roosevelt to provide some help: "I really dont want to go to jail any more. I never been arrested before. I'm really afraid of jail. I do not want to go there again" (September 30, 1940).

Other letters to the CRS complained that the stigma of being on relief resulted in harsh treatment from a variety of government officials. James H. Porter wrote from Fontana, California, to challenge the way state and local officials defined "vagrancy" and used threats of arrest to forcibly relocate migrating workers. Porter explained that he had been arrested for vagrancy and forced to leave town simply because he was a single person looking for work. Noting, "I had a place to sleep, plenty to eat," Porter asked, "Is that law or justice to me?" Porter, told that he would be given a six-month jail sentence if he did not leave town, asked whether he could himself charge the sheriff with a crime for "forcing me out, when I had food and shelter, and out on the hobo for vagrancy" (March 20, 1939).

Not all of the letters that mentioned relief or welfare were supportive of government programs that helped poor or unemployed persons, however. In one of the most mean-spirited letters in the sample, Louis Nally wrote to Murphy to complain about an African American woman in his apartment building. Nally, a self-identified disabled veteran, made claims that resonate with modern political constructions of the stereotype of "welfare queens." Nally emphasized repeatedly that the offending woman and her two children were "on relief" as he rattled off a litany of racially charged complaints about her selling "doped" cigarettes and allowing a white man to stay overnight (June 24, 1939).

Economic Rights and the Right to Employment

The CRS also processed a number of complaints involving the "right" to work, earn a living, or otherwise participate in economic life. In some cases, these claims were about relatively narrow rights. George Ruzicka wrote from New York City to ask whether he had the right to break his employment contract in order to take a higher-paying job (undated, April 1939). Other writers were more expansive in their entitlement claims. Alex Gast of the Gast Brewing Company complained that he had been forced by the bankruptcy trustees to relinquish the presidency of his company. Gast's letter expresses his broad sense of entitlement to government assistance with his business dealings. He bitterly noted that the government did not provide any financial assistance for breweries that were hurt by prohibition: "The Government deprives me of my lawful property without compensation. . . . The Government (R.F.C.) denied my brewery financial aid, that would have been granted in any other industry, when we should have had preferred rights" (December 31, 1940).

Other writers claimed rights with broader application. Irving Amos, a native of Baltimore, had traveled to Delaware, New Jersey, and Pennsylvania looking for work. After running out of money, Amos had been told by Pennsylvania officials that he had to go back to Maryland. The heart of his letter is a series of expansive claims about his right to search for work and secure employment:

> Now as an American citizen don't I have the right to go into any state if I think I can earn a honest decent living for myself and family. . . . According to the laws of our land a man and his family has if I am correct a Perfect right to go where he thinks he can earn a living. Now what I want to know if they can compel me to live in Baltimore and if I want to live somewhere else as I am sick an tired of this Relief and W.P.A. stuff and being compelled to live here if I want to go to some other state or private industry. (July 19, 1939)

In reply, the CRS explained that it could not answer Amos's questions and was not allowed to give legal opinions to anyone but the president (August 1, 1939).

Some writers expressed claims about a right to work or find a job as they described unsuccessful efforts to get themselves off relief. An example is a letter written to Franklin Roosevelt by Hattie Mae Smith of Oak Lawn, Illinois. Smith's letter invokes the Bill of Rights to support her complaint that local authorities refused to issue a permit for her to open a small business. Smith explained that she was living "on relief" with her sister and her sister's "crippled" husband who was unable to work. The family had put together some savings and built an addition onto their home to open a small "tea room" as a source of income. However, when the project was finished, the president of the local village board denied them a permit to open the shop. The letter used language about constitutional rights to support her claim that the government had responsibility to provide economic opportunities. She asked rhetorically: "Under the bill of Rights haven't we a right to earn our own living selling just good food, ice cream, and pop?" (July 18, 1940).

Another writer asserting a right to operate a business was Nathan Fried. Fried claimed that state officials were preventing him from opening a store in Wilmington, Delaware, because his proposed location was in a "restricted area." However, Fried claimed that other stores, including Woolworths, were already operating in the same area. To support his legal claim to government assistance, Fried mentioned the Bill of Rights. He also noted that the existing merchants in the area did not fly the American flag. He remarked, "I would appreciate Justice that I know is Justice than depend on the crooked justice that operates here." Like Hattie Mae Smith, Fried claimed that he was hoping to use the business to support himself and get off relief (February 5, 1940).

Another group of letters making work-related rights claims were complaints about efforts to attack or intimidate workers for union activities. Many letters in this group indicated that government officials were colluding with private employers to intimidate unions, and some did get at least some attention from the CRS. An example is the case of Morris Levin, an attorney who wrote to complain about intimidation in connection with organizing efforts at the Rice-Stix Dry Goods Company in St. James, Missouri. Levin reported that International Ladies' Garment Workers' Union officials had been threatened and that a local marshal and the president of the Chamber of Commerce were working together to run union organizers out of town (September 3, 1940). The CRS did honor Levin's request that they forward the letter to the US attorney in St. Louis.[14] However, there is no indication in the file of a further investigation into the charges.

Another letter, from Frank McCulloch of Chicago, charged that federal officials were interfering with worker rights. McCulloch was the secretary-treasurer of the Workers' Security Federation of the USA, an organization of WPA and unemployed workers that McCulloch described as an alternative to the more "communistic" Workers Alliance. He claimed that one member of his group was detained, questioned by local police and an FBI agent, and warned not to engage in any labor activism in Cairo, Illinois. He declared: "We resent and we protest against this concerted effort of federal and local authorities to prevent unemployed and WPA workers from exercising their legal rights. Such activities border on terrorism an intimidation of the worst sort" (June 26, 1941).

A letter from Joseph Coane of Chicago demonstrates some of the broad-ranging effects of coordinated efforts to suppress union activity. Coane claimed that he had been fired from his job as a police officer after he had given a prolabor pamphlet to a man who turned out to be a friend of the chief of police. Coane later learned that he had been under surveillance by department leadership. The department had targeted Coane because he had refused to join other officers in a violent attack on some striking workers. Coane wrote that he had initially won a lawsuit for reinstatement but then lost an appeal at a higher court.[15] Coane claimed that the appeals court that ruled against him was corrupted by machine politics (July 7, 1939).[16]

Of course, the letters in my sample cannot provide a full overview of the type and volume of complaints about interference with union activity or retaliation against union members. Many persons or organizations would have brought such complaints to the National Labor Relations Board (NLRB) rather than to the White House or Justice Department, so they would not have been processed by the CRS. In some instances, however, writers asked the Justice Department to extend the Wagner Act's protections to workers who were excluded from the law, such as public employees. John Fewkes, for example, wrote to complain about interference with efforts to organize a teachers' union in Chicago. Fewkes acknowledged that the Wagner Act did not cover public school teachers. However, he suggested that the CRS should be interested in interference with teachers' right to organize because the city was violating the "spirit" of the Wagner Act (April 11, 1940).

Like workers' free-speech-related claims, the many claims about rights to work or to organize are met by a smaller number of letters expressing a backlash against worker rights. Forty-four letters gave voice to resentment or anger about union activities that allegedly interfered with rights. Many of the writers expressing resentment about unions articulated their own broad conception of rights to engage in economic activity. A typical example is Morris L. Hall of Westford, Massachusetts, who began by noting that the right to work "is, I believe, generally admitted to be a basic civil liberty in our democratic society." He claimed that any form of picketing was interference with civil liberties because picketing was inherently intimidating. He therefore urged that the CRS to protect the right to work by preventing workers from picketing (March 29, 1939).

A writer named L. G. Goodrich wrote from Clinton, Michigan, to question whether Frank Murphy's public commitment to protecting rights was consistent with his support for worker organizations: "You advocate civil liberty then your action belies the whole of it. Does it mean civil liberty for every boy to be kicked out of a job unless he pays John Lewis the privilege to belong to CIO? Is it civil liberties for a gang of CIO strong arm cohorts to parade with clubs to bull dose and beat down any free man that dares to go to work without their consent? What are you doing to guarantee their rights under the constitution of the US?" (June 8, 1939).

Some writers invoked the Constitution or its framers in support of their antiunion complaints. May Massing said that the Constitution provided the justification for efforts by state officials to impede John Lewis and the United Mine Workers. She wrote: "Thank God for Gov. Chandler who is giving the miners their Constitutional right—the right to work—stop that madman Lewis" (May 19, 1939). Fred Hall wrote to encourage the government to deport Harry Bridges, the president of the International Longshore and Warehouse Union. He complained that the government was not treating immigrant trade unionists harshly enough and insisted that the Constitution's framers would have shared his concerns: "Do you suppose even one single man who signed the Constitution of these United States even dreamed there would come a time when Civil Liberties would be protecting the various branches of the subversive element which is trying desperately by every trick and device to undermine and destroy this free country" (June 3, 1940). A letter from Paul Cowles of Oakland, California, invoked constitutional principles to deny the legitimacy of the Wagner Act (October 9, 1939). Cowles wrote: "The purpose of the strike and picketing TO PREVENT PLANTS FROM OPERATING AND MEN FROM WORKING IS ANARCHISTIC, COMMUNISTIC, AND REVOLUTIONARY notwithstanding the WAGNER ACT insofar as its attempts to abridge the rights of personal liberty GUARANTEED BY OUR CONSTITUTION as the CONSTITUTION STILL STANDS. IT HAS NOT BEEN REPEALED." Cowles complained that the federal government was not prosecuting longshore workers who refused to cross picket lines set up by the Dock Checkers Union's in Newport News, Virginia. His broad sense of entitlement to government legal action to protect his "rights" was not diminished by the fact that the requested government action would presumably interfere with the rights of other people.

Other, less florid letters focused on some of the practical consequences of union activity. Louis Becker, the owner of an interior design company, forwarded to the CRS a letter of protest that he sent to the Illinois Division of Unemployment Compensation. The letter claimed that unions had targeted Becker after he refused their attempts at "extortion" and expressed concern that union power was corrupting local government officials (October 9, 1939). Another example is Walter Spilky, who complained that his efforts to find employment for Chicago's homeless population were being thwarted by unions representing workers who were not US citizens (July 8, 1940).

Positive Free-Speech Rights

In addition to making claims for positive rights related to economic security and work, some writers made claims for positive rights associated with free speech. Such writers went beyond complaining about interference with speech and instead complained that government was not doing enough to make guarantees of free speech meaningful. They then demanded that government take positive steps to empower speakers and make sure their views were heard. Claims of a positive right to free speech are mostly alien to the American constitutional system. The Supreme Court has confined the general phrase "the freedom of speech" in the First Amendment by recognizing rights against government interference but not any entitlements to assistance to make expression meaningful. Nevertheless, some letters articulated a vision of free-speech rights that assigned nonjudicial officials responsibility for taking steps well beyond what judges were willing to do to secure rights to expression and rights to protest.

To justify such demands, writers pointed out that a mere lack of interference from government was no guarantee that government officials would listen to a citizen's voice and provide an appropriate response. Writers also expressed doubts about the value of free speech absent such government assistance. An example is Emily Brunner of Springfield, New Jersey, who complained that a botched vaccination caused her dog to die of rabies. Brunner acknowledged that she had been able to speak out about her veterinarian without encountering any government restraints. She complained, however, that her right to speak had little value because the right had not led to any meaningful response: "for what it has educated me it means specifically nothing" (March 29, 1939). Along the same lines, M. R. Silvernail of New York complained that the right to free speech was "worthless" unless government provided better redress for violations of that right (March 28, 1939). George Richter wrote from Savannah, Georgia, to ask the federal government to intervene after the Georgia state legislature had refused to accept a petition that he had filed (June 16, 1939). Not surprisingly, writers' efforts to convert a right against government interference into a right to be listened to did not get them anywhere with the officials at the CRS.

Voting and Elections

A final group of letters expressed concern about voting and elections. Many of those letters made straightforward complaints about being denied the right to vote. One striking example is a letter to Eleanor Roosevelt from Frances McNutt. McNutt reported that officials in Compton, California, would not allow her father to vote because he could not read or write. McNutt was particularly upset that her father had been "humiliated" by the experience. Her moving letter connects her father's life of hard work and honesty to his right to vote: "I will admit Mrs. Roosevelt, that my father can neither read nor write, but he is a Human Being and has feelings which can be hurt the same as you and I" (August 23, 1939). McNutt's sense of the importance of the right to vote and the personal feelings that people associate with official recognition of rights is echoed in numerous other letters.

In all, thirty-nine letters in the sample of incident letters raised concerns about interference with the right to vote. The range of general complaints was quite broad. Eight letters complained about rules or processes that prevented the names of communist candidates from appearing on ballots. Writers also complained about the failure of states to allow migrant workers to vote (Albert E. Campbell, October 19, 1939; Ida Helpingstein, October 19, 1939; Glen Anderson, October 20, 1939), legislative proposals to prevent relief workers from doing campaign work (John S. Barbara, April 2, 1939), and the effects of the poll tax (Harry B. Flaharty, December 28, 1939).

Rights Claiming and Democracy

The wide variety of broad and imaginative rights-related claims that writers included in their petitions to government officials is one of the most striking things about the letters. The rights claims were expressed through a very conventional form of political participation (writing letters to elected officials), quite often using conventional legalized language about rights or the Constitution. Nevertheless, the conventional elements of the letters clearly did not confine writers to making claims that were conventional in substance. The restless creativity of the letters and the tendency of writers to go beyond officially recognized rights demonstrate that the choice to employ rights talk did not limit people to claims about rights already legitimized through official recognition by judges or rights that were likely to be protected by federal officials. The letters also show how rights are worked into political processes that take place outside of courtrooms and demonstrate that people could quite comfortably inject the language of rights into the process of making political demands on elected officials. Rights, whether real or imagined, were obviously woven quite deeply into the fabric of conventional political processes.

As they made claims regarding specific rights connected to actual incidents, writers also sometimes revealed their general thoughts about the relationship between rights and democratic governance. Consideration of such comments provides a fitting close to this chapter's discussion of the variety of creative rights claims expressed by writers in these everyday encounters with government officials. Writers' comments about democracy make it clear that they did not see rights and rights claiming as being separate from, alternative to, or in conflict with ordinary democratic political processes. In fact, the writers who spoke to the issue all seemed to reject the view, common among legal scholars, that there is an inevitable tension between rights protection and democracy. Scholars often conceptualize rights as limitations on the power of otherwise majoritarian institutions — that is, as "trumps" (to use Dworkin's famous phrase) that are needed to prevent democratic majorities from tyrannizing minorities (Dworkin 1977). The alleged tension between rights and democracy also has roots in institutional understandings of the American separation-of-powers systems. During the last half of the twentieth century, scholars portrayed the capacity of the Supreme Court to protect rights as a "counter-majoritarian" and thus "deviant" part of an otherwise democratic system.[17] As a result, scholars sometimes set up a sharp contrast between ordinary "democratic" politics and guarantees expressed as rights that act as limits on what elected officials can do.[18]

Significantly, this seeming tension between rights and democracy is never expressed in any of the letters to the CRS. Writers who gave voice to their thoughts about rights and democracy invariably saw rights as being consistent with, and often essential to, what they understood and articulated as "democracy." Letter writers were quite comfortable linking "democracy" to protection of rights and in particular to the protection of the rights of unpopular minorities from majority tyranny. For example, when David Ruja wrote to Murphy to protest the prosecution of communist William Schneiderman, he included the following plea: "I believe that civil liberties are the distinguishing mark of American democracy. I believe furthermore, that the Bill of Rights was to apply to the rights of all Americans—or that it will prove a cheat for all. I do not accept the dangerous proposition, now being broadcast, that civil rights can be withheld from this or that dissident minority at the pleasure of those who may have the power to do so" (July 20, 1940). Other examples include a letter from Louise Bransten to President Roosevelt complaining about various attacks on minorities, stating that "the best Americanism is a firm allegiance to the principles of Democracy," which included protection against "anti-minority feeling" (July 1, 1940); a letter from Burrill Freedman of New York complaining about antiunion violence in Rockford Illinois stating: "It appears to me that the majority of the people can never feel quite safe about their rights, unless they see the rights of minorities being protected" (June 26, 1940); and a letter from Andrew Loewi, who argued that protecting New York retailers from anti-Semitic pickets was important not just to protect the economy but also to preserve "ideals of democracy" (April 21, 1939).

Several letters urging the president to veto the anti-alien Smith Bill also commented on democracy and rights. Opponents of the bill often expressed concern that aliens were being targeted as a disfavored minority. Examples include Marguerite Senour, who wrote that supporters of the anti-alien Smith Bill were "trying to destroy American Democracy" and "insult our flag" (June 5, 1940), and Aimo Jamsen of the Finnish Workers Club of Baltimore, who argued that "the defeat of the 'anti-alien' bills is essential to the continued existence of our American democracy" (July 20, 1940).

Other comments about the relationship between rights and democracy can be found in a group of letters that the department received in response to the initial announcement that the attorney general was creating a Civil Liberties Unit. F. J. Smith of the American Association for Economic Freedom pointed out that protection of civil rights is "very necessary in the preservation of our democracy" (March 20, 1939); Harold Carlson of the International Union of Mine, Mill and Smelter Workers in Rodeo, California, saw the CRS as meeting "the needs of our democracy" (March

13, 1939); Orval Brunk connected protection of civil liberties to "national democratic ideals" (September 9, 1939).

In contrast, there is not a single letter in the sample complaining that protecting the rights of minorities or other disempowered persons was somehow inconsistent with "democracy." Even among the many letters expressing hostility to rights protection or arguing that specific rights protections went too far, there is not even one that claims that protection of minority rights is inconsistent with democracy or democratic values, or even that the majority deserves final say over the scope of minority rights. Writers thus did not see efforts to get government attention through novel or imaginative rights claims as a way of short-circuiting democratic processes. They instead viewed the protection of rights as an important government responsibility in a democratic society and the demand for rights protection as a normal part of democratic participation and constitutional citizenship.

The Common Place of Lawyering

*Using Legal and Constitutional Arguments
to Support Novel Civil Rights Claims*

On October 28, 1941, Robert Wright wrote to President Franklin Roosevelt from a jail in Baltimore to complain about an injustice. Wright explained that he was convicted and sent to prison for a burglary that he did not commit. Wright began his letter by noting, "I am friendless, poor, and colored." He proceeded over the course of two pages to provide information about his case and make a desperate plea for help.

Like many people whose letters were processed by the CRS, Wright explained that he did not have specialized knowledge of law: "I have sir, very little knowledge of law. None to speak of." Despite that disclaimer, however, Wright seemed to know quite a bit of about the legal issues in his case. Wright supported his argument by referring to three constitutional provisions and citing four Supreme Court cases. Wright's knowledge of the legal materials allowed him to state confidently that the law had not been followed in his case: "I do know I am illegally in prison. I do know I were not dealt with by law or given any the constitutional rights due me as a human in my case." Significantly, Wright remained confident even though judges had rejected his position more than once. (Wright had been convicted in state court, and his appeal to a lower federal court had failed.) Wright insisted that he lost "not because I haven given facts or true particulars but because I have no attorney to prepare or present my appeal." Wright insisted: "Sir, no court or judge can denied me should I be given a fair review" and "All I am asking is a chance because I am innocence and because no crime has been proven against me."

Even though he knew enough law to cite supportive cases and was confident that his legal position was strong, Wright did not rely exclusively on legal arguments in his letter. Wright instead focused much of the letter on more personal appeals to Roosevelt's conscience. He wrote, for example: "As a human I have a right to know why I am illegally kept in prison. Your Honor. As the father of the United States, I beg thee. Just to have the proceeding of my case read to you and if you can fine anything in that proceeding by law that prove me guilty of this charge in which I am accused I am willing to spend not eight but the rest of my life right here at the hardest labor. All I am asking Sir, is a fair chance as I have not been given one all along." After two weeks without a reply, Wright wrote a second, more urgent letter (November 13, 1941). Wright continued to make his appeal in clear and direct terms: "Please Sir, don't ignore my plead. Every one else has and for that reason I am appealing to you. . . . Sir. I am not writing to you because I want mercy or forgiveness but because I am innocence and because this crime has not been proven against me and because I believe I am entitled to a fair trial." Wright again focused on his lack of resources as the reason he could not get fair treatment:

> I know I cant under the circumstances fight for constitution rights because now I understand that such cost money. I hope I can as a human ask you sir to protect my human rights since I am powerless to help myself other than to appeal to you such as I am trying to do. Sir, I have not the knowledge and other means to put up a letter as should be to you or the U S Supreme Court and I feel, Sir, that my ignorance of such has cause me my eight months fight for my rightful due freedom.

Wright also emphasized that his problems, while of tremendous importance personally, would not require much effort or attention from the president: "I would not be but a very little cause to the state and a very little trouble to you to review the conflicting evidence and testimony presented at my trial."

Wright's letters were attempts to persuade the White House to provide assistance in correcting a perceived injustice. One particularly striking feature of the letters is that Wright combined several distinct rhetorical strategies. Those overlapping strategies create some tension within the letter. Wright says that he needs help because he has no knowledge of law yet then quotes in detail from relevant legal materials. He expresses a realistic understanding that law does not treat everyone equally (rights "cost money"), yet he also says things that suggest an abiding and idealistic faith that law works to ensure justice. He expresses the unwavering conviction that his legal arguments were correct despite having lost in court, yet he also adds a variety of additional persuasive claims that do not appear to have anything to do with his legal position, including efforts to establish his good faith, pleas for pity, and direct appeals to the president's conscience.

Wright's use of a mixture of persuasive strategies is quite typical of the letters in the CRS files. This chapter and the next describe and analyze the broad range of persuasive strategies that writers in my sample used in their letters. The goal of the two chapters is to explore these persuasive strategies in order to address two questions: (1) What were the letter writers' underlying ideas about law and legal processes? and (2) How did their ideas shape the relationship among law, rights, and ordinary politics in these encounters? My approach to those two questions is somewhat indirect. Most writers did not directly state their general ideas about law or unambiguously voice their commitments to law. However, an understanding of writers' underlying ideas and commitments begins to emerge through consideration of the way they constructed arguments, framed pleas, and made choices about what background information to include in their letters.

This chapter looks at writers' legal arguments, and chapter 5 looks at writers' extralegal claims. I organize the legal and extralegal arguments into separate chapters for clarity of presentation in building my interpretive claims. It is essential to understand, however, that individual writers did not choose one or the other type of argument. Rather, almost all the writers combined both types of arguments in the same letters. It is thus crucial that both legal and extralegal arguments be taken into account when answering the two questions that I just posed. Many of the writers' assertions about rights or other legal entitlements would seem hopelessly naive and idealistic if they were isolated from the broader context of the letters in which they appear. Taken at face value, bald assertions about legal rights in the letters would indicate that writers believed rights were absolute, automatically realized except in very unusual circumstances, and ultimately inviolable provided only that the rights bearer brought a breach to the attention of responsible government officials. However, the things writers say about law and rights do not need to be looked at in isolation and taken at face value as expressions of what writers actually believed and expected. Once the legal claims are placed in the context of the nonlegal persuasive claims that writers used, the idealized claims about law and rights in letters begin to look like rhetorical poses, ones that writers understood as being appropriate for making claims on government resources. Idealized claims about law were almost always accompanied by other extralegal persuasive claims and arguments. Those extralegal arguments quite often show that writers understood that their rights were not automatically or routinely protected. Many knew, for example, that realization of rights depended on government officials' discretionary choices about enforcement.

My effort to understand writers' underlying ideas about law by examining the mixture of persuasive strategies involves some creative (and necessarily somewhat tentative) interpretations of letter writers' motives. There is inevitably some guesswork involved in this task. As noted in chapter 1, it is sometimes difficult to determine what writers wanted or expected when they wrote letters. Some appear to have had the entirely instrumental goal of obtaining concrete, material assistance from government officials. Many others, however, gave indications that they did not expect to get much help and wrote to register protest or simply to give voice to their complaints. Uncertainty about motives influences my interpretation of the legal claims. It is possible that writers included claims about law in their letters because they believed such claims would force government officials to make a positive response. However, it is also possible that they included such claims only because they saw assertions about law or rights as assertions of their own dignity, as citizens or as rights bearers. Claims about law might also have been a vehicle for expressing principled defiance toward government officials who writers did not expect to help. The use of legal claims also announced to government officials that citizens could play the legal game, and play it with as much conviction, coherency, and commitment as those officials.

In analyzing writers' strategies, I am trying to understand what connections writers saw between the things they chose to write about and their reasons for writing. Because writers' motives are complicated and difficult to determine, I do not automatically assume that the rhetorical strategies used in letters were efforts to secure individualized patronage. I instead characterize persuasive strategies as efforts to add power and credibility to letters, or as efforts to communicate ideas and relevant information effectively. My minimal assumption, which works for both patronage and protest letters, is that writers made persuasive claims because they hoped to attract attention and give credibility to whatever messages they were trying to send.[1] Note also that by using words like *strategic* or *strategy*, I do not mean to denigrate what the writers were doing. *Strategic* is not meant as an antonym to *sincere*. I mean only to indicate that writers had some reason for writing and that at least some of the things they wrote in their letters were related to their effort to achieve their goals.

This chapter reports on the many types of legal claims in the letters and the facility and skill with which the claims were expressed. Some writers provided detailed and accurate references to relevant statutory or case law. A much larger number of writers invoked law with less mastery. However, even people who got some of the details wrong were able to communicate their demands and ideas with clarity and confidence. Other writers eschewed legal specifics and instead used very general claims about the nature of law or justice. In the rest of this chapter, I first consider some examples of people who directly deployed specific claims about law. I next consider some examples of writers who moved away from official law and made more general persuasive claims about law, constitutionalism, and related political values. I then consider a smaller group of writers who had a much more difficult time engaging legal officials on legal terms. A concluding section considers the important social dimension of the aspirational legal discourses that writers deployed in the letters.

Direct Deployment of Law

People who wrote to the CRS made a wide variety of claims about law and legal processes. While some writers did not attempt to engage the law at all and relied solely on narratives and personal appeals, most writers chose to use at least some legal terminology, most often claims about law, rights, liberties, or the Constitution. Writers were not always able to command the technical details of relevant law. The letters nevertheless demonstrate that a lack of technical expertise did not make it impossible to deploy law as a rhetorical weapon. Writers did not run from law or allow law's obscure and technical character to dampen their demands or protests. They instead deliberately deployed creative claims about law to make their requests or complaints more compelling.

Two explanatory caveats are necessary before turning to my analysis of the legal claims in the letters. First, the finding that people frequently engaged the law in these letters is not a reliable indicator of how often or how well people of the time period engaged with the law in their ordinary lives. Many of the writers were entangled in some formal legal process, such as criminal prosecution and detention, child custody or civil commitment proceedings, or other civil disputes involving contracts or family law.

Since many of the people who wrote were enmeshed in extraordinary circumstances, the letters do not measure the amount of legal knowledge and experience of typical Americans. The letters do, however, speak to the capacity of ordinary people to engage and deploy legal arguments when they are forced by circumstance to do so.

Second, my analysis is not based on some measure of the *effectiveness* of legal arguments or some formal standard for the *quality* of the legal reasoning. It would not make sense to try to evaluate effectiveness based on whether writers received help. For one thing, people wrote for other reasons besides a desire to get help. Moreover, as explained in chapter 2, the lack of federal resources devoted to civil rights meant that the CRS had to refuse the overwhelming majority of complaints no matter what. That fact makes the quality of legal argumentation largely irrelevant. Measuring the quality of legal arguments is not possible because, as noted in chapter 2, official law was itself uncertain on many legal and constitutional questions that were relevant to the issues raised in the letters. Those uncertainties mean there is no objective standard to measure whether a legal argument was valid or not under the legal standards of that era. It is also not clear that the standard for whether a legal argument is good or not should be whether judges of that period (or any period) would have accepted the argument. Many claims in the letters that would have failed before judges in 1939 would fare much better in court today. Ironically, the rejected legal claims in many of the letters seem more valid today than the legal claims made by CRS attorneys in their reply letters and by the judges who heard CRS test cases. (I return to this point in the concluding chapter.)

When I say that writers made quality legal arguments or competent use of legal materials, I mean only that the arguments were coherent, built effectively from the writers' starting premises, and supported by legal materials or metaphors. There are, of course, numerous instances where writers left out crucial information that might well have established a better legal basis for federal intervention. In many cases, those mistakes reflect lack of knowledge rather than lack of capacity to think clearly in legal terms— writers sometimes started with false premises and then constructed arguments using legal materials that would have been quite convincing if their starting premises had been true.

The ubiquity of legal claims in the letters reveals writers' comfortable familiarity with legal rhetoric and their willingness to confront government officials (and often government *attorneys*) with claims about law. With only a few exceptions, the writers who deployed law were not par-

ticularly privileged or specially trained in law. They nevertheless voluntarily, and with seeming comfort and ease, embraced the law as a tool that
could make their claims more persuasive. The frequent and confident use
of legal arguments shows that letter writers were not intimidated by law
and not experiencing law only as an obstacle that distorted perceptions or
made it difficult to articulate novel demands for redress. Law did not work
as an ideologically charged obfuscation that only the most privileged or
well informed could penetrate. Law, conceived broadly, instead provided a
shared cultural resource that writers utilized as they engaged government
officials and communicated the substance and gravity of their concerns.

Writing Back: Directly Challenging Legal Officials' Claims about Law

The cases where it is easiest to see that people were comfortable with
legal arguments and materials are among the substantial group of writers
who wrote back to the CRS after receiving an initial unfavorable reply. As
noted in chapter 2, the brief replies sent by the CRS almost always claimed
that limits on federal jurisdiction made it impossible for the federal government to help. Twelve percent (85 of 710) of the people who reported
incidents wrote back to the CRS to contest claims in the reply letters. Almost all of the people who wrote back challenged the legal claims made by
CRS attorneys when they wrote back. The cases where people responded
directly to the CRS are particularly illuminating because they allow direct
observation of give and take between government lawyers articulating
legal claims and individual claimants seeking help from the government.
Many of these direct challenges to CRS attorneys make it abundantly
clear that writers were not intimidated when government mandarins
made abstract and absolute legal pronouncements to justify contentious
decisions.

Writers who wrote back to the CRS all expressed disappointment at
the department's unwillingness to help, but there is considerable variation
in the tone of the responses. At one extreme is a florid letter from Joseph
Collier of Chicago, who wrote back to report that the CRS's reply letter
was 'enough to drive a man to drink, or to the Communists, or to enquire
at foreign embassies at Washington as to becoming a citizen of another
nation, because I have been utterly ignored and neglected—treated like
a cockroach" (August 12, 1940). More typically, writers eschewed ornate
descriptions of personal reactions and focused on challenging the CRS
using claims about law and the Constitution to challenge the department's

narrow view of its legal responsibilities. For example, after being told to take his complaint about a local school board to state officials, S. J. Murphy of Richmond County, Georgia, wrote back to invoke the Constitution's supremacy clause: "I respectfully contend and insist that the Richmond County Ga. school board has violated first amendment of the federal constitution by abridging freedom of speech and press. Said constitution being the supreme law of the land according to article six. If a body of people violate an article of constitutional law I fail to see where the state has jurisdiction" (April 4, 1939). Morris Hall of Westford, Massachusetts, challenged the CRS by making sophisticated claims about the interplay of statutory law and constitutional principles. Hall first wrote to complain about a picket line interfering with his right to work (March 29, 1939). The department's curt reply mentioned that Congress had created legal protections for pickets in the Wagner Act of 1935 (April 8, 1939). Hall wrote back and claimed that the department had "wittingly or unwittingly overlooked the vital point of my communication." He continued: "My query was directed to something more fundamental than the bare legal authority set forth [in the Wagner Act]. It was an attempt to discover just how comprehensive the so called crusade of the Dept. of Justice in support of civil liberties of our citizens was to be. Are you prepared to challenge the thesis that the right to work is a basic civil liberty? . . . This is not a matter to be passed over lightly by mere reference to a general legislative statute as you will probably see on further reflection" (April 10, 1939). Note that Hall directly rebuffed the department's effort to escape responsibility by classifying his problem as a labor issue falling under the Wagner Act rather than a conflict raising more general constitutional concerns.

Letters such as Hall's reveal that knowledge of constitutional and statutory law sometimes helped letter writers to compose detailed rebuttals of the department's legal claims. The overall record shows, however, that writers did not need to master legal specifics to communicate their disagreements effectively. Consider for example, Henry Kost of Miami, Florida, who wrote directly to President Roosevelt to complain that a local licensing ordinance was interfering with his right to paint signs for a living (November 6, 1941). After the Justice Department told Kost that the matter fell under the jurisdiction of the state of Florida (November 14, 1941), Kost wrote back to the CRS and challenged the government lawyers' ideas about constitutional law. Kost wrote: "The Constitution of the United States gives me the right to pursue happiness, and cartoon drawing is my happiness. The State of Florida made a law that violates the constitution and I want an apology damages via money for violating my rights I want the law cancelled" (November 30, 1941). The right to "pursue happiness" is mentioned in the Declaration of Independence rather than the Constitution, but that technical error does not obscure Kost's effort to connect his claim to core constitutional values.

I noted in chapter 2 that the CRS's use of legal claims in its reply letters appears to be an effort to depoliticize encounters and defuse conflict. In particular, claims about absolute and inflexible limits on jurisdiction depoliticize by masking discretionary choices and allowing government attorneys to avoid direct discussion of the merits or credibility of complaints. However, the instances where people wrote back make it clear that if the CRS was trying to defuse conflict, its effort was unsuccessful. Many of the writers who wrote back to contest legal claims became more defiant, insistent, or resistant in tone.

A vivid example is James Porter, who complained about his arrest for vagrancy in Fontana, California. Porter's claim was that local officials were using trumped-up vagrancy charges to forcibly relocate migrant workers. (Porter had been threatened with a six-month jail sentence if he did not leave town.) When the department wrote back to Porter with the almost comically unhelpful suggestion that he hire a private attorney (April 6, 1939), Porter became more defiant and assertive. Perhaps to reinforce his contempt, he wrote his reply on the back of the letter he had received from the CRS. Porter attempted again to explain his situation:

> How would I be guilty when I am a registered voter . . . I have a place to live in, and I was getting S.R.C. relief $4.88 every 14 days. . . . [I]f this is just law then I am crazy and all people getting relief—as I was, then they are all vagrants also, if not why not? . . . I was not a vagrant, but by arresting me as such, then they actually made a vagrant of me didn't they? And as regards visible means of support—ha ha ha, what a joke—please tell me aside form the idle wealthy folks, then just how many people are there who can show visible means of support for all future time? . . . My arrest was contemptible, and I would like to hear that Mr. Roy E. Beveridge who sentenced me—that they be taught real law and not arrest a person because they don't like his or her looks. (August 4, 1939)

Interestingly, Porter utilizes claims about law and justice as a vehicle for communicating his spirit of defiance even as he is ridiculing legal categories, legal processes, and legal officials such as judges. While his efforts to obtain redress were ultimately futile, his capacity to frame complaints in legal form meant that he could protest assertively against bad treatment without adopting the pose of a powerless victim pleading for help.

There are many other examples of CRS brush-offs inspiring defiant attitudes. In some instances, writers were particularly irritated that the Justice Department told them they had to get help from state or local authorities. An example is Pat Mohr, who wrote to complain that he had been falsely arrested for drunk driving in Detroit and then involuntarily committed for several weeks to a mental institution. Mohr claimed that doctors had refused to allow him to attend a court hearing on his case. After receiving the boilerplate reply from the CRS, Mohr continued to demand help from the department: "As a citizen of the United States, under my constitutional rights I demand that an investigation of my case be made at once and that I be taken to a court and given a fair trial. To date I have been held for 38 days and never been to court. That is absolutely unconstitutional and you know it" (December 2, 1939). John Peters, who wrote a series of letters from St. Louis complaining that he had been cheated out of an inheritance, wrote a second letter to make it clear that he would not be fooled by vague legal claims about jurisdiction. He even added a dig about the department's own legal standards with a reference to the federal investigations of the Pendergast political machine in Kansas City: "As an experienced news correspondent and legal student of the rules of evidence, I can assure you that my evidence is supported by factual coorboration and is as complete as your departments evidence against Pendergast" (May 31, 1939). Elsie Sanders was outraged by the department's reply to her complaint that she was being intimidated because of her efforts to get an alien admitted to the United States. In response to the suggestion that she direct her complaint to the Los Angeles police, she wrote: "No! The local police are NOT for me to go to, because these crooks are never in one place long enough to get caught. They are a ring, and have no addresses." She also explained: "A decent citizen is utterly intimidated, and does not know who to go to for justice, nor how to proceed"(January 19, 1940).

Some writers made statements or gestures to amplify their contempt for the department's legalistic response. When Evangeline Pearson wrote back to contest the CRS's claims, she included a postage stamp so the department could make a "proper reply." (The CRS returned the stamp to her.) When Mary Moloney wrote back to President Roosevelt to repeat her protest against Chicago's conduct in an eminent domain proceeding, she ridiculed the executive branch workers who had told her that her dispute was a "local matter": "Why do you suppose I took the time to write to you Mr. President? I expected you to relay the information to our Mayor something like the following: 'No more money for school purposes until you give Case B203353 a square deal.' I mentioned everything to you in detail as per the enclosed letters" (December 31, 1939). After not receiving a reply to her second letter, Moloney wrote back again to express her contempt for the federal employees who worked for the president and to make it clear that she would not give up. "Really Mr. President. I am surprised that you have such help that they do not want to answer my letter of Dec. 31, 1939. Is your help lazy? . . . [D]id your help think that by not answering my letter I would become tired and just stop writing you" (April 16, 1940). The CRS remained unmoved.

Writing back to the department did not result in people obtaining redress for their grievances. However, as noted in chapter 2, the department did sometimes tell people who wrote back that they could visit their local US attorney's office if they had additional information to support their claim for federal assistance. There is also one case where the department seemed to modify its stance. When John Peters initially complained about fraud that had cost him an inheritance, the department's reply was particularly cold: the letter referred to his "alleged inheritance" and said that there was "obviously" no violation of federal law (May 25, 1939). However, after Peters wrote back to insist that there had been a violation of federal laws against mail fraud, the department wrote a reply that stated: "Your interest in calling this matter to the Department's attention is greatly appreciated" (June 21, 1939). The reply also said that the department was forwarding the complaint to the postal inspector's office. An ongoing barrage of increasingly angry letters from Peters made it clear that he did not get help from the postal inspector and remained unsatisfied (May 31, 1939; June 12, 1939; July 12, 1939).

Technical Training in Law and Learning Law the Hard Way

The next cases to consider are a relatively small group of letter writers who showed some technical mastery of law and relevant legal materials. Some of the letters in this group revealed that the writers had formal training in the law. For example, Anthony Jurich, who wrote about a dispute with the IRS over distillery taxes, offered a sharp legal analysis of his case and included precise references to relevant statutory and case law. Jurich explained in one letter that he had been an assistant attorney general in the Woodrow Wilson administration (September 25, 1939). Jurich, however, is one of only a few writers who claimed to have formal legal training.

A larger number of legally adept letters came from people who had apparently learned about law through recent firsthand experiences rather than formal training. An example is a letter from Harry Reynolds complaining that the divorce laws in Michigan favored women. Reynolds also complained that Michigan's law did not allow him to recover damages from his ex-wife's suitor for "alienation of affection." Reynolds had obviously paid attention to the legal issues during his divorce proceedings. He provided numerous specific citations to provisions in the state's marriage statutes as well as references to court cases (March 14, 1940). Another example is Charles Carpenter, who made a variety of very specific references to South Dakota's laws regarding procedures for involuntary commitment to mental institutions (March 24, 1939). (Carpenter complained that his relatives conspired with state officials to have him committed.) Like Reynolds, Carpenter's ability to deploy technical legal claims appears to have been a response to direct experience with the law. There is no reason to think that such writers had broad knowledge of legal issues other than the ones connected to their own cases. That does not mean, however, that such writers were confined to a narrow understanding of law that could not expand beyond the contours of their limited legal knowledge. Notably, both Reynolds and Carpenter went beyond what they had learned in state proceedings as they presented their claims to federal officials. Reynolds made an argument for federal jurisdiction over his case by referring to several constitutional provisions; Carpenter's letter referred to specific provisions in federal criminal statutes when requesting that the department initiate a civil rights prosecution.

The level of technical facility in letters like Jurich's, Carpenter's, and Reynolds's stands at one end of a broad spectrum. There are a much larger number of letters where writers made less adept efforts at lay lawyering. Many writers offered claims about what "law" said or required that were neither accurate nor likely to prevail in any courtroom. However, even in many cases where the claims were technically flawed, writers still revealed a willingness to at least try to invoke law or legal ideals as a rhetorical tool. The large number of legal claims makes it clear that writers thought it was important and useful to talk about law. The perceived need to do that did not intimidate or silence nonexpert complainants.

Constitution Mining

Writers also showed an ability to find legal materials and incorporate them into their novel arguments. For example, many letter writers creatively engaged with the law by basing their appeals on provisions in the Constitution. These writers apparently obtained a copy of the Constitution before writing and worked to mine its text for clauses that seemed most helpful to their cause. Writers' efforts at constitution mining show that people confronted with problems and seeking a solution from the government could locate legal texts and use them to construct original arguments to support their positions.

Writers usually approached the Constitution's text on its own terms. In many cases, they seemed unaware that the Supreme Court had established interpretive glosses on text that narrowed the reach of some provisions. As a result, the legal arguments in the letters sometimes provide powerful illumination of the way specialized knowledge of Supreme Court doctrine obscures parts of the Constitution's text. For example, many writers were attracted to the promising language of the "privileges and immunities" clause of the Fourteenth Amendment. In contrast, trained constitutional lawyers and political scientists are more likely to instinctively ignore that broad and pregnant clause as a dead letter. Experts see the clause as irrelevant to most rights claims today even though no one seems to believe that the Supreme Court's 1873 argument that killed off the clause provides a correct, or even coherent, account of the text or history of that clause.[2]

Some Constitution miners were quite creative. Robert Grant of Los Angeles sent a telegram complaining that California's 3 percent sales tax violated the Eighth Amendment's ban on cruel and usual punishment and the Thirteenth Amendment's ban on involuntary servitude (March 26, 1940). James Rogers claimed that the requirement that workers on a New Deal building project present birth certificates violated the Constitution's ban on ex post facto laws (June 16, 1940). Another imaginative effort was made by James Minnis, who felt that Michigan was "ruled by outlaws" and blamed an unfair legislative apportionment. Minnis was unable to find a constitutional provision specifically guaranteeing a fair apportionment processes for state legislatures, but he drew attention to the clause in article 2, section 3, giving the president responsibility to take care that the laws be faithfully executed. Minnis also stated: "Under Sec. IV, this smacks of Treason" (September 15, 1939). Also imaginative was V. T. Comer of San Diego, who complained that he had been deprived of his "fundamental Constitutional rights" when civil authorities dissolved his marriage. He claimed that the state court's decision to grant his wife a divorce violated the first amendment's guarantee of religious liberty because his marriage had been established and recognized by the Catholic Church (June 17, 1941). Another imaginative complaint was made by

Vinton Dowis of Saginaw, Michigan. Dowis insisted (at considerable length) that state property taxes were made unconstitutional once the Sixteenth Amendment gave Congress the power to establish a federal income tax (February 14, 1940).

Offbeat constitutional claims were often made with a great deal of conviction. A letter from Harry Smith (August 29, 1939), a "roadside peddler" from Upland, California, argued that local retail licensing fees violated the interstate commerce clause. Smith claimed the local government was usurping powers granted to Congress in the commerce clause. Smith read the clause as giving Congress exclusive authority to regulate interstate commerce. Smith's reading has been, of course, decisively rejected by the Supreme Court, starting with *Gibbons v. Ogden* in 1824 (22 US 1). However, any student of John Marshall's contentious opinion in that case knows that the very open-ended text of the commerce clause in the Constitution does not directly contradict Smith's alternative reading. Smith also anticipated that the Justice Department might raise federalism questions in response to his complaint. Smith thus explained preemptively that he bought merchandise in Chicago and New York to sell in California, "which makes it interstate commerce." Smith also showed at least some awareness of the Supreme Court's constitutional case law, offering a paraphrase of John Marshall's famous claim: "The power to tax is the power to destroy." (The original is in *McCulloch v. Maryland,* 17 US 316, 327 [1819]).

While the accessibility and importance of the Constitution made it an attractive target for mining, a smaller number (61, or 7 percent) of writers also looked to federal statutes to support their claims. Most commonly, writers argued that federal postal laws gave their cases a federal dimension and thus empowered the Justice Department power to act. One example is Harold Brown, who wrote from the Maryland State Penal Farm in Breathedsville to complain that he had been falsely convicted of "housebreaking" (May 30, 1939). Brown claimed that the federal government had the power to intervene because a posted letter had been improperly used as evidence in his case. G. R. Fox of St. Louis invoked the federal Swamp Act and federal laws against mail fraud in a complaint about violations of the property rights of African Americans in the Mississippi Delta (August 20, 1939). A final example is Frank O'Neill, who wrote from Represa, California, to ask for federal protection from a former state prosecutor who was trying to extort money from him (August 27, 1940). (Represa is the mailing address for the Folsom State Prison.) In a second letter,

O'Neill clarified his claim for federal attention by saying that he had been sent threats through the mail (September 26, 1940).

Constitutional and Legal Fantasies

While some writers mined the constitutional or statutory text in search of helpful provisions, others would just make things up. Writers in this group included alleged quotes from the Constitution that do not appear anywhere in the text or referred to statutes or legal principles that did not actually exist. The false quotes are usually recognizable as embellishments of actual constitutional provisions. For example, William Coombs wrote a letter about having his driver's license revoked, claiming: "I have since suffered every indignity it is possible to get and they still refuse to grant me a living" (July 6, 1939). To support his claim for federal intervention, Coombs claimed: "Section five of the constitution reads in Part. 'No citizen shall be deprived of his rights or Privileges without due recourse to law.'" In some cases, writers embellished constitutional text by adding a layer of fake legalese. For example, George Trinckes wrote to complain that California had wrongfully denied him unemployment and veterans benefits because he did not have any dependents. Trinckes, who possessed an expansive understanding of constitutional entitlements invoked "the 14th amendment of the constitution that says, that no Parties or Party, shall Deprive any Party, of Property, or Liberty, without the due Process of Law, and that all Parties have the Equal Rights of the Law" (April 3, 1939). It is striking that the many creative flourishes that Trinckes added to the text of the Fourteenth Amendment did not in any obvious way strengthen his claim for government assistance.

Bertha Baker, who complained to President Roosevelt that state officials had "schemed and lied and railroaded me into a Stockton Calif. Asylum," offered the following account of constitutional rights: "According to the American United States Constitution, I am entitled to service, and to be heard in open court and witnessed deposition, short hand transcripts presented to the Highest Court" (April 17, 1939). Another example is Edward Arps, who wrote from California with a variety of complaints about the constitutionality of the New Deal. One of Arps's claims was: "Article II of the CONSTITUTION says 'To promote and encourage LOYALTY to the U.S. of America, etc.'" Arps claimed that the "tyranny of treason" of government programs "have destroyed our FREEDOM and insulted our CONSTITUTION" (March 28, 1939). Also imaginative was C. B. Tippie of Los

Angeles (May 18, 1941). Tippie complained that the state had suspended his driver's license because he was unable to pay compensation after his car caused an accident. Tippie claimed that the state's process violated a strict constitutional ban on using public power to collect a private debt. Tippie seemed unaware that a constitution that actually contained such a ban would, among other things, make all private contracts unenforceable.

Many writers embellished the Constitution's text in order to provide support for claims related to economic rights. An example is Earl Tucker of Palm City, California, who explained that he manufactured small plaster ornaments and sold them from a stand on the side of the road (December 12, 1940). Tucker explained that California officials had demanded that he pay the state a cash deposit on future sales tax receipts before continuing his tiny operation. Tucker claimed that he could not afford to pay the six-dollar deposit and thus would be forced to stop working and go on relief. Tucker wrote: "Now my understanding is that a citizen can sell there own labor on any street or hi way in any city, town, village or chelment [?] in United States without taxation." Another example is Frank Cox, who wrote to the attorney general from San Gabriel, California, to complain that he had to pay licensing fees to states where he drove his poultry truck (September 24, 1940). Cox noted: "In most all states I have to pay a gasoline tax and the roads are most all built with some Federal aid." Beyond that practical argument, he claimed a constitutional right to move goods freely across state lines: "It seems to me I should be able to stand on the Bill of Rights and go any place in the US which I wished to."

Imagination and Constitutional Values: Recovering the Constitution as a Social Compact

In the examples above, writers made appeals to legal and constitutional texts (real or imagined) to support claims about specific and relatively narrow rights claims. In the next set of cases, writers made more general claims about constitutional values and related responsibilities of both citizens and government. Instead of relying on real or fictitious citations to particular pieces of legal or constitutional text, the writers in this category built their aspirational claims using observations about shared constitutional values, familiar symbols of American democracy, and general observations about American history. Writers drew upon a wide range of symbols and texts from popular constitutional and political culture, including things such as the Declaration of Independence, the Liberty Bell, the Gettysburg Address, and the Statue of Liberty and people like Nathan Hale and Crispus Attucks.

Like the writers who mined or embellished the Constitution, these writers deployed constitutional rhetoric to support claims for rights entitlements that went well beyond what authorities pronounced as official law at the time. However, the writers who made these broader arguments from constitutional culture were also more self-conscious about the expansive nature of their claims. They made it clear that they were expressing visions of what the Constitution could or should be rather than making exaggerated or confused claims about how the Constitution was already working. By invoking constitutional history and national symbols as they protested injustice, these writers also showed that they understood law and constitutionalism as something more than the fixed set of entitlements established through authoritative pronouncements of judges or other government officials. Writers also understood that claims about "law," "rights," or "the Constitution" carry with them a symbolic power and thus help to make protests more vivid and powerful. Interestingly, writers in this group also tended to portray the Constitution as a source of collective obligations for the social good, not simply as a resource for protecting individual entitlements.

Many writers drew upon a broad range of symbols and other resources to tie their particular circumstances to broad and redemptive constitutional visions. One powerful example is a letter sent to the Justice Department from Normal Gould Boswell of Los Angeles (May 1, 1940). Boswell draws upon language from the Constitution, the Declaration of Independence, and the Pledge of Allegiance as part of his complaint regarding criminal prosecutions against providers of alternative medicine. Boswell builds his case by explaining his own accumulated knowledge and experience of American constitutionalism, going back to what he learned as a child:

> In school, I was taught the "American Creed" to *support* the Constitution.
>
> In the Constitution is quoted "God has given men *certain rights which cannot be taken away from them.* Among these are the right to life, the right to *freedom,* and the *right to seek happiness.* We believe these truths need no proof." Further is mentioned certain "unalienable rights, that among these are life, liberty, and the pursuit of happiness." Also in the amendment regarding the 'procedure of trial' "and to be informed of the nature and cause of the accusation" also "to have compulsory process for obtaining witness in his favor."

> Again, in the "Pledge to the Flag"—"I pledge allegiance to my flag and to the Republic for which it stands: one nation, indivisible, with liberty and justice for all." This thus is for everyone.

Boswell then makes a series of creative connections between alternative medicine practices and enumerated constitutional protections for religious liberty.

> Allied with religious freedom is a citizen's right to healing (medical or nonmedical) freedom. Not long ago, the priest was man's doctor. The professional has taken over from the priest, but the doctor and the priest deal in the same, body and soul.
>
> Now here is where I am puzzled. Always believed court procedure was applied according to the principles as laid down by the constitution, upholding liberty and justice for all that a proper charge was made to everyone accused having opportunity to defend himself, presenting his evidence, etc.
>
> Sounded grand to me—yet as I made contact with life noted there were cases where the accused was allowed no defense worthy of the name and even though actually not guilty the accusation was "railroaded" through. . . .
>
> I am very puzzled, a very puzzled citizen. Maybe I am dumb. Maybe different procedures have been sneaked in while the Constitution was not looking.

Boswell does not get all of the details right in his letter. The words he puts in quotation marks are not direct quotes from the Constitution and the pledge to the flag. He borrows ideas expressed in the Declaration of Independence as part of his account of the Constitution. However, such mistakes do not diminish his ability to connect his substantive claims to a resonant vision of core constitutional values. Significantly, Boswell's plea also focuses not on directing attention to an individualized claim but on connecting particular circumstances to a vision of the broader public good.[3]

Many of the writers who wrote to Roosevelt to protest the anti-alien Smith Act invoked constitutional history and broad constitutional values to support their protests. Such letters offered general or practical arguments for preserving important constitutional values. For example, Ruth Wood of Antioch, California, wrote:

> Much of the pride and joy we Americans have for our country rests on the fact that we have a relatively greater measure of civil liberties than most countries.

At least we have a tradition of civil liberties and we do object mightily to alien and sedition acts and criminal syndicalism acts.

Do not slowly kill our incentive to be patriotic by signing such measures as the Smith Bill (H.R. 5138). England and France are going down to defeat because their rule has become essentially fascist. They have abandoned civil liberties. (June 29, 1940)

Bernard Ray invoked a powerful symbol of American values: "The Statue of Liberty stands in the Bay of New York, a symbol of TOLERANCE and JUSTICE to all who enter: Will she too suffer the effects of this act??" (June 24, 1940). Another dramatic attempt to invoke constitutional symbolism to protest the Smith Act came from Marguerite Senour of Los Angeles: "I am a lone woman—but I am one of the People and my voice is the voice of the Mass—and I say to you that the group of men who are trying to destroy Democracy by all sorts of Anti-Alien Bills—those men desecrate the great Hall in which they sit—they insult our flag, they would tear up our Constitution especially Our Bill of Rights and throw it down a sewer. Their names will go down in history as traitors they will be mentioned with loathing and contempt" (June 5, 1940). It might be tempting to dismiss such histrionics because they did not lead to the desired response from the targeted government officials. However, it is still notable and admirable that Senour's pleas are not framed in the oft-criticized terms of *individual* entitlement. Senour claims that her position matches society's shared history and shared commitment to honoring the Constitution, and claims have the broad support of "the Mass."

Writers invoked historical and cultural images for other types of requests. John Flatley, a Boston police officer, protested because he had been disciplined by a board of the police department rather than a regular court (April 24, 1939). Flatley invoked "the men in Concord and Lexington in April 1775" to support his claim for protection under the Bill of Rights. Sometimes historical references were offered as part of more desperate pleading. William Uphoff wrote from the Lee County Jail in Dixon, Illinois, to claim that he was being unjustly imprisoned in a tax case. Uphoff wrote: "please help me now before it is too late, I say, as Patrick Henry, give me liberty or give me death"(August 26, 1939).[4] Other writers invoked historical figures in support of very general principles of justice and morality that were quite distant from the specifics of the Constitution. Joseph Collier, for example, wrote: "When good men such as Washington, Jefferson, and Franklin framed the Constitution and Bill of

Rights, I am sure they intended courtesy and the Golden Rule to be read between the lines" (August 4, 1940).

Creative appeals to constitutional history or values also inspired writers to take a more defiant stance toward government officials. Edward Vocob of Brooklyn referred to a radio address by Frank Murphy announcing the creation of the CRS (March 23, 1939). In his speech, Murphy had mentioned that lawyers for the CRS were conducting legal research to see whether existing statutes could be used to protect civil liberties. Vocob supported the civil rights initiative but did not feel as though the announced measures went far enough:

> Did we get our democracy by such timid, spineless research in the King's law books? . . . I hope I didn't underestimate your talk, but it seems to me that our Constitution is the law which guarantees civil liberties. Therefore, anyone who is a citizen has pledged to uphold and support the Constitution. If an individual or organization causes race or religious hatred they are violating their pledge to protect for all citizens the rights and privileges secured to them by the constitution and they should be held on that condition of fact. Otherwise what good is that kind of democracy.

Like many other writers discussed in this section, Vocob tied his complaint to a sense of common interest and shared constitutional history:

> Democracy is in the saddle in our country. You have the knowledge that anti-Jewish, anti-Catholic, anti-Protestant and anti-labor outfits are working overtime to destroy you and yours—Why wait—prosecute them or they will persecute you.
>
> But if every mental degenerate is allowed to slander, abuse, defame and curse an humble and innocent people because we are the best scapegoats for the anti-democrats then its time to re-examine our foundations and our surroundings.

Another attempt to link the fate of an unpopular minority to the common good was made by Jack Johnstone, chairman of the Illinois state committee of the Communist Party, USA. Johnstone complained that local officials had encouraged a series of vigilante attacks on members of his party. Johnstone forwarded to the Justice Department a letter he had sent to the attorney general of Illinois (August 12, 1940). In the letter, he suggested the attacks called into question the legitimacy of elected government: "These are the desperate acts of a political machine frantically trying to maintain power. If the Democratic Party cannot win the elections without the votes of the Communists, then it has no right to the offices involved." Interestingly, Johnstone did not simply catalog a series of rights-related entitlement claims. He instead articulated a number of more practical reasons for protecting minority political rights. In particular, Johnstone tried to connect protection of minorities in the United States with the country's inevitable entry into the war in Europe and the broader effects that interference with political minorities would have on that effort. He claimed: "Officials of labor unions and other progressive organizations are alarmed at what seems to be a program of public officials to destroy democracy at home, while pretending that democracy abroad is their main concern." Johnstone also connected his plea to specific constitutional protections, claiming: "The United States Constitution and Bill of Rights have been ripped to shreds in the act of setting this unreasonably high bail" and claiming that the "victims" of state oppression had been "held for many weeks . . . in a filthy and abominable jail during the height of a heat wave . . . without due process of law." Johnstone then returned to his broader theme of the general good: "Continued violations of the constitutional and legal rights of the people lays the foundation for fascism, which America detests."

Many other writers who complained of racial discrimination or attacks on religious or political minorities referred pointedly to the looming war in Europe. In these cases, writers made a forward-looking appeal to American values. Writers characterized the war as an effort to defend constitutional values and thus as an opportunity to reaffirm a sense of shared commitment to those values. In some instances, references to the war in Europe led to expansive claims about equality and racial justice. A letter from J. Yamaguchi, who identified himself as a member of the Japanese Citizen's League, provides a good example: "Will you please be kind to give us your sincere explanation about the Japanese boys who are born in this County and have entitled the same privilege to the government jobs, which just as other races, by the U.S. Constitution. But only the Japanese American born citizen are rejected from the government works. Why so treated discriminary? I have three boys eligible to bear guns for America's defence. But eldest boy was reject to join marines, also to work in air-craft shop. Our Japanese Citizen's League wishing to hear from you definite answer about the matter before election day" (October 27, 1940). Yamaguchi did not know that conditions would soon become much worse for Japanese Americans.

Another writer who connected the war effort to constitutional issues of equality was Henry Johnson of Chicago, who wrote to complain about racial discrimination at the WPA. Johnson tried to establish the importance of his claim by writing of past and future sacrifices made by African Americans during wars. Johnson wrote: "No one national group has a better military record than ours. Not one of us has betrayed this country. In fact one of us was the first (Crispus Attucks) to give his life in rebellion against taxation without representation against King George. Certainly no race deserves more military recognizance. You yourself did promote one of our military leaders, but not for meritorious service, but as political vote getting move. In the Navy we are relegated to menial labor duties—yet we are expected to give our lives if needs be to defend DEMOCRACY" (April 25, 1941). Johnson also reminded the president of the "the insidious treatment accorded to the colored folk" during the last war.

Another letter that used the war to develop a constitutional claim of common purpose came from Charles Jones of Los Angeles. Jones made a direct link between the treatment of racial minorities and the willingness of African Americans to take part in any war effort:

> I am writing you for help for my people! We are living in a country of freedom but the Negro does not get that what is call freedom. We are the same as the white race the only difference is that we are dark we cannot help that but we do not get freedom because of that we are call not good enough. . . . If they would be a next war what do you think the negro would think when ask to go he would think that he would be fighting for a country that is a hell to him. (February 7, 1940)

These letters about war show that framing novel demands in terms of American constitutional values need not fuel a trend toward docile, conservative, or conventional claims.

The relationship between the federal government and the states was another topic that inspired many writers to make broad claims about constitutional values and constitutional history. Many writers patiently explained why the federal government needed power to intervene in disputes that CRS attorneys saw as falling solely within the jurisdiction of the states. In particular, writers argued that the federal government needed to intervene in cases where local and state officials violated constitutionally protected rights. Many of the writers who offered arguments on this issue were victims of state and local officials whose power was not adequately checked under state law. The arguments about the need for federal intervention are particularly important because they directly confront the constitutional basis for the CRS's claims of limited jurisdiction.

One example is George Runyan, the writer from Lansing, Michigan, who got into trouble with a state judge for criticizing a Chrysler dealership that had sold him a lemon (December 28, 1939). At the request of the dealership, a state judge had slapped Runyan with a injunction to prevent him from posting signs that were critical of the dealership. Runyan was not pleased when the CRS wrote back and told him that the department had no jurisdiction to help him with his complaint about being "defrauded" by the dealership. The CRS reply also stated that Runyan had "ample opportunity" to pursue a remedy in state courts with the aid of private counsel (January 12, 1940). Runyan quickly wrote back to the CRS, insisting that the issue was not fraud but a "conspiracy between the used car dealer and a Judge of the Circuit Court." He explained: "Due to the fact that their combined acts does violate the Federal constitution it was my belief that some agency higher up than the local government would have to take a hand in the matter if my civil rights were to be protected" (April 2, 1940). Runyan supported this plea for outside intervention by reiterating that the dealer was involved in a corrupt "racket" with local government officials, including judges.

Herbert Shenkin argued in favor of federal intervention to alleviate conditions in state insane asylums. Shenkin's comments about federal powers to protect rights demonstrate a sophisticated understanding of the difference between the promises in black-letter law and the practical realities faced by the federal government: "Theoretically, the Federal Government can intervene whenever any citizen is being deprived of his liberty without due process of law. Practically, the Federal Government will not deal with isolated matters; it will leave such things to the several states. If a situation becomes general, however, and the Federal Government has reason to believe that the states are not protecting the liberty of its citizens then the Federal Government should take action. This is a sound, and considering the nature of our system of government, a necessary doctrine" (March 29, 1943). Mr. Shenkin was one of the few writers who identified himself as an attorney. He said that he had worked for the Federal Housing Administration before being committed to an asylum in Pennsylvania.

Another example is Mary Moloney, the writer who ridiculed the CRS's response to her complaint about her dispute with the city of Chicago. The city government was forcibly acquiring a lot Moloney owned in order to build a school. Moloney's first letter claimed that biased local courts had set a low price for the property in eminent domain proceedings (November 16, 1939). Her core contention was that the federal government had to intervene because the state government was itself part of the problem. After not receiving a quick reply, Moloney wrote a second letter noting that the local government was using federal funds to finance the new the school (December 6, 1939). The department then replied by claiming that the administration of local projects built with federal funds was "a matter solely within the jurisdiction of the City of Chicago and its action in this regard cannot be questioned by the Federal Government" (December 12, 1939). Moloney quickly wrote back to challenge that disingenuous claim about state spending of federal funds (December 31, 1939). She noted that the federal government often used its spending power to influence decisions by state and local governments. Moloney recalled how Roosevelt's interior secretary, Harold Ickes, had used financial pressure to control the way Chicago officials built a federally funded subway line: "Mr. Ickes refused to lend money to Chicago unless Chicago did what he wanted relative to the construction of said project. It is a local affair but still Mr. Ickes said to Chicago 'you will do it my way or no money.' Those may not be his words but the meaning is about the same." Moloney seemed to understand that even in cases where the Constitution limits direct federal intervention in state matters, the federal government retained numerous weapons to influence state officials.

Henry Johnson also built a case for federal intervention by pointing out inconsistencies in the administration's response to different issues. His wide-ranging letter about discrimination at the WPA included a discussion of lynching and federal power. Johnson noted that there had been creative efforts to expand federal jurisdiction in other policy areas and challenged Roosevelt by questioning his priorities: "I still remember the decimation of the kidnapping menace. You thoroughly put the screws on that. It so happens that the deprivation of life and property without due process of the law is condemned by the CONSTITUTION. Giving you the power Mr. President to act any time a lynching threatens or occurs. Do you think Sir that The nations 'G' men are better employed safeguarding some rich person from being separated from his ill gotten wealth or protecting some poor black from a blood thirsty mob" (April 25, 1941).

Thurman Reed Rigdon, whose letter from a jail in Rockville, Maryland, is discussed in chapter 3, took a more scattershot approach that combined claims about federal power with claims about the impending war (May 2, 1942). Rigdon made some preemptive counterclaims about federal power because he anticipated that the Justice Department would tell him that he had to take his dispute to state officials: "I know you are going to say that is a state proposition and the Federal government does not get into state affairs." To support his expansive interpretation of federal power, Rigdon wrote: "I know you are a federal agency but it is the federal agency who is supose to look after its forty eight subsidiaries." He cited the Fifth and Fourteenth Amendments to support that claim. In connection with the war, he argued that "we today are asking the peoples of every state to fight for and to preserve" the relevant constitutional principles. Rigdon continued: "There is surely some way to keep a few rotten crooked grafting, thieving politicians from wrecking and trampling disparaging and ignoring the very thing you and the rest of the representatives of the people are asking us to protect with our very lives." Rigdon also buttressed his claim for federal attention by claiming that many of the state's police officers had not turned in their income tax returns and had not reported money that they stole from prisoners as taxable income.

Staggered by the Law: Legal Traps and Legalese

Before turning to some conclusions about the way writers deployed legal and constitutional arguments, it is important to acknowledge that some writers had a more difficult time in encounters with law than the writers used as examples so far. I have given many examples where writers sought out law and legalized language as a rhetorical resource or otherwise indicated that they were not paralyzed by the perceived need to make legal claims. In contrast, a smaller group of writers appeared much less comfortable using legal language and had more difficulty communicating legal information coherently. Most of these writers did not voluntarily seek out the law as a rhetorical resource. They wrote because they were caught in some significant and immediate legal difficulty. Their claims about law were attempts to explain their pressing problems rather than efforts to construct creative arguments for government attention to their problems. The writers considered in this final grouping provide some vivid illustrations of the way law's technical obscurity can sometimes complicate the obstacles faced by people caught in legal traps. The letters in this group also present some of the most heartbreaking stories in the CRS files. Many of these writers were quite poor and lacked basic facility with written language. Nevertheless, even in this group, writers managed to make claims about law and to assert legal entitlement, albeit will less facility than some of the writers considered thus far.

A first example of a writer who seemed overmatched in the face of a legal and bureaucratic nightmare is Maeta Perry, who wrote to President Roosevelt for help with her son, J.C., who was being held in a Florida prison. Perry explained that J.C. had been arrested a few weeks earlier on a "charge of liften ira ellis tire." She claimed officers had executed a search warrant at her home but were unable to find allegedly stolen goods. She also described a frustrating and ultimately unsuccessful journey to visit her son in jail: "they had me to lose three days down there expecting them to Bring him out an they slips him." Perry also claimed that authorities were taking advantage of the fact that she lacked the resources to fight effectively: "I has no money to hire a lawer are I would an they new that very well." She closed her letter with the following plea: "I am a poor wites woman an has no help at all But J.C. Perry an we both is sick Rite now he sick in Jail an me out" (June 14, 1939). Perry wrote back to the Justice Department more than two years later to update her plea with the claim that her son had been transferred to a state hospital, but she again did not get any help from the department (December 7, 1942).

Perry's letters are among the most difficult in the CRS files to understand. The handwriting is often illegible, and the odd grammar, diction, and spelling leave some passages incomprehensible. Perry included a line that suggests that she was self-conscious about her inability to plea effectively: "i hope you will be able to under stand this Bad hand rite" (June 14, 1939). Nevertheless, Perry still managed to communicate important information that drew attention to some constitutional issues that provided a potential basis for federal intervention. Her first letter claimed that the police had never found or presented any evidence and that her son had not been allowed to contact witnesses who would have supported his case.

In some cases, writers did not know enough about the structure of government to even know what to request. Lucy Potter wrote to the attorney general from Chicago to explain that she had been injured when the ceiling of her apartment had collapsed and was no longer able to work as a dressmaker. Potter indicated that she needed and wanted help but did not seem to have any idea of what form of help to request or what legal basis the federal government might have for intervening (July 16, 1939). Other writers seemed quite confused about the organizational structure of government. Pearl Squires Olsen's letter complaining about a "dope peddling" sheriff of Townsend Township, Michigan, ended with a request that the attorney general send a "secret service man" to remove the sheriff (March 11, 1939). (The Secret Service is part of the Commerce Department.) When Virginia Lambert wrote her complaint about rampant corruption in Pineville, West Virginia, the only request she could articulate was that President Roosevelt "send an operator here" to solve the problem (April 7, 1939).

Some writers signaled their struggles with legal technicalities by slipping into an odd and nonidiomatic dialect that appears to be an awkward effort to emulate the detached formality of legal language. Sometimes this oddly formal language would appear in passages that talked about the law, but not in other parts of the same letter. Sometimes such clumsy efforts to simulate legalese make it difficult to understand complaints. The champion of odd legal diction was a writer who identified himself as "poor Bob Zagonel" of Girard, Kansas. Zagonel's letter complained about the losses he suffered under a bad sharecropping contract (February 14, 1939). While Zagonel may not have been a native English speaker, his efforts to communicate with the government seem to suffer from a more complicated problem. His letter is full of overly complicated words and clauses that make little sense. An attached postscript to the letter uses an odd, left-justified margin to achieve an oddness that is poetic:

> They are indelicate.
> I please for indemnification. I get been inculcate frequent time.
> I want respect to Constitution and bills of right and to the true poor man and get paid by law.
> Him offend us in many way and many time before we give to him few reply.
> (February 14, 1939)

Sometimes the resort to odd formalities appears to have been prompted by legal language in the CRS's reply letters. For example, Regina Wallace wrote back to challenge the CRS after getting an unfavorable reply to her complaint about being detained unlawfully by state officials. Wallace wrote back with a second letter that contained oddly formal diction ("whereas," "wherein") and strained verbal constructions that were not present in several other letters that she wrote to the White House and other federal and local government offices. Referring to the department's reply letter, Wallace wrote, "Whereas you have therein stated that the matter which I described is one of local concern and redress should be sought from the government of my State, wherein the alleged injustice occurred. I therefore entreat you to be gracious enough to help me, and refer to me the channels in Jurisdiction over my problem" (May 19, 1939). While such efforts did not prompt government officials to provide help, they do at least show that law's technical complexity and formality, while perhaps intimidating, did not intimidate everyone into silence.

The Social Dimension of Individual Rights Claims

Beyond the handful of writers who had a particularly difficult time with legal claims and argumentation, the full sample of letters reveals that a much larger number of people were comfortable deploying legal rhetoric and arguments in support of petitions for help and letters of protest. Few of the writers had any formal training in law. When they attempted to make legal arguments, most writers were not able to state all the relevant technical details with complete precision. Nevertheless, writers were able to invoke particular principles of official law and make broader claims about justice or constitutionalism.

A few characteristics of the way law is discussed in the letters are worth emphasizing because they appear to contradict some common assumptions about the inaccessibility and obscurity of law and legal arguments. First, writers were not typically intimidated by law or the need to use legal language or dispute legal outcomes. Writers typically stated their legal claims with confidence, even when making claims that contradicted what government authorities had told them about law. Most strikingly, a substantial number of writers wrote back to challenge directly the legal claims made by government attorneys. The people who wrote back to the CRS were clearly not willing to take the claims in the CRS reply letters at face value and did not accept those claims as valid justification for the government's refusal to provide help. It is, of course, not possible to know what the people who did not write back thought about the CRS's reply letters. Nevertheless, the broader context of legal claims in the letters makes it clear that the finding that a large number of people did not write back does not indicate that a large number of people simply accepted the CRS's claims about law. There are many other reasons people would not write back. Many of those who did not write back expressed their legal positions with confidence or defiance that makes it seem quite unlikely that they would be convinced by the CRS's curt replies. Many others wrote to the CRS in order to challenge legal claims made by other legal authorities, such as state judges or local government officials. In contrast, there is no direct evidence of anyone being willing to accept automatically what the CRS or any other officials offered as a legitimate accounting of law.

Second, the decision to deploy legal rhetoric did not confine writers' demands to the quite narrow range of rights protections that were available at that time in official law. Together with the letters discussed in chapter 3, the ones considered in this chapter show that writers used legal rhetoric to argue creatively for a broad range of entitlements that government authorities would not recognize. They also used legal and constitutional language to defend a considerably expanded vision of government responsibilities to protect new rights and to provide redress when state officials violated rights or failed to protect rights. It is thus clear that official law was not establishing the boundaries of legitimacy for claims about rights or other legal entitlements in these political encounters.

Third, many of the novel positions taken by writers who offered expansive ideas about rights and, in particular, ideas about the appropriate institutional basis for rights protection, have been vindicated by time. Again and again, writers complained that state and local officials were not living up to federal standards established in the Constitution. Writers also pointedly noted that local abuses could only be stopped if the federal government played some oversight role. In the decades since 1939, the institutional capacity of the federal government to protect rights has expanded dramatically. That expansion reflects the development of a broad consensus that federal power to protect rights had to grow if the Constitution's promises of substantive rights and equal protection were to become meaningful. Well before those changes occurred, many of the people who wrote to the CRS seemed to understand the practical problems that demanded such an expansion of federal power to protect rights. The letter writers who made these efforts to deploy legal claims in support of federal power seem, in retrospect, to be well out ahead of the government officials who offered only rote recitation of the crabbed interpretations of federal power favored by the ancien regime.

A fourth and final observation regarding the use of legal and rights claims deserves a bit more discussion. A thread that runs through many of the letters is that writers emphasized common fate, shared values across communities, and a related sense of shared responsibility to support claims for rights protection. This finding is surprising. Many critics of rights rhetoric and associated legal remedies worry that resorting to rights talk inevitably leads claimants to pose as isolated individuals in pursuit of *individual* entitlements and thus also to eschew broader collective efforts to pursue more general and potentially transformative change (e.g., Tushnet 1984; Glendon 1991, chapter 3). However, in the CRS letters the use of legal language and rights claims quite often led people in the opposite direction, toward a more social orientation.

Letter writers were more likely to emphasize shared constitutional values and responsibilities than they were to make claims of purely individualized entitlement. Moreover, writers quite often defended their claims for *new* rights by emphasizing that the conditions they faced as individuals also had broader harmful effects on other people. Writers seemed to expect that expressing the sociality of their predicaments would make their claims more persuasive to government officials. Many writers conceded, for example, that their own case would not be worthy of government attention if not for underlying problems that gave the case a broader, public dimension. Writers also tried to strengthen their claim for help by arguing that federal government attention to their single case would indirectly help many other similarly situated people.

Thus the writers' choice to engage in a politics of rights did not lead them to focus inward. People who used rights claims as they tried to persuade government officials looked past their individual circumstance to think about how other people might be in similar straits and how their own fate was linked to the problems of other people. The letters show how aspirational rights rhetoric can have a significant social and political dimension even when deployed by individual claimants seeking vindication of individual rights.

A typical example of the social pose adopted by rights claimants is in a letter written by Edna Reynolds, who claimed that her husband was unjustly in prison. Reynolds wrote: "It may not be of grave national importance that James H. Reynolds is now confined in the Leavenworth Penitentiary, that incident is important only to him, but the illegal method used by Government Officials to impede his defense and secure conviction are a matter of grave national concern, in that if such procedure be permitted to become a substitute for duly enacted law and the American theory of justice, then no citizen is secure in his Constitutional rights" (March 18, 1940). Reynolds also focused on claims about systematic problems: "unimportant citizens without funds to engage interested competent counsel are helpless against the techniques practiced by appointed individual government officials" who "impede the defense of persons they accuse of crime by placing their will and self made rules above the law and above the Constitution." Reynolds also claimed that the problems that had led to her husband's incarceration had broad-reaching effects that went beyond the criminal justice system to society at large and the political system. She noted that word of people being subjected to "Kangaroo proceedings" led more people to support "subversive organizations of various types that purport to offer a better protection for un-important citizens."

In a wide variety of cases, writers tried to persuade government officials to give them attention by broadening the scope of complaints beyond themselves. William Gillespie, an accountant from Baltimore who had been convicted of securities fraud, wrote to Eleanor Roosevelt: "[Y]ou might be interested in this case . . . not only for the good it will do for me personally, but principally, and of paramount importance, that some other person may be spared a similar fate at the hands of unscrupulous people" (January 17, 1940). Thomas Jones, writing for a local of the Brotherhood of Painters, Decorators, and Paperhangers of America, reported that local police had conspired with "union busters" to attack a group of glaziers at a Detroit tavern. Jones argued that a failure to intervene would cause the problem of corrupt police to spread: "If they are successful in their endeavors in Michigan, I am of the opinion that they could be successful in any other part of our country" (June 24, 1939). Thomas McHugh, an employee of the Alcohol Tax Unit of the IRS in Lodi, California, wrote to complain that he had been punished by his superiors for trying to investigate tax evasion in the wine industry. Writing "primarily as a citizen of the United States," McHugh stated: "While I am concerned in this instance with my one case only, it is not singular nor exceptional and there are at least ten men in the Northern part of this District, and perhaps an equal number in the Southern half, whom have suffered abuses . . . have had their rights violated, too, and been discriminated against and intimidated" (September 16, 1939). William Kosma, who wrote from Michigan to complain about the Ford Motor Company, relied on a very general claim about the need to protect constitutional rights: "I write in defense of the U.S. Constitution. If I said nothing it could pave the way for the deprivation of constitutional rights of others in the future, and I for my part am willing to die if necessary to keep that great manifestation of human enlightenment above class or sect" (February 20, 1940). In other cases, writers could point to more direct benefits of federal intervention and investigation. William Smith, an embalmer from Chicago who was beaten and railroaded by police in Hialeah, Florida, stated: "I am sure that once an investigation is started there will be many more people come forth and tell of similar circumstances." Smith also spoke to the need to prevent future rights violation: "These men should be brought to justice before they can harm more people" (January 16, 1940).

The war in Europe, once again, emerges as a theme in some letters where rights claimants broadened the scope of their claim. Edward Olmstead, who wrote from Michigan in 1939 to complain about the procedures that had led to his commitment to the Ypsilanti State Hospital argued that "unless we look into such things and uproot them, we will shortly find our nation like the European nations which are under the despotic reign of mentally incompetent rulers" (October 7, 1939). Allen Applegarth, who wrote from Berkeley, California, in 1939 to complain about efforts to revoke the citizenship of communist leader William Schneiderman, wrote that "there is no place for repressive acts of this sort which stimulate wartime hysteria and endanger the peace and democracy of the American people" (March 19, 1939). Andrew Loewi, who wrote to report that his furniture store in Manhattan had been targeted by anti-Semitic pickets, claimed repeatedly that he was concerned not about his own injury but the broader implication of such action. Loewi worried that the picketers were part of a growing fascist movement and that failure to protect the ideals of democracy could be a "fatal" blunder for the United States (April 21, 1939).

The efforts by letter writers to make their letters more persuasive by broadening their complaints beyond their own cases, along with the assuredness with which people used legal claims and argued creatively for as yet unrecognized rights, result in a relatively optimistic picture of rights claiming as a rhetorical strategy in everyday political encounters. Writers often seemed emboldened by the choice of legal rhetoric and appropriated symbolic language of law, rights, or the Constitution in the service of novel and creative entitlement claims. Legal discourses about rights thus appear here as a resource that ordinary people use to understand and express grievances and to strengthen claims for the attention of reluctant government officials. Legal language quite often helped to make complaints more vivid or powerful.

A key question that remains to be answered is how well the people who made creative legal claims understood the limitations of rights claiming as a tool for obtaining material redress of grievances. That question can be answered only after consideration of the extralegal persuasive claims in the letters. Those claims are reviewed in the next chapter.

CHAPTER FIVE

Underlying Commitments of Rights Claiming

Extralegal Persuasive Claims and Citizen Understandings of Law

Everybody knows, everybody knows
That's how it goes
Everybody knows.
—Leonard Cohen

The discussion of legal and constitutional claims in chapter 4 shows the important role of legal claims and arguments in letters to the CRS. Taken in isolation, the frequent resort to legal arguments might be interpreted as a sign that writers had broad faith that law was some objective, timeless force in society that operated independently of human agency and choice. The legal claims give voice to a faith that responding government officials are compelled to fulfill the promises of entitlements expressed in the Constitution and other sources of official law. The tendency of writers to frame demands in a legalized language of law, rights, and the Constitution thus seems to suggest that letter writers believed in what Scheingold (2004) called the "myth of rights." The rights claims in the letters also seem to show that faith in myths about law was remarkably resilient: even many writers who were trapped in bad experiences with legal processes expressed legal claims in an idealized form that suggests an underlying faith that justice would prevail in the end. If such faith in legal myths is widespread, the myths presumably have political significance in that they may blind people to the gap between law's ideals and promises and the reality of the way law usually works.

The appearance of broad faith in legal ideals also calls into question my claims in chapter 4 about the quality of writers' legal arguments. I argued that writers were surprisingly sophisticated and comfortable when making legal assertions to government officials and often quite sophisticated when drawing on legal materials to construct arguments. Yet it is more difficult to claim that writers were sophisticated, adept, or realistic if writers also had very unrealistic expectations about the likely consequences of their assertions about rights. Any faith that credible assertions of rights would somehow compel government officials to respond favorably seems hopelessly naive and unrealistic. Even writers who made accurate claims to entitlements that were recognized in official law did not get favorable attention from the federal government.

The apparent tension between writers' habitual and comfortable deployment of legal claims and their apparently naive faith in law disappears, however, if the legalized discourses in the letters are considered in light of other nonlegal claims and arguments. Almost all the writers who made legal claims supplemented those claims with other, extralegal persuasive claims. Those extralegal claims reveal that writers who gave voice to idealized formulations of law did not believe that those claims could stand alone and make their letters persuasive. The content of those extralegal claims also quite often reveals that the faith in law that writers seemed to be expressing when they made legal claims was conditional and quite limited.

For example, writers who portrayed law as some objective or transcendent force that was beyond agency routinely included other claims that reveal that they understood that law alone would not force responsible government officials to take action to protect rights. The extralegal claims often reveal directly the writers' understanding that responding officials would be exercising discretion and that their choices could be influenced by factors other than law. Thus the appeal to rights or constitutional ideals does not imply that writers had faith that such ideals had always or even often prevailed. Of course, my claim that most writers had only limited faith in law is only plausible if there is some way to make sense of the finding that so many writers made idealized claims that seemed to express such faith. Unfortunately, however, the explanation for the idealized claims is not always apparent in the letters. Nevertheless, there is also nothing in the letters that confirms that the people who wrote were deluded about the power or objectivity of law. In the broader context of the extralegal claims, it seems more likely that writers used rights claims and constitutional claims because they understood that the language of law and rights had rhetorical power in American political culture. Many writers said things to show that they understood the language of law as a medium through which government power is both justified and contested.

Considering the legal claims in light of the extralegal claims also draws attention to a fascinating feature of the exchanges recorded in the CRS correspondence: both letter writers and the responding government officials appear to have been operating with the expectation that language of rights and law would resonate with the intended audience for their letters. Those expectations led both sides of the exchanges to use legal discourses to communicate ideas, but the strategies of communication were different for the CRS officials than for the letter writers. The use of legal claims by CRS officials suggests that those officials expected letter writers to recognize talk of law as a shared medium for communicating claims about legitimacy in political interactions. Their expectations about their audience appear to have been right on target. Even the letter writers who expressed disagreement with the CRS's claims understood that the CRS was using claims about jurisdiction to try to justify its response. Meanwhile, the people who wrote letters also recognized that law provided a shared language of legitimacy and also expected their claims to be recognizable and meaningful to their audience of government officials. The letter writers also used legal discourses to take advantage of the fact that government officials also recognized that law was important and had commitments to legal ideals. Writers leveraged law's cultural significance and symbolic power to make broad claims for new entitlements. Instead of just making claims about the legitimacy of existing arrangements, letter writers used legal discourses to communicate more general ideals and aspirations about political and social life.

There was thus a *mutual* recognition of legal discourses as a powerful and resonant means of communicating and building understanding. Significantly, that shared recognition also gave both sides reason to voice absolute and idealized formulations of law even when they were not fully committed to those formulations. In chapter 2, I pointed out that CRS officials were not fully committed to the absolute claims about federal jurisdiction that were expressed in the CRS's reply letters. After all, CRS attorneys were almost simultaneously arguing in appellate courts and law reviews that those limits were wrong and had to be changed. That they nevertheless made such claims in the reply letters demonstrates that legal officials will adopt different poses toward law in different contexts. The people who wrote letters also adopted multiple poses, often in the same transaction. Writers made idealized and absolute claims that suggested faith in law while simultaneously writing other things that betrayed the limits of their faith. The apparent compulsion to deploy legal ideals thus not only reveals their recognition of the power of legal discourses but also provides the source of their capacity to resist legitimating claims from government officials.

Hattie Mae Smith provides a good starting place for thinking about the way extralegal claims reveal limits in underlying faith. Smith is the woman who claimed that her family had a "right to earn our own living selling just good food, ice cream, and pop" (July 18, 1940). (Smith's complaint about a zoning decision that prevented her from opening a small store is discussed in chapter 3.) Taken in isolation, assertions like Smith's seem like precisely the kind of exaggerated rights claims that skeptics would pounce on as evidence that rights talk produces a distorted and unrealistic understanding of how law and politics actually work. Critics of rights discourses claim that exaggerated formulations of rights are problematic because absolute language masks the bargaining processes through which government officials inevitably *balance* rights-related entitlements against competing claims (Glendon 1991, chapter 3). However, in Smith's case, the evidence suggests that her own understanding of rights and law is more complicated than the rhetorical flourish about her "right to sell ice cream" seems to suggest. Smith's rights claim is embedded in a lengthy letter that ultimately reveals that she was not in the grip of some myth of absolute rights. Claiming a "right" to sell ice cream was a way for Smith to communicate a particularly sharp sense of her perception of injustice and entitlement. However, instead of relying exclusively on the legalized claim, she devoted most of her letter to making other kinds of persuasive claims.

Hattie Mae Smith primarily tried to persuade government officials to give attention to her case by giving details about her character and personal hardships. She wrote in detail about the difficulty her family was facing, her need to support members of her family who were unable to work themselves, and her problems finding appropriate work. She also attested to her own character to show that she was worthy of the government's limited attention. She stated, for example, "I never handled any lickor in my life. I hate the stuff," even though her story had nothing at all to do with alcohol. These extralegal details did not affect the legal status of her rights claim and would have been irrelevant and unnecessary if the right to sell ice cream and pop was an automatic legal entitlement. The fact that Smith included extralegal claims indicates that she expected responding government officials to be making a choice about how to respond to her plea and that she believed their choice would be influenced by nonlegal factors.

The ubiquity of extralegal persuasive claims in the letters suggests that, far from having an unrelenting faith in law, writers understood that government officials quite often made choices that left rights unprotected. Writers also showed that they could maintain their own ideas about morality and justice and resist the messages of legitimacy embedded in authoritative pronouncements of official law. Writers sometimes stated quite directly that they did not see official law as the relevant standard of justice or legitimacy. Other writers revealed their skepticism indirectly when they offered visions of law, justice, or constitutional democracy that they distinguished from the actual outcomes afforded by official law. Such writers were appropriating the rhetoric of law to make claims about how things *should* be or *were supposed* to be, but they were not losing sight of how actual practices of official law fell short of legal ideals.[1]

To be clear, I am not claiming here that writers were always conscious of the tension between their legal and extralegal claims or that writers were consciously making a point about the discretion exercised by government officials. It is difficult to pin down each individual's level of awareness with precision. My analysis in this chapter is based instead on the observation that it would make little sense for writers to make so many extralegal persuasive claims unless they (1) believed that the government officials who would respond to their claims about rights were exercising discretion and (2) believed that the choices made by those officials were not fully controlled by legal considerations. Those two underlying beliefs express the limits of writers' faith in core legal ideals. In pointing out those limits, I am avoiding the stronger assumption that writers consciously made an analytic connection between official discretion and their extralegal claims. Writers who included personal information and other types of extralegal persuasive claims may not have all deliberated carefully about why they were making certain kinds of claims and not others. In many cases, the content of the letters seems to reflect writers' efforts to follow familiar cultural repertoires or scripts that are commonly used and expected when people are asking for help from strangers or speaking to government officials. Writers thus may not have consciously recognized that there was a tension between their idealized rights claims and their more realistic efforts to influence official discretion with extralegal claims. Nevertheless, the habit of adding extralegal claims to the letters shows that the pull of myths of rights and other legal ideals was not all-powerful or unlimited. The letters reveal, at a minimum, that the cultural repertoires and scripts that led people to use idealized legal language had to compete and coexist with other cultural practices that recognize law's limitations and thus provide a means for articulating resistance to law's claims of legitimacy.[2] Even if some people were following the scripts mechanically and without a great deal of thought or reflection, they were still following at least one script that exposed their awareness of law's limitations and thus the limits of their own faith in law. The decision to deploy law thus did not mean that law became a totalizing or colonizing force that crowded out other ideas or inhibited the expression of alternative claims. Writers moved quite freely between legal and nonlegal sources of normative ideals as they constructed persuasive claims.

The letters also show the importance of contextualizing claims about the disciplining power of legal rhetoric. Recitation of certain elements of official law's idealized claims of equal treatment or justice does not mean that people are fully committed to legal values or believe that such claims describe some underlying reality. As a result, scholars cannot understand people's underlying beliefs and commitments by simply tallying the idealized legal claims that they express in surveys or interviews or when they are observed in particular kinds of social interactions. The strength of people's underlying commitments has to be tested against a broader context of other ideals that they express and in light of the choices people make when they are forced to deal directly with problems or obstacles created by legal processes. That full context is, of course, very difficult to observe. The letters used in this study provide one valuable window onto the political impact of legal commitments because they allow observation of how people articulate and act on their legal commitments in practical situations where they seek attention from government officials.

I divide the evidence considered here into two parts. First, I consider a variety of extralegal persuasive claims that writers used to establish that they deserved attention from the government officials. These types of claims were ubiquitous in the letters, including many letters where writers made detailed legal arguments. I argue that such claims indirectly reveal the limits of writers' faith in law. I then consider some writers who offered more direct expressions of their awareness of the way law worked. Although such expressions were not as ubiquitous as extralegal efforts at persuasion, the writers who made direct claims almost invariably expressed a realistic understanding of law's shortcomings rather than a naive faith in myths of rights.

Indirect Expressions of Awareness: Persuasion, Worthiness, and Official Discretion

Writers who wanted help almost invariably supplemented their assertions about legal entitlements with extralegal claims. I call claims extralegal when they were not connected with or relevant to the writer's expressed legal grounds (real or imagined) for the complaint.[3] Writers who made extralegal claims were apparently trying to persuade responding government officials to give attention to their case. Writers often persuaded by portraying their claim as particularly *important* and worthy of attention. Writers also emphasized the egregiousness of what had occurred or emphasized the costs that would result if the government chose not to help.

The variety of extralegal claims in the letters is quite broad, and individual writers often made quite a large number of extralegal claims. Writers most often included claims about their character, social position, or immediate circumstances. Some writers also made direct appeals to the conscience or honor of responding government officials. Writers also made assertions about personal hardship, pleas for pity, and claims for patronage based on political service or loyalty.

A series of letters from Zella Morrison of Port Huron, Michigan, provides an initial example. Her letters show how writers used extralegal claims to persuade and illustrate how some writers would use quite a wide variety of claims. Morrison, who was also known as "Madam Zola," wrote several letters to Attorney General Frank Murphy and one to President Roosevelt after she was convicted of violating a local law against fortune-telling. Morrison had been fined twenty-five dollars, placed on probation, and warned that she would be sent to jail if she continued to tell fortunes. She complained that the court's ruling left her unable to earn a living. Morrison asked the attorney general to provide her with legal advice on her case and to "send two private investigators till I prove to you what is going on in our Police Dept Here" (April 19, 1939).

Although Morrison's letter to the attorney general was an effort to seek help with legal problems, Morrison did not clearly articulate a legal basis for the federal government to intervene in her dispute with local authorities. Her complaint was quite different in that regard from most other letters from people who had been charged with crimes. She did not claim that she had not violated the law or that her trial had been tainted by constitutional violations. She did claim to have been "framed by our Police Chief." However, her claim of being "framed" was only that the police had caught her through an undercover investigation. (She reported that a police officer had paid two women to come to her house and pretend that they were looking for "spiritual advice.") Her letter acknowledged that she regularly read fortunes in exchange for "donations."

While Morrison did not elaborate a legal position in much detail, her often quite lengthy letters did include many other types of persuasive claims. She made a variety of claims related to her personal status and character, as well as claims about the misplaced priorities of the police. In her first letter, Morrison wrote, "I have lived here all my life and am a taxpayer," claimed to be "a relative to our president," and indicated that she was religious. (She even included the name and address of her priest.) Morrison also made detailed claims about the severity of the personal problems that resulted from her criminal conviction: "My husband has not worked a day since the Bridge has been completed . . . this frame up has placed us on the welfare of 4.20 for 2 weeks we are nearly starving on this amount" (April 19, 1939).

In an uncommon move, the CRS's reply to Morrison's first letter urged her to "immediately pursue an appeal to the highest court in your state." The reply letter also invited her to provide more information related to the legal basis for her complaint: "If you have been intimidated in the exercise of any Federal rights, although not indicated in your letter, it is further suggested that you seek an interview with the United States Attorney in Detroit . . . and bring the evidence of such intimidation to his attention" (May 2, 1939). Morrison apparently did visit with officials at that office but was not satisfied by their answer. She wrote three additional letters to the Justice Department and president (May 5, 1939; May 31, 1939; June 6, 1939). Even though the CRS had urged her to articulate a *legal* claim about a violation of a federal right, Morrison's letters continued to focus on personal attributes and circumstances. She mentioned that she had been rebuffed by an FBI agent in Detroit but did not attempt to articulate or challenge the reasons for his refusal to help. Her letters instead repeated her initial extralegal claims and amplified them with additional details. (She mentioned that her father had once been a sergeant in the police force and clarified: "I am a relative to our president Franklin Roosevelt on my mother side" [May 5, 1939].) She did not try to strengthen her claims for federal attention by establishing that she had been "intimidated in the exercise of any Federal rights."

Given that the department had invited Morrison to bring a claim of a federal rights violation, Morrison's failure to attempt to make a rights claim is unusual. Other people in my sample who wrote back to the department after such an invitation usually made some attempt to strengthen their legal position. Morrison could have claimed that laws against fortune-telling violated her right to free speech or perhaps her right to free exercise of religion. However, she never made such claims. It may be that Morrison did not know enough about the Constitution to make legal claims effectively or that she simply decided that she had no basis for making any legitimate legal claim.

It might be tempting to further conclude that Morrison's real problem was a poor understanding of law and governmental processes. She otherwise would have known that she was wasting her time by writing to federal officials. She did not seem to know that no federally protected rights had been violated in her case and did not know that the federal government lacked the resources to provide help in most cases involving violations of real rights. However, things appear to be more complicated than such an explanation implies. Morrison's letters ultimately show that while she may have been a charlatan, she was not a fool. Morrison did not have a specialist's grasp of the legal issues relevant to her case, but the strategies that she pursued in her letters nevertheless reveal someone with a fairly sophisticated understanding of how law and legal processes work. Morrison was not a helpless and naive supplicant with a strong faith in the power of law to compel officials to produce justice. Morrison understood quite well that the realization of legal entitlements was highly contingent and that law alone would not dictate the federal government's response.

In particular, Morrison correctly understood that both the cause and potential solution to her problems lay with discretionary choices by government officials charged with enforcing the law. Morrison directly called attention to discretionary choices made by local officials who decided to direct police and prosecutorial resources toward enforcing the law against fortune-telling. She complained about the way the local police and prosecutor exercised discretion, and she critiqued their underlying priorities. Her critique was based on moral and political rather than legal claims. Morrison complained that it was wrong for the police to target "good honest people also taxpayers" because "there is so many other things of so much more importance that really need to be done to keep our city respectful and clean" (May 5, 1939). To sharpen her complaint about police priorities, Morrison noted that other fortune-tellers were "doing the same thing," charging even more money and "paying for their homes this way." She asked, "Why should they crucify me when the officers know that my husband had not worked for a year and that I was trying to get along with one Boarder at 8.00 per week and keeping off the welfare this way" (May 5, 1939). Morrison also included a newspaper clipping that reported on her case. The article also questioned the priorities of a police force that targeted fortune-tellers.

Morrison was also aware that the federal officials who would respond to her letter would also be making discretionary decisions. She reveals that awareness indirectly, through the strategies she used to persuade those federal officials to give attention to her case. As already noted, she made a variety of persuasive claims about her character and the hardships she faced. One of her later letters employed an additional strategy by making a more personal plea to Brien McMahon, the assistant attorney general who had signed the CRS's initial reply letter. She appealed to McMahon's honor and patriotism, telling him that "you would be doing one mighty wonderful thing for your country" by deciding to provide help (May 31, 1939). Morrison also showed that she understood that securing help from federal officials would be an uphill struggle because of competing demands for their attention. She stated in her letter to the president: "Mr. Roosevelt you no doubt get hundred of such letters" (June 6, 1939).

Personal Character

The full sample of letters includes an astounding variety of extralegal claims and arguments. The most pervasive strategy, as already illustrated in the cases of Zella Morrison and Hattie Mae Smith, was to make claims about personal character. The claims about character seem to have been offered to show that a person whose rights had been violated was a worthy rights bearer with a case that warranted use of scarce government resources for protecting rights.

A few additional examples can help to illustrate the range of claims about character and status. W. E. Bullard, who wrote to complain that he had been beaten while canvassing door to door as a Jehovah's Witness in Fairview, Oklahoma, wrote: "I have lived in this County for a period of 47 years, or since a ten your old boy, have paid taxes since I was 21 years of age, both me and my wife and both of our parents were born in these United States and are entitled to the protection it's laws guarantees to it's citizens. . . . Both my people, and I are law abiding citizens, and entitled to the confidence and protection that the Constitution of these United States offers it's citizens, and am asking for nothing more" (September

22, 1941). Louise Leonard, who complained that her nephew had been framed and jailed by corrupt officials in Hyattsville, Maryland, reported that her nephew was "a very fine young lad, just twenty-one years of age." She continued: "He does not smoke, or drink intoxicating liquors. He is however, engaged to a very lovely young lady, now attending Trinity College here in Washington." Leonard added that the "incident has almost caused the death of his dear Mother, such humiliation" (January 29, 1941). Josephine O'Neal, who complained about her brother's wrongful conviction for rape, wrote: "My brother John Cleveland is 30 years of age and is a citizen of the U.S. and has work and made an honest living for himself since he has been of age" (September 10, 1939). Edward Olmstead, who wanted his rights restored after being released from an asylum, identified himself as "a resident of the City of Detroit, since June 3rd, 1929, never having been on the public welfare rolls, or arrested for any crime within its borders" (October 7, 1939). Alvina Douglas, who wrote a heartbreaking letter about a daughter who was in prison for murder in Michigan, wrote: "Betty wasn't the pampered darling of a wealthy family nor was she the daughter of a college professor but just a happy, vivacious, carefree young woman of the middle class. She came from a home of culture and refinement; her father before he died many years ago was a medic in Detroit and he gave unsparingly to charitable organizations" (February 12, 1940). Douglas complained that the prosecutor had "hurled all the insulting wrath and fury he could assume at her" and had "tainted her character, and made her appear as a disreputable, common, cheap, tawdry mistress." As a final flourish, Douglas added that Betty's life sentence "reminded me of Pilate sentencing our Lord to the cross" (February 12, 1940).

Writers made some offbeat claims to attest to their character. Virginia Dryer, who complained about a dog-licensing ordinance in Pontiac, Michigan, noted that she was a champion dog breeder with "eleven blue ribbons" (March 17, 1939). Mrs. O. P. McCoy of Tonasket, Washington, who complained that rising water costs had led to a foreclosure on her family farm, noted that the apples from her farm had fewer worms than other area apples (March 31, 1939). There was also considerable variation in how high writers aimed when they made claims about status. Jacob Kind wrote that a friend who had been unjustly committed to a mental institution had "received his education in the public schools, won a scholarship to—and worked his way through—a major university of this country" and had become "an honorable member of an honorable profession, a reputable accountant" (April 13, 1939). In contrast, a nurse named Eleanor

Watjus claimed, rather modestly, "I passed the State Board Examination above a mediocre level" (February 10, 1941).

In most cases, the claims about status were unrelated not just to the law but to the subject matter of the complaint. Writers used claims about status primarily to establish their own worthiness or to dramatize the importance of their claims for attention. Frances McKoney, who complained about a false arrest that led to the death of several of her dogs, wrote: "I have always stood for civil liberties. My great, great Grandfather fought with Washington to win these liberties, and I am willing to give my life fighting to retain them. You may think this Washington affair is a 'little' affair to be making such a squawk about, but 'Great Oaks From Little Acorns Grow' " (December 26, 1940). Many other writers claimed worthiness because of bloodlines or familial connections. In a letter about youth participation in politics, Anton Vedral claimed to be a descendant of Nathan Hale (July 3, 1939). Marie James, who complained that she was no longer able to play ball with her dog in her yard after San Francisco widened her street, noted that she was the widow of an army veteran who had been shot in the Spanish-American War (June 19, 1939). Many other writers could not claim such specific pedigree but still asserted that they were citizens with deep roots on American soil, apparently to make a contrast with less worthy recent immigrants. Unsurprisingly, efforts to invoke nativism occasionally turned ugly. For example, a letter from Louis Sheppard complained that he had been fined $1,000 by three police officers and a "Jew lawyer" after he had killed a "drunk girl" while driving. Sheppard asserted: "I am white, my people have been in this country for a couple of generations, also a taxpayer. What right has any Jew to restrict my liberties" (September 11, 1940).

In other instances, the claims of status were appended without much explanation or obvious connection to reports or legal claims in the letters. William Harvey, who wrote from Los Angeles to complain that his rights were being violated by a Chinese gang, noted that he was a "Gold Star Mother's son" (August 7, 1939). Louis Nally, who wrote from Chicago to complain that an African American neighbor "on relief" was living the high life, made a point of noting: "I am a disabled World War Veteran" (June 24, 1939). Harry Dollowing of Baltimore, who complained that CBS radio had violated his rights by broadcasting his name, wrote: "I am a citizen, voter, of this Constitution (high school graduate) honest, sober, Law-Abiding" (October 20, 1939). Gertrude Notes, who wrote to complain about the legal troubles of a friend, began her letter by noting that she was "an American citizen, a daughter of the Eastern Star, a mother and grandmother who has lived in Washington D.C. for thirty years" (March 12, 1939).

Not all the letter writers could claim to be angels. The circumstances of some complaints meant that writers could not tell their stories without admitting some past wrongdoing or mistake. Such writers would often preemptively acknowledge the black marks on their records and then add some assurances about the overall worthiness of their claims. An example of such a preemptive claim is in a letter from Mrs. Roy McDonald. McDonald provided a detailed, moving, and at times gruesome account of the murder of her husband by police officials in Junction City, Arkansas. At the very beginning of her narrative, McDonald acknowledged: "My husband was slightly intoxicated at the time when arrested." She repeatedly emphasized, however, that he did not do anything wrong. He "made no resistance," yet was nevertheless tortured, beaten, garroted, paraded through town by the mayor, and eventually burned beyond recognition in a mysterious jail fire. The letter also noted that he was "from a good and substantial family" and had three children (October 11, 1944).

Some writers with blemished records made more extended efforts to explain problems and try to turn them into positive attributes. Samuel King's long and fascinating letter to Frank Murphy (May 16, 1939) provides an example. King, an African American CIO organizer, explained that he had recently escaped from prison in Alabama after a lengthy odyssey through the criminal justice systems of several southern states. King had been organizing small-business and farm cooperatives in Alabama when government officials framed him and sent him to jail. King claimed that the police were acting at the behest of white business owners who felt threatened by his organizing activities. He had escaped from custody after being warned that he was about to be murdered in prison.

Many of the claims in the letter reveal that King was concerned that the Justice Department would not find his story credible or worthy of attention. King thus used a variety of tactics to reassure the department of his reliability. Early in the letter, King acknowledged that there was "one black mark against my records." He claimed that he was convicted of a felony for unlawfully possessing a pistol when he was seventeen and sentenced to one to two years in prison. However, King tried to turn the experience into something positive, noting that experience in jail had changed him in a constructive way. He noted that he had learned in jail that "all criminals are suckers" and insisted that he was determined to stay on the right side of the law: "I wouldn't have ever gone to prison again if selfish people hadn't forced me" (May 16, 1939).

King followed this acknowledgement with a more philosophical reflection on his character development. He recounted a boyhood story about confronting his father in defense of one of his playmates: "I answered him by asking him why he and other neighbors didn't help that boy be a better boy by aiding his widow mother who had he and four other children to care for. And to this day I don't see it as my relatives see it, hence our relationship isn't the best." King concluded his letter with a biblical defense of his actions: "I am using my conclusion to beg you not to chide me for the method I used to escape death, 'twas my only alternative. I do not feel ashamed of having used it, for David feigned insanity (I Samuel 21–13) to save his live when he was helpless at the hands of Achish the King of Gath" (May 16, 1939).

In addition to making claims about their own good character, many writers made claims about the bad character of their adversaries. Thomas McHugh, an IRS employee who claimed that he had been retaliated against for whistle-blowing, claimed that his supervisor spoke "in a mean and sarcastic tongue, and his choicest words of derision are given to those men the country has honored" and that the "personal history of this man is bound up with pettiness and meanness" (September 16, 1939). Douglas Dorner complained that a WPA supervisor who had disciplined him was a "lesser-ranking official" and "a recent arrival to our shores" who "obviously . . . lack[ed] the good sound judgment which is characteristic of American Democracy" (March 9, 1939).

While it was quite common for letter writers to include some information about personal character, there is no evidence in the files that such information ever convinced CRS officials to provide help to a letter writer. That does not mean, however, that writers' efforts to establish their good character were misguided. There is clear evidence in some case files that judgments about character did influence discretionary decisions of the CRS. There are some instances where officials lost interest in cases after learning about flaws in a complainants' character. For example, in 1945, the CRS began investigating a case of police brutality and false arrest in Gadsden, Alabama. The CRS had both the FBI and the local US attorney look into the case. An FBI investigation corroborated the reports of the unlawful detention and beating of an African American woman named Marie Johnson. (The police were trying to extract information regarding a third party.) However, the department quickly dropped the case after the

FBI also reported that Johnson's reputation was "average" and that she had previously been arrested on liquor charges.[4] Another example is Velva Wise, who wrote a series of letters to both the Justice Department and to J. Edgar Hoover complaining about police corruption in Little Rock, Arkansas. Wise said that women were "being framed and picked up for things they do not do" (January 16, 1942) and that she "saw almost 50 women persecuted . . . for things they had not committed" (July 13, 1942). When Hoover forwarded one letter to the Justice Department for instruction, he included a cover memo indicating that the FBI had a file on Wise, who had earlier faced charges of immorality and habitual prostitution (March 5, 1942). Assistant Attorney General Berge quickly wrote back to Hoover instructing him to ignore Wise's letters (March 11, 1942).

Of course, there are legitimate practical reasons for the prosecution-oriented CRS to be concerned about the character of persons who claimed rights violations. The success of any criminal civil rights prosecution would be influenced by the status and character of the victim of a crime. In some of the cases that the CRS did prosecute, CRS attorneys had difficulty with jurors who were inclined to be more sympathetic to the perpetrators of rights violations than the targets (Carr 1947, 138–42). My point here is not that character should not matter in the exercise of official discretion. It is that the letter writers' compulsion to provide reassurances about character makes it clear that letter writers were aware that government officials would be concerned about their worthiness as rights bearers, not just the legal status of their rights claims.

"At the Breaking Point, and Unable to Stand the Strain Any Longer": *Pleas for Pity*

A closely related persuasive strategy was to emphasize that difficult or dire circumstances had created a desperate need for help. The extralegal claims in this group often read as efforts to persuade responding government officials by generating sympathy or pity. In comparison to the claims about character, the claims of hardship were more often directly connected to the circumstances giving rise to the complaint. For example, many writers described in detail the hardships that resulted from alleged rights violations in order to demonstrate how much they needed federal assistance. Consider again Zella Morrison. She noted that she had been supporting herself and her husband with the "donations" she accepted for her card readings. She said the donations had "kept us living" and that she and her husband were now "terribly up against it" and about to lose their electric appliances to creditors. Morrison further noted, "I am a little attractive but it don't seem to get me work" (June 6, 1939).

Quite a few writers followed Morrison's strategy of emphasizing how rights violations or other legal problems had hurt the ability of people or families to support themselves. For example, G. Haltzbander of Pine Bluff, Arkansas, wrote to Eleanor Roosevelt, complaining about her son's false arrest and imprisonment by local officials. Haltzbander wrote: "Lady isn't there some way you can get that Federal charge lifted then I can get him out here on a parole and he can come home and help me, as my health is no good, and I am passed 55 my husband is passed 72, so you see we are not young people and haven't got money, so I trust in the lord you understand, my conditions, I have read so many good deeds you have done" (February 10, 1941). Marie James, the war widow who complained that San Francisco had widened her street, wrote: "I have no other income than $20 a month pension am 60 years old, have been in very poor health for 10 years" (June 19, 1939). In some cases, the description of hardship was powerful and compelling even when the underlying claim was weak or unclear. Lulua Hughes, for example, wrote to complain that threats were being made against her, a boarder, and her two daughters. Hughes, whose husband had recently committed suicide, wrote a particularly desperate letter but could not describe the threats in detail or report clearly about who was making them. However, she did clearly articulate the difficult circumstances of her life raising two daughters:

> My youngest girl age 17 years has a cripple foot and leg as she had infantile paralysis when she was small. I have never done anything wrong in my life and to have to go through this. I know we can't stand much more of this as the strain will break us down if nothing else does. . . . Won't you please help us. All we ask is to be left alone and let us live this down the best we can. . . . Let me have a chance to work and make our living. If things were peaceful I could support my girls. As I am a cook a first class cook can get work any time if I was able to leave my home. (August 28, 1939)

The sadness of the plea did not go unnoticed by CRS staff. A line added to the boilerplate reply stated: "It is deeply regretted . . . that we are unable to be of service" (September 14, 1939).

Another writer who tried to persuade with a heartbreaking story was Mary Deming, of Mt. Pleasant, Michigan. Deming's son had been in prison for eleven years. He had agreed to plead guilty in exchange of a promise of an eighteen-month sentence. Deming's lengthy letter mixed descriptions of the hardships her son faced, claims that her own health was deteriorating, and direct appeals to the conscience of government decision makers. One passage begins with an account of the day authorities had come to remove her son from her home: "Jake Melman stopped at hour house with him here in Mt. Pleasant the morning he took him a way to prison. I was crying clinging to Claude bidding him good but Melman said to me don't worry Mrs Deming Claude will be out in 18 months any way. That 18 months has run in to 11 long years." She continued: "*Please* try to get him out. Something *must* be done. It seems I wont live to see my boy back home with his family. I am 70 years old and Broken hearted. Justice must be done . . . he surely has been Punished enough." A letter presenting the opposite situation came from eighteen-year-old Cecil Stevens of Baltimore, who reported that authorities had removed his mother from his home. Stevens explained that his mother had gone to visit a doctor for a "nervous" ailment. That afternoon, he received a visit from a doctor who reported that she had been committed to a mental institution. Stevens reported that he was dependent upon his mother and that the news "left me completely astounded" because "Mother seemed to be the normal, intimate person that I have always known." He focused much of his plea on explaining the effect that his mother's absence had on him: "My whole destiny depends on this one thing . . . during the last year and a half I have been very very unhappy, distressed, and unsettled." He added, "I aspire to enter college, but it will never remain in view unless I can clear up this case" (September 3, 1939).

Claims for attention based on hardship were sometimes made using considerable rhetorical flourish. Nicolaas Steelink, who complained that he was still facing hardships several decades after his imprisonment for violating antisyndicalism laws, wrote: "Tears are falling on this handwriting as I think of all the humiliation my family has had to suffer!" (January 13, 1941). Alvina Douglas wrote that her daughter's trial was "the most unjust, most ridiculous, most heartrending and breaking in the entire state of Michigan" (February 12, 1940). Some writers targeted government officials with claims that expressed demands in very personal terms. When Seth Plummer wrote to President Roosevelt to complain on behalf of a friend who had been committed to a state hospital, he made the following appeal: "Put your mother in this poor womans place. Wouldn't she cry her eyes out under similar conditions?" (September 10, 1939). In her letter about false arrest, Frances McKoney wrote: "How would you like your Daughter jerked up and treated this way. They had the Gaul to take my picture and fingerprint me. I have been given a Jail record by being here. My Christmas has been ruined. I am an innocent person" (December 26, 1940). Writers sometimes freely mixed pleas for pity with more idealized claims about American values or history. Molly Mollison wrote to President Roosevelt from Florida to complain that the police were forcing her to leave Miami Beach after she had been involved in a series of fistfights with another young woman in a dispute over a bathing suit. Mollison explained that she "had not one soul to defend me" and that she wanted to get a lawyer because she "wanted to get justice." In pursuit of that goal, her letter primarily focused on a set of dramatic appeals to Roosevelt:

> Dear Dear Mr President! I am writing you this as a poor American Citizen. . . . I was told that I could not live in the city of Miami Beach . . . cause I've no money looking for work. I was living in a hotel 10 dollars a week my mother was sending me I am a very nervous person.
>
>   I wasn't given a chance to prove myself I am a good girl 26 years old and oh mister President Bleave me I wish would you pleas make Fla an American city. . . . [L]ove and Justice for all sick and poor. God Bless America Please President Please. (January 12, 1940)

Another frequent strategy was to emphasize that a favorable response to the letter was a writers' last remaining hope for obtaining relief. Eleanor Blake McNamara, who wrote to complain about the performance of corrupt lawyers in a foreclosure proceeding, stated: "I'm told I must have nerves of steel, but I feel now, that they are at the breaking point, and unable to stand the strain any longer." McNamara explained: "I'm appealing to you the Attorney General of the United States, with jurisdiction over the Courts, and lawyers as my last hope to save my property, and restore my peace of mind" (August 23, 1939).

Flattery and Political Affiliation

Another strategy for gaining attention was to flatter government officials or claim past political support. An example is Douglas Dorner of New York City, who quoted the Fourteenth Amendment in his complaint about a dispute with his WPA employer. Dorner reported that he was a "good Democratic district captain." He also called Frank Murphy a "noble and upright man" and urged: "I am more than sure a great man like you cannot fail to give me a complete satisfaction" (March 9, 1939). Thomas McHugh, who wrote about retaliation from his IRS work supervisors, made repeated mention of Murphy's expressed commitment to protecting civil rights, and cited specific federal civil rights statutes. He also wrote: "This is my story—and I am giving it to you in my sincere and fervent hope it shall deserve your thoughtful consideration and may bring action. And I am giving it to you because of my personal faith in your integrity as a man and the one man in the political life of our country in this time to whom men of all political faiths give their faith for that personal attribute" (September 16, 1939). A less polished but more self-conscious effort at flattery came from Bernice Yendick, a fourteen-year-old from Detroit who wrote to the president: "Please help me. I have know you probily get lots of letters like mine and you answer them with a lot of thought because you must be a fine man by the looks of your kind face. This is not just flattery to make you decide in my favor. It's the truth because I wouldn't lie to you" (October 10, 1939). Yendick's long letter was a request for help in a dispute with some of the children in her neighborhood.

Writers also made claims about various forms of political service. James Porter, who wrote from California to complain of his arrest on a vagrancy charge, was one of many writers who noted that he had voted for FDR (March 20, 1939). Louise Leonard noted that her unjustly incarcerated nephew had purchased tickets to Roosevelt's inauguration (January 29, 1941). One writer offered a particularly dramatic political tribute. Lambert Gerin, who asked for protection after he had been attacked by the CIO in LaGrange, Illinois, concluded his telegram by stating: "Incidentally, Franklin, We had twins born on January 1st. The names are Franklin Delano Roosevelt and Eleanor Roosevelt Gerin" (January 11, 1941).

Documentary Evidence and Literary References

Another frequent strategy for establishing the credibility or worthiness of complainants was to include documentary material to support or amplify claims in the letters. One hundred thirty-seven writers, 19 percent of those who reported incidents, enclosed some sort of supporting documentation. These materials included newspaper clippings, court papers, or letters from other government officials. Quite often, these materials were efforts to establish the truthfulness of accounts. One example is William C. Smith, who wrote from Chicago to protest his false drunk driving arrest in

Hialeah, Florida. Smith included with his letter a statement from a Florida doctor stating that he had been treated for injuries resulting from blows to his head (January 16, 1940). In cases like Smith's, the materials might be counted as legal rather than extralegal because they were efforts to display an evidentiary basis for a legal claim. In many cases, however, the materials are better classified as extralegal efforts at persuasion rather than attempts to provide admissible evidence. For example, when John Stoddard wrote to complain that James Morrin, the president of the ironworkers union, was a racketeer, he included a photograph of Morrin as proof. Stoddard explained: "I am sure after you have given careful consideration to the enclosed picture of him, you will agree that he has one of the most repulsive faces to be found outside of a prison" (March 7, 1939). Frances McKoney included in her letter a newspaper clipping of a photograph of a distraught father looking over his son's corpse following the German invasion of the Netherlands. She wrote on the photo: "I had to stand and watch three brutal policemen murder my dogs" (December 26, 1940).

Other writers made their claims more vivid or memorable by using literary or biblical references as rhetorical flourishes. Literary references in the letters ranged from Gilbert and Sullivan (Jacob Kind, April 13, 1939) to Shakespeare (Samuel King, May 16, 1939) to George Hurley's curious reworking of Adelaide Pollard's hymn "Have Thine Own Way, Lord":

> Have thine own way, Land Company
> Have thine own way
> Thou art the Potter
> We are the clay. (January 15, 1941)

Literary references were not usually efforts to communicate factual information. They were sometimes used for humor, for emphasis, or perhaps to demonstrate worthiness by putting the writers' cultural sophistication on display.

"Pimps and Panderers, Who Lay Feeding in the Public Pork Barrel": Getting Personal and Demanding Help

A final type of persuasive strategy used by letter writers is more difficult to categorize precisely but emerges as a distinctive category across the full sample of letters. In these instances, writers tried to forestall an unfavorable exercise of discretion by making a preemptive comment about the character of the government official responding to the letter. The letters in this group were pointed, defiant, and sometimes downright nasty. Writers would challenge government officials by raising issues of honor (e.g., by calling them cowards) or integrity (e.g., by claiming they were violating an oath of office). An example is a letter from Paul Cowles demanding that the federal government prosecute labor leaders who were interfering with his rights. Cowles attempted to provoke the department by saying that if it did not prosecute the labor leaders he was attacking, they were duty bound to prosecute him for making false accusations. Cowles wrote to Frank Murphy: "If you do not prosecute the parties I have named, or me, then I and all of those who know, can only conclude that YOU ARE A MORAL AND POLITICAL COWARD" (October 9, 1939). Another example is John Peters, who wrote a series of letters about losing an inheritance because of the "larcenous and felonious actions by a double-dealing shyster-politico lawyer named John Nangle" (May 7, 1939). When he wrote back to dispute the CRS's initial boilerplate reply, Peters made a personal attack on Welly Hopkins, the acting assistant attorney general for the Criminal Division who signed the CRS's reply. "As my charges of mail fraud are based upon prime principles of Federal Law and legal good faith, I am sorry to find that Attorney General Murphy and you, yourself, are indifferent to them, or for unexplained reasons, simply following wrongful, illogical, and illegal avenues of judgment, that might also lead you to consider the amount involved, four hundred and twenty-five dollars, as too small for you to concern yourselves with." That claim was just the warm up. Peters continued:

> Now Mr. Hopkins, if you refuse . . . to perform your duty and expose this rotten mess, I cannot help but conclude that . . . the present National Administration of Justice has degenerated into the supine attitude of assuming the same innocent trappings as are employed in vice-bred and ridden 'clip joints,' while your officials, including Attorney General Murphy and yourself, naturally also assume the unsavory positions of pimps and panderers, who lay feeding in the public pork barrel. Needless to say, I hope this unfavorable conclusion will not prove out to be true in this case, Mr. Hopkins. (June 12, 1939)

Peters wrote two other letters attacking Hopkins. In one, he mixed metaphors at warp speed.

> I think that you have become so over-ripe in this matter that you simply stink! . . . If you can tighten your belt and try to girdle yourself in the vicinity where your intestinal fortitude should be, let your lack of guts become bulwarked

by all of your innate courage and the corset you can make of your belt. . . . I am and have become emotionally aroused to extreme lengths in my efforts to get this business brought to a proper head, and let me tell you Hopkins that I will bring it to that head.

As for you, Welly Hopkins, you stepped into this picture for the Attorney General. You and Mr. Murphy had better delouse yourselves and try to come clean. (July 21, 1939)

Another example is a writer who signed her name as Ever Joy to a se-ries of letters to the department about a corrupt New York official named Flatto. After her first letter was rejected with a boilerplate response letter, Joy wrote: "I am going to hold you personally responsible until I have released to me all that belong to me . . . you are under oath and paid to see me have the protection guaranteed to us to protect our property and businesses. . . . I shall expect service from you at once, according to your oath. I am surprised that you would waste my time and yours sending me your letter of March 27, telling me to go to the local authorities" (April 6, 1939). Some writers tried to turn the name of the "Justice" Department into a rhetorical weapon as they demanded a response. An example is Layle Lane, who wrote from Pennsylvania to complain that a man named Elijah Harris had been framed and sent to a prison camp in Everglades, Florida. Lane claimed: "A department of justice whose chief activity is chasing kidnappers or running down income tax evasions is unworthy the name of department of justice" (June 26, 1939). More caustic and sweep-ing was Alex Gast, the brewery owner who had lost control of his company in a bankruptcy proceeding. Gast concluded his letter with the following florid expression of his anger: "In view of the foregoing conditions and circumstances the Government is contemptible, it is vicious, it is so vile that it can have no just claim to existence" (December 31, 1940).

Direct Claims about Understanding Legal Process

The finding that letter writers were so frequently preoccupied with estab-lishing their own character or worthiness provides indirect evidence that writers did not have faith that their legalized claims of rights and other entitlements would force government officials to make a favorable re-sponse. They instead understood that the realization of legal entitlements depended on discretionary decisions by government officials. Clearer evidence of writers' awareness of the way the law works in practice can be found in a subset of letters where writers spoke more directly about their ideas or expectations concerning law. Although these claims were not as ubiquitous as efforts to establish character or worthiness, they do provide additional illustrations that writers could make legal claims and draw on legal rhetoric without developing unrealistic expectations or losing sight of law's many practical limitations.

What Would Happen to the Letters

A first, basic question related to writers' understanding of law and legal processes is whether letter writers had realistic expectations about who would read their letters and how the letters would be processed. This question seems particularly important given that, as noted above, some writers made very personal pleas to the conscience of high-level individuals in government. Did writers actually believe that Franklin Roosevelt would personally read their letters and make the decision about how to respond? Or did they more realistically understand that their letter would be processed through a bureaucracy in which low-level officials would decide how to respond in individual cases?

Many of the letters that were addressed to individuals like Franklin Roosevelt or the attorney general gave clear indications that writers understood that they were addressing a bureaucratic institution rather than an individual. Many such letters began with the salutation "Gentlemen," for example. But there were also many writers who framed their pleas as though they were speaking directly to named high officials like the president or attorney general. However, that does not mean the writers actually believed that such officials would be the ones who read their letters. It is also possible that such writers were simply adopting a conventional posture to frame such a request. Writers may have expressed a comfortable familiarity with Roosevelt in particular because of the popularity and intimacy of his fireside chats.[5] Many letters from Michigan also addressed Frank Murphy, the former governor and mayor of Detroit, in quite familiar terms. In most cases, there is no way to determine whether writers were adopting a pose by writing as though speaking directly to a top official. However, some writers did include comments to indicate their expectations about how their letters would be processed. Almost all the writers who made such comments seemed to understand that their letters were unlikely to reach the president, first lady, or attorney general.

A few writers seemed to hold out hope that their letters would reach the president but also made it clear that they knew they were facing long odds. An example is Raymond McKee, a convicted white-collar criminal who complained to Attorney General Murphy about societal discrimination against ex-convicts. He began his letter:

> Dear Sir,
> There was a time when a letter directed to the head of virtually any Federal department would reach him, so long as it was not frivolous and deserved consideration. I hope, somewhat against my judgment, this will reach you. (April 29, 1939)

Some writers made efforts to overcome anticipated bureaucratic obstacles. At one stage in his lengthy struggle to attract attention from the president, Harry Reynolds wrote to Senator J. Prentice Brown, asking him to hand a letter to Roosevelt, explaining: "The contents are of such a personal nature that diversion by one of the many secretarys would be fatal to this writer's patriotic cause" (March 14, 1940). Other writers expressed their recognition that the president was too busy for claims like theirs even as they launched into pointed and personal appeals to the president's conscience. Seth Plummer, the man who wrote to get help for a neighbor who had been committed to a mental hospital, wrote: "I know you have lots of important things on your mind and this may seem a small matter to you, but you will save a poor woman from the torture of hell and possibly her life if you act at once" (September 10, 1939). Just one writer comes close to expressing directly the belief that the president would personally handle the letter. That writer was an anonymous opponent of the Smith Act who signed the letter to Roosevelt "An alien with first paper waiting to become a Citizen." The writer included a note with the letter addressed to "My dear Secretary to the President" asking that the letter be read aloud to the busy president (June 25, 1940). Other writers who expressed their expectations all seemed to understand that letters like theirs did not normally reach top-ranking officials.

Law, Money, and Power: Understanding Structural Biases of Legal Process

There are other cases where writers made claims that show clearly that they had a good understanding of how legal processes create systematic advantages and disadvantages. Writers complained that they had lost out because they did not have the resources to defend themselves in legal proceedings and recognized that they needed assistance from government officials to protect their rights. Significantly, writers did not simply make the relatively banal assertion that wealth was an advantage or that wealth dictated legal outcomes. Writers instead made more specific claims that identified recurrent and structural features of legal processes that prevented law from fulfilling its legitimating promise of equal justice. Some writers pinpointed the same structural features that socio-legal scholars have pointed to when trying to explain why the "haves" come out ahead (Galanter 1974).

A first example that illustrates a capacity to identify structural problems is a letter from Georgiana Wines of Los Gatos, California, discussed in chapter 3. Wines used a multidimensional attack to try to get help from the president in her dispute with the Ford Motor Company. Ford had sold her a lemon and then repossessed the car after she stopped making payments to protest Ford's failure to pay the cost of repairs. Wines claimed that her rights as a citizen had been violated and claimed more generally that the president needed to recognize how "the big corporations of our country unjustly take from those who are unable to defend their rights." Wines also made some of the standard claims about character and hardship, noting that her problems were "no fault of mine" and that she was a "woman alone" who could not earn a living without a properly working car (April 18, 1939). However, Wines went beyond those standard claims to articulate a range of critiques of the legal procedures that give advantages to corporations and create barriers that prevent ordinary people from obtaining legal redress. Wines ultimately expressed frustration with legal remedies and sought out political alternatives to legal action as she grappled with her ideas for combating corporate power.

In particular, Wines complained that the cost of legal action made it easy for corporations to ignore the legitimate legal claims of an individual consumer. She reported that she had sought legal help and found that "the lawyers say it will cost more to bring an action against the Ford Company than it is worth." Wines also noted: "I am quite sure there are many people likewise who are at the mercy of the millions of dollars of Ford Motor Company." She thus suggested that with legal avenues blocked, the solution was to generate publicity that would help to unite the otherwise isolated consumers who were helpless against Ford and force Ford to treat consumers more fairly. She wrote: "I told the Seattle Branch of the Ford Company that for the sake of others also, I was going to give my case publicity." However, she also worried that it would be difficult to get publicity: "The newspapers are not likely to do anything because they get large advertising from the Ford Motor Company." She also worried that Ford would retaliate if she was able to carry out her threat of generating publicity, telling the president that "in case anything should happen that I am gotten rid of you might read between the lines."

Wines's letter sought help from the president but did not make a specific request regarding what the president might do to assist her efforts to target corporations with adverse publicity. She urged the president to "try to protect those who can't fight back for their rights in the Ford Motor Co + perhaps other large corporations" and thanked him for "whatever interest of it is possible for you" (April 18, 1939). Given that her general plea was to the president, Wines was likely puzzled when she received a reply from the Justice Department. The reply letter stated, "The Matters of which you complain do not come within the jurisdiction of this Department," which must have seemed strangely irrelevant to Wines. It also suggested, rather unhelpfully, that she "seek the advice of private counsel to determine what steps should be taken in redress of your grievances" (May 15, 1939).

Many other writers explained law's failure to live up to its promises of rights and equality by making specific structural critiques. In some instances, writers would juxtapose claims about law's shortcomings with idealized claims about law that seemed oblivious to such problems. The result was sometimes an unresolved tension between idealism and skepticism. Consider again the case of another writer with a dispute with an automobile manufacturer: George Runyan. As noted in chapter 4, Runyan complained that a local judge had slapped him with an injunction and threatened his job after he publicly criticized the car dealership that had sold him a lemon. In his letter, Runyan claimed that his case was part of a broader pattern of collusion between local business "racketeers" and judges. Such claims appear to betray a jaded cynicism about the alleged impartiality of law and judges. However, as noted in chapter 3, Runyan also expressed what appears to be genuine surprise that a judge would side with business interests and issue such an outrageous restraint on "free speech." He also seemed to have broad faith that the federal government could restore justice by choosing to take action. Runyan pointedly asked whether there was "any remedy to get protection for a poor worker who buys a used car that don't have money enough to protect himself from the action of a swindling dealer who gets a Circuit Court Judges to threaten said victim with confiscation of all of his property unless he ceases to tell the public the true facts about the deal in which he was swindled" (December 28, 1939). In this case, Runyan seemed to understand that the judge who issued the ex parte order favored the car company over a modest citizen who lacked the resources to press his concerns effectively in court. However, Runyan's plea to the federal government can be read as evidence that he still believed that there was some chance that legal processes could still produce the right outcome in the end.

Molly Mollison, the woman involved in the dispute over a bathing suit in Miami Beach, provides another example of the uneasy tension between idealism and realism. Mollison stated that she was unable to protect her rights because her adversary had more resources than she did: "Well it so happens that this women had 40 dollars on her I had none. and I was jailed and not allowed to telpone for 72 Hours and she was she got 50 dollars bond. I stayed in jail. I was taken to Court and she was allowed to bring a witness I was not I had not one soul to defend me I want to get a lawer. I wanted to get justice. I am not Guilty of such a crime. . . . I wasn't allowed to defend myself" (January 12, 1940). Mollison thus articulates structural biases as a reason for her predicament: The problem was not that the legal rules were not neutral but that legal institutions and processes made it difficult to obtain legal redress. However, like Runyan, Mollison also wrote things suggesting that she was quite surprised to encounter unfair treatment and retained some faith in the power of American legal ideals. Mollison also expressed concern that the actions taken by local officials were inconsistent with her idealized expectations of the treatment she deserved as "an American citizen" and asked the president to "defend Americanism." Of course, it is not possible to tell whether Mollison was sincerely committed to the ideals and expectations that she expressed in the letter. It is also possible that the claims of surprise and expressions of ideals were a pose adopted to dramatize the importance of her plea.

The letters from Runyan and Mollison provide a reminder that the letters do not yield evidence that allows a definitive assessment of letter writers' faith and beliefs. It might be argued, contrary to my claims, that the fact that so many writers felt the need to make legal claims ultimately demonstrates that most had strong faith in law. The problem with such a claim is that there is nothing in the letters to actually support the conclusion that there is some broad underlying faith. Most writers gave at least some indirect indication that they lacked faith in law's impartiality, while almost none gave voice to an unconditional faith in law. It might still be objected that my findings about limited faith in law are distorted by the fact that my sample from complaint letters includes many people who were facing very difficult personal circumstances and many people who had recently had bad experience with law. However, my sample also includes many letters from people who were not trapped in such difficult circumstances and yet still expressed doubts about legal ideals. Moreover, even if there is widespread faith in law among the unsampled population of people who have never had a bad firsthand experience with law (if such people even exist), the letters make it clear that many people's faith in law is not very resilient. While some disgruntled writers told stories about losing faith, their letters reveal that even if such faith existed, it was fragile enough to be shattered by a single bad experience.

There are also some cases where people expressed their skeptical views about law quite directly. Some writers dropped all pretense of faith and expressed quite strongly their skepticism about law or their awareness that law did not fulfill its promises. Such skepticism was not necessarily linked to cynicism. Writers who expressed skepticism about how law worked were often hopeful that problems with legal processes could be fixed or alleviated by government action. Some interesting examples of this type of letter can be found among a handful of letters that responded to news stories about the creation of the CRS. Several letters expressed support for Murphy's decision to create the new unit and devote federal resources to protecting rights and liberties. One reason writers gave for supporting the move was a belief that government resources were needed to help offset the existing structural biases in law. For example, a postcard from F. B. Dodge told Murphy that Californians "appreciate the creation of your new department—the liberty unit." Dodge explained that people believed that "the law should apply to the higher financial brackets as well as the lower" and that the "average person has neither the time or money to bring pressure to offset the enormous pressure that the moneyed group exerts." Dodge hoped that attention and scrutiny from the federal government could make California "more in the line of Government for the people" (June 12, 1939).

Other writers who expressed ideas about biases in law may not have been aware of the formation of the CRS. G. F. Harrington, who first wrote to the Department of Education, asked pointedly whether there was any federal office that could help people to overcome cost barriers that made it difficult to secure the promise of rights and law. Harrington wrote: "Is

there any department of the Federal Government that can and will investigate and act in violations of constitutional rights of citizens by local politicians; without the prohibitive expense of high priced lawyers and court
actions? In other words, what chance has the 'under dog'?" Harrington
also indicated the need for such a department by providing a general account of law's failure: "My present viewpoint is that there are many laws
now enforced against poor persons depriving them of life, liberty, and
property for the sole reason that they have not the money to obtain legal
protection. This colossal racket of grinding out law, lawyers, and courts
has, it seems, at long last bound, gagged, and almost strangled 'Justice'"
(February 25, 1940). Harrington's actual reason for writing was not just
the figurative "under dog" but actual dogs: he felt that Los Angeles' dog-
licensing ordinance violated the Constitution.

Some writers made quite specific claims about why it was difficult to
use law or litigation as a tool for producing social change or challenging
entrenched power. One important practical limitation of litigation is that a
person presenting a legal challenge needs to have standing to bring a case
to court. In some instances, bringing cases can be quite costly to individual
plaintiffs because participation in the case can create risk of criminal prosecution or civil penalties. (Perhaps the most famous instance is the long
struggle that eventually produced the landmark *Griswold v. Connecticut,*
381 US 479 [1965]). In that case, the Supreme Court struck down a Connecticut law that banned birth control. After the Supreme Court rebuffed
earlier challenges based on appellants' standing to bring the claim, a group
of activists and doctors had to provoke state officials to arrest them for
violating the archaic law (Garrow 1994, chapters 1–4). The difficulty of
creating appropriate legal challenges to unconstitutional practices was not
lost on letter writers. Thomas Lindsay, for example, wrote from Wollas-
ton, Massachusetts, to complain about a tax collection "racket" being run
by his local government. Lindsay claimed that the town tax collector had
sent him a warrant for his arrest because he had failed to pay a tax on his
automobile. Lindsay complained that the local official was a "little Hitler"
who was threatening "liberty" and using the federal mails to collect an
unjust tax. Lindsay wrote that he was tempted to continue his defiance and
allow himself to be arrested so that he could challenge the constitutionality of the collection procedures in court. However, he had decided instead
to pay the tax under protest to avoid the obvious inconvenience of arrest
and detention. Lindsay urged the attorney general to recognize that his
office had the "duty to see that all laws and statutes are in keeping with

the federal constitution" because citizens should not have to sacrifice their own liberty to challenge unconstitutional practices (January 23, 1940).

Writers also commented on the practical problems created by uncertainty of law and gaps in statutory rules. E. F. Croft, a shipboard radio operator who wrote from San Francisco, developed a solid understanding of Justice Brandeis's famous insight that "in most matters it is more important that the applicable rule of law be settled than that it be settled right" (*Burnet v. Coronado Oil & Gas Co.*, 285 US 393, 406 [1932]). Croft wrote that the NLRB was investigating his claim that he had been fired from a steamship for his labor union activity. Croft contacted the attorney general's office regarding a subsidiary matter that was preventing him from working while his case was pending. Croft hoped to determine whether his former supervisor could legally refuse to provide a performance evaluation on his federal radio licensing form. Croft explained that instead of marking his performance as "satisfactory" or "unsatisfactory," the supervisor wrote "D.R." on the form. The supervisor said he was indicating "decision reserved." Croft stated: "I have never seen such an entry in my more than 10 years under license at sea." He also explained that a missing evaluation was even worse than an "unsatisfactory" evaluation because he could not get licensed for new work without an evaluation from his previous employer. He wrote: "I don't mind anyone coming right out and stating that I am satisfactory or unsatisfactory nor do I mind them not writing it on my license. I am proud of service and ability as a first class operator. All I wish is my rights as an American citizen by birth, free from the taint of Communism, proud of our history and the Constitution I look to for protection. . . . [I]f a Master or Employer deems an employee unsatisfactory to him he should be prepared to state so frankly and without reservation." Croft also suspected that the supervisor was trying to blacklist him for his union membership. He expected that a prospective employer encountering the mysterious "D.R." notation would write to the former supervisor and that the former supervisor would send "a letter confidentially stating that I am an undesirable American citizen because I belong to a labor union" (March 28, 1939).

Croft's letter described in detail a frustrating odyssey through numerous federal agencies as he tried to determine the legality of the supervisor's refusal to make an evaluation. He first visited the office of the US Shipping Commissioner in San Francisco. He said that one of the commissioners told him that the captain of a ship was bound to give a satisfactory or unsatisfactory evaluation and agreed that "D.R." was "a *very odd* endorsement." However, Croft reported that the office "would make no statement" indicating that the refusal to evaluate was unlawful. Croft next went to the US Bureau of Marine Inspection and Navigation. He reported, "They too would not or could not commit themselves along any definite lines. . . . [T]hey advised me that the license did not come under the jurisdiction of the US Department of Commerce." The bureau told him he had to get an answer from the Federal Communications Commission (FCC). So Croft went next to the FCC. He reported: "At the office I ran into the indefinite statements. No one knew, no one had any authority to say one way or another and there didn't seem to be anything in the law that says one way or another nor had there been any test case before that they could base action on so I was left with the status quo." Croft made it clear that he did not believe that there was a clear answer to his legal question in official law. He concluded by noting, "I am not sure whether there are any iron bound rules in respect to the aforementioned points in question." He indicated that because the law was uncertain about which agency had authority to decide, the attorney general's office should help him to obtain some definitive ruling that would help him to decide how to proceed (March 28, 1939). The department refused that request and told Croft that he should bring his complaint to yet another agency, the NLRB.

Law versus Morality

I noted in chapter 2 that one possible reason CRS attorneys relied on legal claims in reply letters was that legal claims can legitimate contentious outcomes. Such legitimation works, however, only if people are inclined to equate what government officials recognize as "law" with what is right or just. The letters that people wrote to the CRS raise doubts about whether that condition was met. Some of the letters did mix language about what was right with fairly idealized claims about law. More frequently, however, writers consciously articulated claims about what was right or moral in order to compare unjust outcomes produced by official law to other, more just possibilities.

It can be quite difficult to sort out writers' attitudes about the relationship between law and morality. Once again, there is a tension in many of the letters. Writers would portray law as an ideal linked to justice but then elsewhere make it clear that they understood that law routinely fell short of such ideals. Thus, even when writers express a vision of law that equates what was (or should be) legal with what is right, such claims do not mean that writers saw a *necessary* connection between official law and morality.

Samuel King, the African American labor organizer who wrote to report his escape from a prison camp in Alabama, provides one striking
example of the tension in some of the letters in this group. King made a variety of claims that suggest he retained an idealized view of official law and
connected law to ideas about justice and legitimacy. However, King also
included a variety of statements about law, legal processes, and legal history that distinguished official law from what he was willing to recognize
as "justice." For example, he began his letter by distinguishing the formal
legal proceedings in Alabama that had led to his imprisonment from what
he thought a real, legitimate law would look like. "Although you're the
law, I'm telling you that I'm a fugitive; not a fugitive from law and order
but a fugitive [from] outlaws and disorder. My objective is, contact the law,
get the ear of men who realize that justice is the only thing that places man
above the brute, men who realize that civilization would have been lost
in the entanglement of the ages had not justice been done and men who
realize that each age requires changes and each change requires a more
flexible justice." He also suggested that abuse of the law was a constant
occurrence that had to be vigilantly fought against, and he asserted that
government officials determined to do bad things could continually ma-
nipulate the law. "Everytime you fine people make a law to prevent 'em
from taking the advantage of the less fortunate, they dig deeper into their
trick bag and get a new trick, one that the law doesn't include." However,
King also expressed at least some optimism that law was progressing toward more just outcomes: "Personally about the best American method
I can think of is watch 'em close, detect every new trick and give it a legal
rating and make it a felony. In a course of time they'll run out of tricks and
fall in line." As an example of his concerns, King related the story of two
black farmers who were committed to an insane asylum and then forced
to do agricultural work. King believed that the state government was turning to insane asylums as a source of forced labor in the aftermath of the
CRS's antipeonage campaign. (He called the asylum a "ruse to avoid being
punished for peonage.") King also explained that he had been arrested on
phony charges of robbery only because southern authorities had "about . . .
worn the rape trick out." He noted that "10 yrs-ago that would been their
ace in the hold" (May 16, 1939).

Another way that writers indicated their awareness of a distinction between law and morality was by commenting directly on the symbolic power
of legal rhetoric. In particular, writers complained that official pronouncements of law portrayed unjust outcomes as legitimate. Writers sometimes
noted that people, particularly government officials, used claims about

what is "legal" as a tool for masking injustice. Writers complained that incorrect accusations of illegality created a stigma of immorality and worried that calling unjust activities "legal" could make those activities appear legitimate. Such writers seemed to understand that the impact of law went beyond law's direct effect on outcomes to law's indirect effects as a carrier of ideological messages about legitimacy.

Consider, for example, E. V. Pease, who wrote to Attorney General Jackson to complain that Delaware was "flagrantly ignoring the provisions of the Bill of Rights" by flogging prisoners in state custody. Pease was particularly appalled at a report that there were eighty-five witnesses to state prisoners being whipped. In making her case for federal intervention, Pease noted that the legitimating power of law and legal authority was itself a cause of deteriorating conditions in prisons: "If such an abomination be permitted in any state, hypocritically cloaked as lawful, is it logical to presume that equally and perhaps death-dealing atrocities will now be perpetrated minus the hypocritical cloaking?" (March 18, 1940). George Runyan made a similar point: "Of course, anyone feels badly enough about being swindled on a used car deal, but when the courts turn around and protect the swindler, that is much worse and some action should be taken to stop this un American practice" (January 28, 1939).

Nicolaas Steelink of Los Angeles provided a particularly powerful articulation of his concerns about the radiating effects of law on perceptions of legitimacy. Steelink wrote to Eleanor Roosevelt in response to a newspaper column where she had argued that the public's level of patriotism was dependent on maintaining the public's faith that the government had a firm commitment to justice. Steelink had been convicted many years earlier of "criminal syndicalism" because he was a member of the "Wobblies" (the Industrial Workers of the World). Steelink, who had served a sentence in San Quentin, remained quite bitter about the damage the ordeal had done to himself and his family. Steelink told Eleanor Roosevelt that despite his having served his sentence, "[s]ociety officially is still holding the finger of scorn against me" because he had a criminal record. He noted that California's governor had begun issuing pardons to a few convicted Wobblies, but he complained that the procedure for obtaining one required the person to make a formal request and that the pardons did not acknowledge the state's wrongdoing. Steelink insisted, "I, for one, will never *ask* for a pardon," and he demanded that the legislature pass more sweeping legislation fully repudiating the "trumped up" prosecutions based on the "standardized testimony of pimps and prostitutes." He also insisted that financial redress be provided to the people who were targeted.

Steelink felt he would continue to suffer without full acknowledgement and official repudiation of past policies (January 13, 1941).

Steelink recognized the symbolic power of legal pronouncements but did not naively equate official legal outcomes with justice or morality. Other dejected writers expressed their frustration with legal processes by declaring directly that they had lost all faith in law. An example is V. T. Comer, who complained that corruption in the San Francisco Court system had affected his divorce case. Comer showed some signs of an initial faith in the myth of rights. He claimed that his "fundamental constitutional rights" had been violated and said that he began the legal process with "enough confidence in the integrity of our courts to believe that the matter would be thrown out" once the judge "knew all the facts." As with many other writers, however, Comer's initial faith did not prove very resilient. He claimed to have learned that the courts were a "pat racket" and suggested that "corrupt conditions . . . must prevail in this community of San Francisco to breed such flagrant disregard of the rights of its citizens." In the end, he declared defiantly that he was not fooled by the masks created by official law: "I refuse to give countenance, either directly or indirectly, to any dirty racket no matter how legally it may be disguised" (June 17, 1941).

Numerous other writers indicated directly that formal guarantees of rights were not producing real protections or benefits. Bernard Glick, who wrote to protest the long history of fixed elections in Hoboken, New Jersey, declared that "civil rights are as extinct as the Dodo" (March 30, 1939). In one of his letters, Harry Reynolds invoked the idea of a "myth" of rights as he explained that his experiences left him without faith in the power and legitimacy of law: "I have lived to see everything in the line of Civil Rights disgarded, and I think that secondary to keeping us from starving will be the putting back into our American Life those rights that at present are a myth. We can't be Americans without them" (March 12, 1940). In his final letter, Reynolds indicated that he was tired of fighting for his claimed rights and ready to give up: "I am going to take the advice I have been giving to others and move out of Michigan and hunt me up a good place to fish" (March 24, 1940). M. R. Silvernail, who wrote from Albany, New York, responded quite pointedly after hearing Murphy announce the formation of the CRS. Silvernail, who had heard Murphy urge citizens to "watch out" for rights violations, wrote to claim that it did little good to "watch out" if there were no effective means of redress for rights violations (March 28, 1939). A final example, one offering a more general condemnation of law, is from Roy Schwing. Schwing complained that California's emergency legislation during the Depression had hurt some of his investments and violated the Constitution's contracts clause. After reporting that his lawyers had advised him to drop his case, Schwing wrote: "My answer was that the lawyers were more concerned that law violators succeed than that what was right be upheld; that law violators could only succeed with the aid of lawyers; and since there was most money in evasion of the law, that the legal profession was essentially dishonest" (March 5, 1939).

Other writers referenced the link between law and morality less directly by claiming that an otherwise reasonable law was producing bad outcomes in a particular case. Writers in this group would acknowledge that government officials were following the letter of the law. However, they claimed that certain features of their own case meant that rigidly following the law would produce an unjust outcome. In some cases, writers claimed that a particular application of an otherwise just law would be self-defeating because it would produce outcomes that contradicted the underlying purpose that justified the law. Other writers drew attention to remote but harmful consequences of a law and argued that such consequences provided grounds for limiting its application. Claims of this sort show that writers were willing to challenge law as unjust even in cases where they would acknowledge that official law had been followed.

An example is a letter from Louis Becker, who forwarded to the Justice Department a letter he had sent to the Division of Unemployment Compensation in Illinois. Becker, a painting contractor, complained that union corruption had led to an adverse finding in a dispute over compensation of his employees. Becker acknowledged that officials had followed the law. However, he complained that their rigid adherence to the law was facilitating the corruption: "The fact that the Division of Unemployment Compensation chooses to interpret the letter of the law to subversive ends in place of interpreting the spirit of the law toward constructive ends causes me to request the rehabilitation of these mentioned departments by supplanting federal control." Becker self-consciously appealed beyond the law to a higher legal and moral standard. He explained that he was forwarding his complaint to several federal offices "in deeply rooted trust that somewhere in these offices in the United States there yet exists a bond of honor, justice and Constitutional Spirit" (October 9, 1939).

While Becker gave voice to general conceptions of "justice" and "Constitutional Spirit," other writers made more detailed utilitarian arguments. In some cases, the utilitarian claims were just straightforward pleas for attention on grounds that something good would happen if the federal government provided help. For example, Mary Moloney claimed that helping Chicago landowners get more money in eminent domain proceedings would boost the economy because recipients would quickly spend the extra money on Christmas presents (December 6, 1939). Other kinds of utilitarian arguments spoke to the link between law and legitimacy by suggesting that the link was severed if a law failed to serve the greater good. Writers quite often challenged existing and proposed laws on grounds that their harmful effects undermined their claim to legitimacy. Writers who made these claims indicated their belief that the link between law and legitimacy is contingent rather than automatic.

The cases where utilitarian claims indicate the clearest separation between law and morality are ones where writers acknowledge that a law is generally justified but argue that rigid application of the law in their particular case would produce injustice. An example is Virginia Dryer, who wrote to complain about an ordinance in Pontiac, Michigan, that prevented people from owning more than two dogs. Dryer argued that if the purpose of the law was to ensure that dogs were well treated and well cared for, the city should exempt professional dog breeders since they were much more likely to treat their dogs well (March 17, 1939). According to Dryer, the failure of the state to provide a sensible exception for dog breeders created an injustice that warranted a federal remedy.

Other writers argued that particular legal rules were unjust because of their bad consequences. For example, Veronica McCormick wrote from Hollywood, California, to complain about a severe beating her brother had endured during a false arrest for drunkenness. Her brother's injuries were so severe that he had to have a leg amputated. McCormick complained about a state law that immunized the city and police department from lawsuits over police brutality. That law made it impossible for her brother to recover damages related to the beating. McCormick offered a practical argument to show that such a legal shield was wrong and unjust: the shield allowed and encouraged police officers to behave badly. "Don't you think that Law protects the Police and encourages them to use their fists and abuse too freely merely to satisfy their own selfish selves and motives knowing that their conduct will not cost the city and his superiors anything. In other words he can do as he pleases and what can you do about it, that's that. Don't you think the government should be interested in changing the law?" (August 5, 1941). To make a case for federal intervention, McCormick also mentioned that California had recently absorbed many people from out of state who were needed for work in factories making war supplies. McCormick suggested that the coming war effort could be hindered if such workers were scared off by unchecked police brutality.

A letter from Martha Nakielski argued in favor creating a new legal shield rather than dismantling an existing one. Nakielski, an employee at a clothing factory, reported that a coworker had been fired after testifying at the criminal trial of a supervisor who had attacked a fellow worker. Nakielski argued that the courts would not be able to conduct criminal trials effectively if witnesses were not shielded from such recrimination (April 15, 1939).

Writers also made utilitarian arguments about consequences of laws when they wrote to urge Roosevelt to veto bills. For example, Pearl Buffo of Pittsburg, California, urged Roosevelt to veto the Smith Bill because it "is not something to promote calm and sane views among the 8,000,000 other aliens in this country who are abiding by its laws, supporting its Constitution, and in by far the greatest majority of cases, preparing themselves to become useful citizens here" (July 9, 1940). Other writers focused more narrowly on the costs of particular laws, and suggested that laws were unjust when those costs outweighed any benefits. Harry Smith, the street peddler from California whose claims about the contracts clause are discussed in chapter 4, also made more practical arguments against the state's licensing requirements. Smith argued that the licensing fees made it too difficult for traveling salespeople to conduct business: "As I only stay in a town from two days to a week I can't pay license in every town." Smith also argued that the application of the ordinance in his case served no legitimate purpose, arguing that the ordinance "makes no distinction between meat and vegetables (which could be unsanitary) peddlers and merchandise peddlers" (August 29, 1939). Another more tragic example is a letter from Lonnie Griffith of Klamath Falls, Oregon. Griffith complained that the state had taken custody of his two sons. Griffith, who was on relief and having difficulty supporting his family, acknowledged that the state had an interest in conserving the resources needed for relief efforts. However, he argued that the state was ultimately hurting its interest by removing children from homes. Griffith noted that it would ultimately cost the state more to remove and then care for his two sons than it would to provide Griffith with additional support that would allow him to care for them himself (March 30, 1939).

Not all the writers who questioned the policy judgments underlying government applications of law were as disadvantaged as Lonnie Griffith. Some writers in relatively privileged circumstances also complained about instances where following the law was counterproductive or against the long-term public interest. One theme was that market interventions aimed at relieving the effects of the Depression were unjust interferences with private investments and private contracts. For example, Julia Smith wrote to complain about the compensation she received in an eminent domain proceeding. She wrote to President Roosevelt: "Will you please instruct the City of Miami to pay an adequate sum for my Lot—I feel sure you would not want me to lose my property and my money. I have been waiting Ten Years to realize a profit on my investment—and now they threaten to take my PROPERTY and my MONEY" (October 28, 1939).

Max Brown, president of the Mel-o-Toast bakery in Pine Bluff, Arkansas, played a different card. Brown argued that his company had been "forced" to sign a contract with a union and that the result was a wage increase "beyond our ability to pay and remain in business." Brown, whose Mel-o-Toast letterhead boasted that his product was "union made," asked the Justice Department whether he could hold up his payroll and demand an adjustment that would protect his "legal rights" and continue his business (June 17, 1939). The basis of Brown's claim of unfairness was that the union was asking his company to pay the same wages as more efficient competitors with automated production facilities. Nothing in Brown's letter suggests that the contract was invalid or that the union had behaved illegally. Brown was asking for an adjustment on the basis of what he felt would be more just and fair than the terms of his legal contract with his workers. A sadder example of an effort to protect property by asking for an adjustment to legal remedies can be found in the letter from Mrs. O. P. McCoy, the apple farmer who boasted that her apples were relatively worm-free. McCoy told a story of her efforts to negotiate a debt owed to the directors to the Oroville Tonasket Irrigation Project. McCoy reported that she and her husband had purchased their farm in 1927 and managed to make it profitable for a decade. Unfortunately, Mr. McCoy had shattered his backbone in an accident on the farm, and as a result the couple, who were in their sixties, could no longer manage the entire thirty-four acre farm. Mrs. McCoy reported that they had invested more than $6,000 in the farm and owed just $1,750. The couple had tried unsuccessfully to reach an agreement with their creditors to sell off first half and then three-quarters of their land. The McCoy's wanted primarily to keep the part of the farm that included their home. They also offered to pay back the entire remaining amount in four annual payments. The creditors rejected that offer and ordered the couple to vacate their home. McCoy did not deny that the officials and creditors were acting within the law. She admitted: "Technically, these men seem to have the power to dispossess the people under this project no matter how much we have poured into it or how little the company holds against us." However, McCoy felt that she and her husband still had a moral claim to keep the farm. She noted that she and her husband had made numerous improvements to make the farm profitable and that they had built their farmhouse "with our own money and our own *hands.*" She also noted that they were "behind with our water rent, owing to lack of fair prices for apples due to conditions throughout the country with which you are familiar." Given these conditions, McCoy insisted that "justice" required a better outcome for them than the one dictated by legal technicalities (March 31, 1939).

At the beginning of chapter 4, I argued that the ideas behind the legal arguments in the letters to the CRS have to be interpreted in the full context of the many different types of legal and extralegal arguments and claims that appear in the letters. Chapter 4 shows that people quite frequently made legal arguments containing somewhat idealized legal language. This chapter, in contrast, has shown that many writers who deployed idealized legal rhetoric did so with a realistic understanding of law's many practical shortcomings. That awareness gave them capacity to resist or reject the normative claims embedded in legal rhetoric. The implications of these findings are explored in more detail in the concluding chapter.

CHAPTER SIX

In Defense of Extravagant Rights Talk

Please assume that I know whereof I speak.
—Harry Reynolds to O. John Rogge, March 2, 1940

I began this book by noting that most scholars of popular legal discourses are critical of the American propensity to use a legalized language of rights and skeptical about the effectiveness of rights claiming. In concluding, I note first that there are some characteristics of the encounters recorded in the CRS correspondence that do seem to match claims made by such critical scholars. Most strikingly, if they are judged as efforts to obtain help, the many attempts by letter writers' to deploy law in these everyday political encounters were spectacularly unsuccessful. Despite this finding, I have nevertheless constructed an account of popular legal discourses that leaves more room for optimism than in more critical accounts. I have shown that many of the people who wrote letters made competent use of legal materials and engaged with legal discourses as they advanced novel claims. I have also argued that writers were able to deploy idealized legal language without losing sight of the fact that law did not live up to its expressed ideals and without succumbing to official law's claim to set some objective or universal standard for justice or legitimacy. Writers quite often used legal languages of rights or the Constitution to express grievances and make demands that went beyond anything recognized in official law.

Even accepting these conclusions, there is still reason to worry. The letters reveal that there was a widespread compulsion to think and communicate using legalized discourses when engaging with government officials. The role of law in the encounters was, at best, a mixed bag. Letter writers *often* used legalized discourses, and *sometimes* made powerful legal arguments, but government officials *almost always* deployed law when they tried to justify their refusals to provide help. Those officials deployed law not to advance rights but to kill off people's efforts to appropriate legal language in support of aspirational claims.[1] Moreover, even though many writers were able to challenge official articulations of law by offering alternative visions, their efforts do not seem to have contributed directly to any positive or lasting change. Not only did they fail to get help, their articulation of alternative visions failed to change the Justice Department's understanding of federal responsibilities for protecting constitutional rights. The political act of writing letters did not coalesce into any broader movement that could have exercised more political power.

Despite these limitations, there are other elements of the exchanges that should give pause to anyone who is convinced that official promises of rights are necessarily hollow and that rights-based political strategies are ineffectual or constraining. For one thing, the stories in many of the letters reveal conditions that make it difficult to reject rights categorically as a tool for making meaningful social and political advances. Since 1939, the United States has seen an enormous expansion of legal entitlements that are formally recognized as rights. A network of new federal civil rights statutes has supplanted the few scattered provisions of Reconstruction-era laws used by the CRS. Those statutes promise new legal protections against rights violations associated with race, sex, religion, and disability. In addition, the Supreme Court has abandoned or relaxed many of the doctrines that limited the reach of federal power to protect rights. Most famously, *Brown v. Board of Education* (347 US 483 [1954]) rejected the separate-but-equal doctrine that gave constitutional support to racial segregation. Equally important, there has also been a significant expansion in institutional capacities to protect rights. When the letters in my sample were written, the tiny CRS was the only federal office dedicated to protecting rights. Today, there is an entire division at the Justice Department devoted to civil rights, as well as numerous other federal regulatory offices devoted to rights protection in the workplace, in housing, and in education, as well as many other new agencies at the state and local level.

There remains much to criticize about the web of rights protection in place today. Access to remedies for rights violations are still quite limited, and the range of rights promised in law is still narrow. The dismantling of legal segregation stopped short of ending systems of local funding that preserve sharp inequalities in educational opportunity. The expansion of rights-protecting bureaucracies has not solved fundamental problems like huge disparities in wealth and lack of access to economic opportunity and adequate health care. Many of the problems of inequity now seem to be getting worse rather than better. Such conditions fuel some well-warranted skepticism about rights, law, and litigation. Nevertheless, looking at the conditions faced by individuals around 1939 also provides a reminder that ongoing problems should not lead to denials of real progress. I am comfortable saying that the United States is now a less unjust society than it was when the letters to the CRS were written and am comfortable saying that the expansions in meaningful rights protections are part of the reason. If it happened today, it is much more likely that the police officer who murdered Private Thomas Broadus on a Baltimore street would have been investigated, prosecuted, and perhaps even punished. As a result, incidents like that one are now less likely to happen. That is a good thing.

Nevertheless, recognizing that creating meaningful institutional protections for rights can sometimes make things better does not lead directly to the conclusion that it is valuable to have a political culture that compels people to articulate demands on government by using legalized discourses. Whatever the value of real rights protections, the widespread use of rights language in popular demands on government raises pressing questions about the consequences of such practices and habits: What is gained and what is lost in a society where people develop a propensity to formulate demands on government by making legalized claims and to habitually translate grievances into a universalized language of individual rights? What underlying problems produce a political system where government officials routinely respond to desperate pleas for help by making abstract claims about law? What kinds of interests are likely to be privileged, or made invisible, in such a political culture? Are the large majority of people who lack an expert's understanding of law and legal remedies made particularly vulnerable by the pervasive talk of law?

Rights in Courts and Rights in Everyday Politics

The letters to the CRS, limited to a narrow time frame within a particular political context, cannot provide definitive answers to general questions about rights, law, and political culture. Nevertheless, by providing a picture of how individuals deploy legal claims in everyday political encounters, the letters do yield some insights that are helpful to general reflections on the politics of rights. Perhaps most importantly, the letters reveal how deeply talk of law and rights is woven into everyday political activity and engagement, not just legal processes in courtrooms before judges. Much scholarship on rights focuses, understandably, on rights claiming in connection with litigation or other ways of seeking legal remedies before judges. That focus makes sense, given that courts have often been visible protectors of rights, perhaps most famously in connection with the NAACP's legal campaign against segregation. The NAACP's use of constitutional litigation to sidestep broken-down and unresponsive electoral processes inspired efforts by other groups to use rights-based litigation to produce social change. Some of the resulting Supreme Court rulings induced a good deal of hand-wringing in the legal academy and led a generation of constitutional scholars to follow Bickel (1962, 16) in portraying the Supreme Court as a "deviant" and "countermajoritarian" institution (see also Wechsler 1959). Many scholars have subsequently focused exclusively on courts as the place where rights are established and conceive litigation around rights as a mechanism for protecting disfavored minorities from the outcomes of electoral processes. Scholars also sometimes imagine that efforts to pursue rights in court are a distraction from more "pure" forms of electoral politics that are less constrained by talk of law and rights (see, e.g., Spann 1993, chapter 6; Tushnet 1984).

More recently, some scholars have begun challenging the institutional understandings that led to the close associations between allegedly countermajoritarian courts and minority rights (see, e.g., Graber 1993, Lovell 2003; Powe 2000). The Supreme Court's more recent conservatism has also helped to make it clearer in retrospect that the model of the court as a liberal protector of the rights of disfavored minorities was inspired largely by the Warren court, a short-lived aberration from a very different institutional norm (Lemieux and Lovell 2008; Lemieux and Watkins 2008; Martens 2007). Moreover, scholars now understand that the court's apparent activism during the 1950s and 1960s was not, as scholars like Bickel worried, the result of the Supreme Court's being all-powerful and isolated from political controls. Liberal judicial activism was consequential only to the degree that it had strong (if sometimes tacit) support of elected officials and their appointed administrators (Powe 2000; Bell 1980). More generally, the idea that rights are best advanced by judges because of their capacity to stand up to majority tyranny is, to be blunt, silly. Even sympathetic judges will have a difficult time broadly enforcing legal protections for rights unless other branches create the institutional capacities necessary to make promises of rights protection meaningful.

These broad claims about constitutional politics are illustrated in the background constitutional issues that shaped the CRS's activities. The CRS tried to exercise federal power granted in the Civil War amendments, the most important structural advances for rights in American constitutional history. Those amendments, created by elected officials and ratified or assented to by the people, targeted earlier Supreme Court decisions that had rejected claims of rights and established doctrines that severely constrained the reach of rights protections (e.g., *Baron v. Baltimore,* 32 US 243 [1833]; *Dred Scott v. Sandford,* 60 US 393 [1857]). When the CRS was formed, more than seven decades after the Civil War, most of the core constitutional guarantees expressed in the Civil War amendments had become empty promises. The Supreme Court, far from protecting rights, collaborated actively in the processes that had dismantled the statutory and constitutional protections created during Reconstruction (Nieman 1991, chapters 4 and 5). Even after the CRS was formed, the Supreme Court continued its pattern of narrowing rather than advancing rights. In the crucial CRS test case *Screws v. United States,* the court obstructed novel efforts by more electorally accountable officials to restore federal rights protections.

My point is not that the courts are never rights protectors. There have been some notable instances when American courts have recognized and protected "rights" that would not have been protected by elected officials, such as the recent decision finding a constitutional right for corporations to make direct expenditures in electoral campaigns (*Citizens United v. Federal Election Commission,* 558 US ___ [2010]). Nevertheless, the pronounced pattern is that rights protections are more often created and expanded *outside* of courts by elected officials. Congress has created many crucial rights protections through statutes without much prior judicial support. These include protections against race and sex discrimination in education, housing, and the workplace; protections for the rights of disabled persons; and almost all privacy rights (e.g., in banking, telecommunications, medical, and educational records). Such statutory rights have more often been narrowed than broadened by judicial interpretations. Moreover, the most innovative doctrines developed by the Rehnquist and Roberts courts have involved not protection of minority rights from majority tyranny but reversals of efforts by electoral majorities to expand protections for minority rights. (See, e.g., *United States v. Morrison,* 529 US 598 [2000]; *City of Boerne v. Flores,* 521 US 507 [1997]; *Parents Involved v. Seattle School District No. 1,* 551 US 701 [2007]. See also Noonan 2002; Tushnet 2003; Mezey 2005.)

Rights are typically realized only through coordinated political and legal activity involving all three branches of government. Judges are necessarily important players in the processes that shape rights protections, but they are not the sole or even the most important players.[2] It is thus not surprising that rights discourses permeate more conventional forms of political participation like writing letters to elected officials. As a result, the impact of legal discourses cannot be assayed without looking beyond litigation campaigns to see how such discourses facilitate or constrain everyday political encounters *outside* of courtrooms.

Assessing Popular Rights Discourses

While I do not claim that popular rights discourses are an unqualified good, my exploration of the CRS letters as everyday political encounters has shown that the actual political practice of rights claiming does not work in a way that matches the central claims of more skeptical and critical scholars. One important issue is the origins of popular obsessions with rights. Mary Ann Glendon, the most widely read critic of rights discourses in United States, locates the origins of a America's "extravagant" rights talk in the Supreme Court's response to the civil rights movement of the 1950s and 1960s (1991, 5–7). Strikingly, however, the letters to the CRS show that people were already articulating novel (and sometimes, perhaps, extravagant) rights claims well before the era of expansive Supreme Court rulings that Glendon identifies. Glendon's mistake is to investigate the nature of an allegedly extravagant popular rights dialect by looking primarily at changes in Supreme Court doctrines. The letters to the CRS show, however, that Supreme Court case reporters are not the place to look if one wants to understand *popular* rights discourses. Most of the expansive claims for rights in the letters had no resonance at all in the court's case law. In some cases, the inspiration for novel claims appears instead to have been ideas that were rattling around in debates on economic policy of that era. Ultimately, however, the letters demonstrate that neither Supreme Court rulings nor elite discourses of ordinary politics provide a reliable indication of what kinds of rights claims are being imagined and articulated by ordinary people. Scholars hoping to understand popular rights discourses or the impact of rights ideology cannot reliably use judicial opinions or other elite discourses as a substitute for actually observing how ordinary people actually use and talk about rights.

The letters also challenge critics who see the popular use of rights and legal discourses as a sign of idealism, confusion, delusion, complacency, or acquiescence. The letters show that many people with a fairly realistic understandings of the limitations of existing rights protections would nevertheless make exaggerated rights claims. Although writers often articulated rights as absolute and self-executing entitlements, such writers seemed to understand that government officials have to balance rights claims with competing interests and make discretionary choices about where to direct limited resources. The rights discourse in the letters also did not, as Glendon claims, force claimants to express a "hyper-individualism" that focused on the "lone rights bearer," while ignoring the more complex social dimensions of governance (Glendon 1991, chapter 3). People who made aspirational claims to legal entitlements quite often supported those claims not by insisting that they were entitled as individuals but by establishing the broader social dimensions of their predicament or claiming that attention to their case would produce widespread benefits.

The findings here also raise doubts about the claims that other critical scholars have made about the ideological dimensions of legal discourse (e.g., Tushnet 1984; Gabel and Kennedy 1984). Critics of rights as ideology have been correct to suggest that legal officials who produce legal discourses take advantage of the rhetorical link between law and legitimacy. The letters record many exchanges where CRS officials tried to justify refusals to provide help by making claims about law. However, the letters also reveal that looking only at the legal discourses provided by government authorities does not provide a reliable picture of how ordinary people receive and respond to such claims. When the ideological claims made by legal authorities are considered side by side with the things people wrote in letters, it appears as though the CRS's efforts to deploy law as a legitimating ideology were quite often completely unsuccessful. Many people actively rejected and resisted the CRS's version of law.

More generally, the letters show that people who invoked law in support of their claims were not in the grip of law's ideological messages. Writers did not see law as a "brooding omnipresence in the sky"[3] that would, by itself, determine the outcome of their cases. They realized that the law left responding officials with a great deal of discretion. The letters also show, repeatedly, that people did not automatically accede to official declarations of law. Nor did the boundaries of official law set an outer limit on writers' demands. Many writers rejected official law's claim to be the standard for legitimate, just, or moral outcomes. Some offered alternative visions of justice that they believed the law should bend to fulfill. In the face of sometimes startling official indifference, legal discourse became a vehicle for defiantly asserting individual dignity or directly expressing resistance to authoritative renderings of law.

The findings here also challenge the claim that legal discourses have a hegemonic power to make existing arrangements seem inevitable or invisible. In these political encounters, outcomes supported by official law did not go uncontested, and the structural biases of legal processes did not go unnoticed. Law was not a totalizing force or even a primary determinant of what people experienced or expressed as injustice. In the letters, law was almost always in competition with other sources of normative resources (on this point, see Sarat and Kearns 1995, 22; Ewick and Silbey 1998, 22). Writers who chose to deploy law were able to move freely in and out of legal discourses and thus to deploy a variety of legal and nonlegal rhetorical weapons to claim the attention of government officials. Writers combined legal and constitutional claims with claims drawn from a variety of cultural resources, including claims about religion, basic ideas of fairness and reciprocity connected to a presumed social compact, and occasionally ideas from literature and other arts.

The ability of writers to combine law with other normative discourses meant that legal discourses were more malleable and less confining than many critical scholars have claimed. The choice to deploy legal language in these political encounters did not limit claims to entitlements that were already recognized in law. Even though there were few meaningful legal protections for rights at that time, people freely adapted rights talk, constitutional ideals, and other legalized language to support claims for a wide variety of entitlements, many of them quite baffling to the government attorneys responsible for executing civil rights law. The habit of using rights discourses also did not appear to determine or constrain people's sense of grievance. People expressed grievances about incidents that were not recognized as wrongs in official law and demanded entitlements that government officials were unwilling to provide. Instead of adapting or narrowing their sense of grievance to match official law, many people instead bent various elements of law and legal language so that they could express their complaints in legalized terms.

These findings resonate with the work of legal theorists who have defended rights discourses as a potentially powerful way of expressing aspirations without inducing commitments to law's own version of legitimacy or justice, particularly work by legal scholars who work on critical race theory (Williams 1991; Matsuda 1989; Crenshaw 1988). The findings also resonate with the work of many socio-legal scholars who have explored rights consciousness empirically. For example, landmark studies of working-class people who pursue legal remedies for grievances (Merry 1990), rights-based litigation campaigns (McCann 1994), and reactions to new statutory rights (Engel and Munger 2003) have also found variable and complex patterns of behavior and attitudes toward law. They have not found unwavering faith in law or broad belief in a monolithic "myth of rights." For example, in his study of the pay equity movement, McCann measured the ongoing legacy of reform litigation through interviews with activists and workers who took part in surrounding political campaigns. Even through judges ultimately rejected the key legal claims of the activists, McCann found that participation in litigation-oriented political campaigns had altered "the expectations of potential activists that already apparent injustices might realistically be challenged at a particular point in time" (89). Participation in the campaigns gave people a heightened sense of entitlement and helped to create solidarity and other resources that could be used in ongoing political struggles (276). McCann concludes that the assumption that citizens' imaginations will be limited by a politics built through a discourse of individualist rights "ignores a broad range of alternative rights claims developed by citizens in actual struggles" (302).

My findings about the willingness of writers to deploy legal language to support claims for novel entitlements and to resist the legal claims of responding government authorities reinforce and extend these earlier findings in several important ways. The frequency with which writers expressed broad and aspirational rights claims reveals that there is more fluidity in popular concepts of rights than has been established in earlier accounts. Many studies of legal mobilization have focused on people who are actively involved in organized movements (McCann 1994; Polletta 2000; Luker 1984; Anderson 2004) or people who are among the intended beneficiaries of civil rights laws that had already been enacted (Engel and Munger 2003; Bumiller 1988; Marshall 2003). In contrast, this study discovers a great deal of creative rights claiming among people who were isolated in their predicaments and lacking any institutional or organizational support.

The letters to the CRS also seem to reveal more robust forms of rights claiming, engagement, and resistance than found in studies of legal consciousness of individuals outside of organized movements (see, e.g., Merry 1990; Ewick and Silbey 1998; Nielson 2004; Gilliom 2001; Engel and Engel 2010). I also find a very different relationship between institutional recognition of rights and people's willingness to support rights claims. In her exploration of individual rights consciousness in a variety of international human rights contexts, Merry (2006) found that

> vulnerable individuals' willingness to adopt a rights framework depends in part on the way institutions respond to their rights claims. If their claims are treated as unimportant, unreasonable, or insignificant, they are less likely to take a rights approach to their problems. On the other hand, if their experience of claiming rights is positive, in that the institutional actors support and validate these claims, they are more likely to see themselves as rights-bearing subjects and to claim rights in the next crisis. The case study of women in Hawai'i shows that the support of the courts, the police, and advocates is crucial to transforming their consciousness of themselves as having rights. Poor women think of themselves as having rights only when powerful institutions treat them as if they do. (215)

The people who wrote letters to the CRS in 1939–41 behaved very differently than the women Merry interviewed in Hawaii and Hong Kong. The letter writers articulated rights claims even when those claims had no institutional support. Many continued to press their demands even after government officials had directly rejected their claims. My finding that people facing economic hardships will articulate novel claims of entitlement in terms of rights also contrasts with findings by Gilliom (2001), who found little interest in privacy rights among low-income women in Appalachia. Of course, the sample of people in my study is much different than in Merry's and Gilliom's. Not all the people who wrote were poor, and those who were did not always articulate claims in terms of rights. Nevertheless, the letters do show that at least some people have the capacity to deploy rights talk and other legal discourses as they make demands on government officials even when there is almost no legal or institutional support for their claims. That finding is particularly striking because this study focuses on an era when there was very little support for rights in existing law. Even in a very unsupportive context, I find that isolated people freely invented legalized claims of entitlement. That finding reveals that the conditions under which people will articulate novel rights claims are broader than the ones identified in existing scholarship.[4]

Legal Discourses, Faith, and Resistance

The findings here suggest a need to reconsider existing conceptual and empirical tools for thinking about the underlying beliefs, understandings, and commitments of people who are observed reciting idealized claims about law or rights. In a masterful review of socio-legal and historical scholarship on legal consciousness, Susan Silbey (2005) notes that the drive to investigate legal consciousness originally developed out of a desire to explain why people maintained faith in law despite law's widespread failure to live up to its own legitimating ideals. As Silbey explains, scholars turned to concepts like hegemony and ideology because they wanted to understand why the public maintained "unrelenting faith in and support for legal institutions" (326). My study of the CRS letters suggests, however, that scholars who wish to understand law as ideology should step back and actively question the assumption that people have a great deal of faith in law or unwavering belief in legal ideals. The claim that such faith existed was not very well grounded empirically when socio-legal scholarship on legal consciousness took off in the 1990s.[5] Moreover, the claim of unrelenting faith has ultimately not received much support in the now quite large body of relevant socio-legal scholarship. Notable studies by Merry (1990), McCann (1994), Ewick and Silbey (1998), Engel and Munger (2003), and Nielsen (2004) find that people express familiarity with legal ideals, but they uncover nothing like unrelenting or unconditional faith in law and legal institutions.

The most important study of legal consciousness among ordinary people is Ewick and Silbey's *The Common Place of Law* (1998). Using more than four hundred open-ended interviews with a representative sample of New Jersey residents, Ewick and Silbey demonstrate that people quite often talk about law as they explain how they negotiated their social worlds. Ewick and Silbey were able to identify three very different types of stories about law that people used to describe everyday experiences. None of those three types involves any necessary or straightforward commitment to the legitimacy of law. The type that comes closest, which they call "before the law," does involve stories that drew on idealized notions of law as an objective force that exists outside of human agency. However, people who told "before the law" stories also told the other two types of stories, each of which contests the characterization of law as objective. Moreover, while the "before the law" stories often portray law as powerful and inescapable, the people telling such stories did not inevitably also portray law as legitimate or just. Very few of the respondents' statements quoted in the book appear to express unqualified acceptance of law's legitimacy.

What the socio-legal studies do find is that claims about law are voiced in a wide variety of contexts to describe a wide range of experiences. That finding confirms that legal discourses resonate powerfully in American culture. However, the popularity and resonance of a very malleable legal discourse does not necessarily indicate that people unconditionally accept law's embedded ideological claims of legitimacy. On the contrary, empirical studies seem to show consistently that the reach of law's normative allure is limited. People express their familiarity with legal ideals, but the consistent empirical finding is that law's ideological messages are not always accepted or left uncontested. Scholars instead find that law's claims to legitimacy compete and combine with alternative normative frameworks of justice and morality.

Curiously, however, these consistent findings have not seemed to dampen scholarly concerns about the constraining and disciplining effects of law's ideological dimension. Socio-legal scholars have remained concerned about law as a legitimating ideology and continue to connect law to hegemonic power. Part of the reason may be that most of the studies of ordinary people, that is, people who are not in organized movements, uncover very little use of law or active resistance to law. Engel and Munger (2003) found that none of the people with disabilities who they interviewed actively pursued legal remedies for discrimination. In their much broader sample, Ewick and Silbey (1998) also found little direct resistance to law. One of the three common stories about law that they identified allowed people to express resistant attitudes toward law, but the reported acts of resistance were quite modest and limited. People told stories of minor evasions or subterfuges that were hidden and went largely unnoticed by authorities wielding legal power, not stories of open defiance of law that might weaken law's institutional power (1998, 48–49, chapter 6; 2003).

The absence of more direct resistance appears to have led socio-legal scholars to continue to link legality to legitimation, deference, and hegemony. The failure to uncover more defiance and resistance seems particularly puzzling given that many socio-legal studies of legal consciousness have focused on populations that face unjust conditions or difficult personal obstacles. It is thus quite striking to find an almost universal failure to resist directly and actively. Even when legal resources are available for addressing problems, people are reluctant to use them. The puzzling failure to contest the injustice of difficult conditions demands explanation, and the tendency of people to talk about everyday problems using metaphors borrowed from law provides one tempting answer. The pervasiveness of legal discourses raises the possibility that the legitimating reassurances of legal ideologies lead people to downplay experienced injustice and thus to acquiesce in legal ordering. That conclusion does not leap out of the data, however. For example, as noted above, Ewick and Silbey did not find that people expressed unconditional commitments to legal ideals. Much like the letter writers in this study, the people in their study who gave voice to legal ideals also expressed contradictory ideas that seem to contest those ideals. Nevertheless, perhaps because people did not act more decisively on their more resistant ideas, Ewick and Silbey conclude that the contradictory ideas that they uncovered are ultimately reconciled in a way that reinforces law's stability and hegemonic power (1998, chapter 7).

My study of the letters provides a striking contrast. The letters to the CRS reveal how legal discourses are deployed among a much more actively resistant population, one that expressly challenged authoritative declarations of law and directed those challenges openly to legal authorities. I am also able to observe directly the way the writers expressed themselves while making protests. I find many people who refused to acquiesce to authoritative expressions of law's legitimacy. Strikingly, even writers who were quite defiant used legal language and metaphors and often also gave voice to law's legitimating ideals. That finding severs the causal link between ideology and acquiescence. If both resistant people and people who choose not to resist traffic in legal ideology, legal ideology no longer seems like a factor that explains low levels of resistance in other populations.

More broadly, the letters in this study suggest a need to recalibrate methodological tools that scholars use to identify public faith in law and their susceptibility to the ideological claims of legitimacy expressed through official law. The letters contain many broad and idealized claims about law, rights, and the Constitution. However, the letters also show, again and again, that the presence of such claims does not necessarily indicate that the people who made them had broad or unrelenting faith in law or that they believed in the literal truth of the idealized claims they articulated. Thus, our challenge as scholars is not to explain the persistence of "unrelenting" faith in law but to understand why people with real doubts about law's efficacy continue to regard legal ideas and legal rituals as meaningful and important.

To understand fully the impact of the habitual use of legal claims in the letters, it is necessary to understand why people directed such claims to government officials and what they were trying to accomplish by using them. The letters show that whatever the reason was, it was not unconditional faith in official law. The content of the letters does not, however, point to any simple alternative answers. The letters do suggest a variety of alternative reasons people might deploy legal rhetoric when making political demands. Some writers used legal discourse to dramatize the gap between legal ideals and reality. Others used claims about law to display their cultural literacy and thus to demonstrate that they deserved a thoughtful response from a government attorney. In some cases, writers may simply have been following their own uncertain understandings about what kinds of displays were appropriate when asking for help or addressing persons in power.

Writers might also have invoked legal ideals with the hope that the ideals they were voicing were important to the self-understandings of the powerful people they addressed in their letters. Writers may have hoped that people in power could be influenced by their own commitment to such ideals. The writers may well have been correct to think that responding officials would have such commitments. One revealing finding about these exchanges is that the people who expressed the most unqualified commitments to law's normative and ideological dimensions were not the people who wrote in with claims but the government lawyers who responded. Those government officials were often forced to make decisions to refuse requests from people in very difficult circumstances. Given the discomfort that such choices are likely to create, those attorneys had reason to convince *themselves* that they lacked discretion, even if they could not convince the letter writers. The tendency of conflicted legal officials to use claims about law to hide discretion from themselves has been noted by other scholars and observers. An example is Robert Cover's (1975) study of antebellum judges who opposed slavery but nevertheless made proslavery rulings. Cover showed that legal officials faced with difficult moral choices resolved internal conflicts by retreating into legal formalism. The judges Cover studied used law to convince themselves that they had no choice but to side with people who claimed ownership of persons they identified as escaped slaves. The formalisms could never convince the people who were being held as slaves that the judges' choices were legitimate or just, but the formalized claims about law could help judges to reconcile their own internal moral conflicts. Another example is in Helen Prejean's account of conversations with legal authorities who oversaw and carried out executions. Those officials also used claims about law's constraints to deny that they had any choice but to participate in executions, even as they admitted that they saw the legal process as morally suspect (1993, 101–6). Prejean thus shows that one pathology of law is that it allows legal officials to convince themselves that they are not responsible for their own lethal actions (see also Sarat 2001).

Many of the people who wrote letters to the CRS seemed to have a similar insight about the way government officials used claims about law. Because they understood that commitments to law helped government officials manage their duties, they hoped that there was at least some chance that such officials would be responsive to efforts to invoke legal ideals. In some cases, writers tried to directly disrupt the comforting effect of law on official denials of responsibility. Those writers pointedly insisted that law left government officials with discretion and thus that they were personally responsible for their choices.

There are thus many possible explanations for the widespread habit of using legalized discourses besides a widespread faith in law. Because it is usually not possible to determine with confidence what led writers to use legal claims in individual cases, it is not always possible to pick out one reason as the most important or most common. Undoubtedly, different people had different reasons for using legal discourse, and some may have had multiple reasons. Nevertheless, there is also no reason to assume that people who articulate legal ideals have faith in law that makes them susceptible to law's ideological messages of legitimacy and thus prone to acquiescence.[6]

Power and Compelled Discourses

In reaching these conclusions about the use of legalized discourses, I do not mean to suggest that the widespread compulsion to articulate familiar bits and pieces of legal rhetoric is always harmless or inconsequential or that the habit of using claims about law, rights, and the Constitution was completely costless. The frequent recitation of idealized claims may not, by itself, demonstrate that people had faith in law or believed in the literal truth of idealized expressions of legal justification. However, the observable habit of using legalized language while making political appeals does show that people believed it was important and useful to deploy law in those contexts. The resulting habit of speaking to government officials in legalized terms is in itself a signal of the power of those legal discourses.

As a result, some observers might continue to insist that the CRS letters ultimately confirm the constraining or disciplining power of legal ideology. Skeptics might still argue that I have not uncovered real resistance to law but only verbalized resistance to certain legal ideals. In the end, the letter writers yielded to the compulsion to speak in the preferred legitimating language of their rulers and thus ultimately confirmed their subject status. Even if people hint that they do not buy into law's own idealized claims of legitimacy, the fact that they nevertheless parrot those claims becomes a striking manifestation of the power of law. They are, at a minimum, buying into the broader practice of using legal discourses to express grievances and thus reinforcing the importance of those discourses. Even when writers openly rejected proclamations of law from legal authorities as a normative standard, they nevertheless helped to reify legal categories and the central place of law in society by giving in to the habit of engaging officials using legalized discourses. Perhaps what they needed to do instead was to abandon legal discourse altogether and try some different approach.

It is not possible to categorically dismiss these kinds of concerns. Compelling people to say certain things or to speak in certain ways can certainly be a means of exercising power or forcing people to signal that they are subject to power. The habit of deploying legal claims shows that even resistant writers were not completely free of the pull of law. However, it is also important to recognize that not all discursive habits and compulsions are equally constraining. The degree to which power can be exercised through a compulsion to speak in a particular way depends largely on the nature of the discourse and the mechanisms that create and maintain the habit of using that discourse.

In the case of the letters considered here, there is good reason to question whether the habit of using rights discourses had particularly significant reifying, constraining, or disciplining effects. To see some of the limits to the power of the rights discourses in the letters, it is instructive to compare the letters written to the CRS to a different example of compelled participation in a discursive practice: Lisa Wedeen's study of the cult of Hafiz al-Asad in Syria (1999). Wedeen shows that people in Syria routinely watched and engaged in ritualistic incantations of exaggerated praise for Asad. She argues that the practice of giving in to the ritual had a powerful disciplining effect on the Syrian population and that those disciplining effects occurred even though people did not believe that the ritual claims of praise were true. For example, people did not literally believe that Asad was, among other things, Syria's "premier pharmacist" (1). Rather, the cult was "soft" and "nontotalizing." Its effect was "not to induce charisma or belief, but rather to elicit outward signs of obedience" (29). The widespread practice of uttering absurd pronouncements of praise became a powerful manifestation of Asad's ability to control people and thus helped to reinforce his power. As Wedeen explains: "The cult of Hafiz al-Asad does not simply depend for its efficacy on other mechanisms of enforcement; rather, *the cult is itself such a mechanism*" (145).

The example from Syria shows that compelled discourse can, in some cases, be a mechanism of power and control even if people do not believe the underlying messages expressed through the discourse. However, the example also provides a sharp contrast to the kind of compulsion revealed in my study of the CRS letters. While the cult in Syria did not require strict adherence to a specified script, the discourse was still far less open ended and elastic than the legal discourses deployed in the letters. People in Syria did not have the option, within the compelled discourse, of pointing out publicly that Asad was not, in fact, the premier pharmacist in Syria. In contrast, the legal discourses that appear in the CRS letters provided considerably more space for creative contestation and resistance. The letter writers deployed legal discourses to contradict authoritative pronouncements of law. Writers routinely refused to bind themselves to the legal categories and rules scripted by judges and other legal officials. The legal rights and entitlements that writers associated with particular issues were not always the same ones that government legal officials recognized as relevant.

Moreover, the Syrian practice described by Wedeen contributed to domination precisely because it compelled people to communicate only praise for Asad, however that praise might be expressed and whether or not the speaker believed the communicated message. Wedeen does discuss various mechanisms of everyday resistance, mechanisms that enabled people to use humor to call attention to the unreality of the official messages (chapter 4).[7] However, as Wedeen explains, people engaged in the transgressions were no longer using the official discourse as they engaged in resistance.

In comparison to the people compelled to praise Asad, it is striking that the people who wrote to the CRS were able to adopt legal language to call attention to law's shortcomings and to construct their own alternative versions of law or constitutionalism. People also used open-ended legal discourses to announce their rejection of law's normative claim to legitimacy. Unlike the people in Syria, the writers also made such claims directly and unambiguously. They also sent them in written form to government officials. Many writers responded to official accounts of law by insisting that their own unofficial version of law was correct or more just.

When legal discourses are put to such purposes, the deployment of such discourse does not, in itself, signal the speaker's submission to organized power and official violence. A discourse with enough flexibility to become a vehicle for direct contestation is not going to be a very effective tool of social control or mechanism for legitimating existing practices. If people appropriate such a discourse to challenge legal authority, they are not signaling docile acceptance of legal authority.

Thus the habit of using legal discourses in the letters is not a manifestation of power and control in the same way as the cult of Asad. If letter writers were "buying into law," they were doing so at a heavily discounted price. The flexibility of legal discourses also helps to explain the enduring appeal of legal myths. It is precisely because the discourse can bend to accommodate competing visions that it maintains its currency even in the absence of consensus on what is legitimate or just.[8]

Real Resistance, Real Acquiescence, and Real Violence

The stories told in some of the CRS letters also show that scholars need to look beyond the way law works as ideology to consider other, more concrete forms of power that inhibit resistance. Considering the role of other forms of power, particularly coercive violence, is important because readers might otherwise hesitate to recognize letters asking government officials for help as a robust form of resistance to legal ideology. Skeptical readers might still insist that letter writers' failure to do more than write letters is itself a sign of deference to or acquiescence in the existing order.

My response to such claims follows a strategy that is similar to the response that critical race theorists have made to critiques of antidiscrimination law (e.g., Crenshaw 1988). Efforts to use relatively conventional legal remedies, or to assert novel rights using the conventional form of protest letters, have to be evaluated with a realistic understanding of what other options are available to people. People sometimes face coercive conditions that make more dramatic responses impossible or counterproductive.

Many of the stories in the letters to the CRS reveal some important reasons letter writers did not resist unjust conditions in more powerful or consequential ways, reasons that have nothing directly to do with law's power as a legitimating ideology. One crucial factor was that many of the people who wrote to the CRS were writing as isolated individuals who were confronting hardships without any institutional or organizational support. Whether or not people accepted the fairness of their legal and political system, there was usually very little that they could do about it. As Georgiana Wines understood when she wrote to complain about her Ford automobile, individual consumers had little chance of building and exercising collective power, even when many other people faced similar problems. Wines did not have any way to identify similarly situated and similarly motivated people. The fact that Wines acted as an individual and made a futile request to government legal officials was not the cause of her failure to improve her situation but a symptom of the political system's failure to give meaningful voice to many of its citizens' concerns.

Isolation and lack of resources were by no means the only factors that prevented people from mounting more direct and meaningful resistance to perceived injustice. The institutional and social system that created some of the most disturbing incidents reported in the CRS letters was maintained not by using ideology to create acquiescence but through organized lethal violence. Much of that violence was organized through law itself. It is crucial to recognize how this background threat of violence can discourage overt acts of resistance by individuals. In a pathbreaking 1986 article on law and violence, Robert Cover pointed out that the appearance of widespread acquiescence to law is an illusion. Much of what looks like voluntary compliance based on deference to law's legitimacy is ultimately the result of law's capacity to unleash a vast array of institutional mechanisms of lethal violence on people who refuse to comply. Those mechanisms become invisible to scholars because they do not often need to be unleashed. The widespread awareness of organized violence normally means that the violence does not actually need to be deployed. Cover draws attention to law's violence in order to challenge scholars who saw widespread compliance with law as voluntary and a sign of shared commitments to legal values. To other scholars, compliance seemed like consent, which in turn seemed like a sign of law's ideological power to maintain shared commitments and induce voluntary compliance and acquiescence. Cover's evocative insight was that the credible threat of violence is always a crucial, if ordinarily hidden, part of the social world shaped by law. The need for such organized violence is itself a clear manifestation of the limits on consensus and shared commitments.[9]

Letters to the CRS contain stories that reveal the effect that the threat of legal violence had on people's capacity to resist. For example, consider again another writer who was sold a lemon by a car dealer, George Runyan. Instead of writing a letter to the Justice Department as Georgiana Wines did, Runyan first publicized his complaint in a way that threatened the dealer's business. The company responded by enlisting the aid of a legal actor, a local judge. The judge then threatened to unleash law's organized violence to separate Runyan from his property and livelihood if he continued to publicly protest or resist.

Other stories in the letters add complexity to Cover's account of law's official violence. Some letters show that in addition to the official violence organized directly through legal mechanisms, it is also important to consider both violent lawlessness by state officials and state tolerance of extralegal violence as mechanisms of control and power. Among other things, the threat of such violence can prevent people from more actively resisting unjust conditions. The CRS files provide some instructive examples of how extralegal violence affected a few people who engaged in acts of resistance that were more bold and direct than writing letters to federal officials or the White House. One example is Roxanna Harris, who grew tired of watching Baltimore police officers beating her fellow citizens and yelled out her window that a group of police officers should stop "disturbing the peace." The police responded by forcing the eighty-year-old Harris from her home and holding her overnight in jail. Harris was set free the next day but remained quite shaken and quite upset that the police would not return a flashlight they had taken from her. Two other examples of resistance led to more tragic consequences. Private Thomas Broadus decided not to back down when a racist police officer tried to demean him on a crowded public street. The officer responded by beating Private Broadus with a club and then murdering him by shooting him twice in the back.

Robert Hall, the man who stood up to the corrupt Sheriff Screws, also paid a very high price for resistance. Hall challenged the sheriff through a legal process and participated in an organization of black citizens aimed at improving conditions in Baker County, Georgia. Sheriff Screws responded by gathering a drunken gang that that conspired to murder Hall. They purported to "arrest" Hall for using a fabricated warrant for a crime that never occurred. The sheriff and his friends dragged Hall from his home in the middle of the night, drove him in shackles to a public gathering place in the center of town, and spent more than thirty minutes beating Hall's head into a bloody pulp with clubs and blackjacks (Troutt 1999). Such acts were carried out as public spectacles and perpetrated by persons clothed with state authority. The people who did such things were encouraged by their confidence that they could get away with it. Ordinary people of that era understood that such things could and did happen. Their realistic and informed understanding of the way power is exercised through legal and extralegal violence does far more to explain the low incidence of active resistance than the habit of using legal discourses to articulate aspirations.[10]

More generally, evaluating the political impact of the habit of using legalized discourses requires a realistic understanding of available alternatives. When people respond to injustice by articulating legalized claims to an unresponsive government agency, it may look on the surface as though they are acquiescing to the normative categories of legal discourse that purport to guide such agencies. However, people were writing in a context in which people's basic rights were routinely violated. They were writing in a time of severe economic hardship that left them vulnerable to the largely unchecked power of relief, mental health, and social welfare officials. In such a context, it is not an act of acquiescence or cooptation for people to tell government officials that they ought to live up to their own expressed ideals.

The Value of Popular Aspirations for Constitutional Rights

I have argued so far that the letters provide reason to question claims that rights critics have made regarding some of the negative consequences of popular legal discourses. The rights discourses used in the letters were malleable enough to support a wide variety of novel claims, and writers who deployed legal and constitutional discourses drew on the rhetorical power of legal ideals while still resisting law's claims to legitimacy. Nevertheless, there remains reason to be skeptical of the value of the popular rights claiming on display in the letters to the CRS. Even if the legal discourses did not create the expected harms, skeptics might still question whether the legalized claims had any real benefits.

Such skepticism deserves to be taken seriously. Given that very few of the letter writers received any material benefits in response to their letters, I expect many readers to remain puzzled about why I have labored at such length to show that writers made competent and realistic use of legal arguments. The content of the claims and responses might tempt some readers to conclude that the primary lesson that the letters teach is that Americans are stunningly ignorant. The writers did not understand the law, the Constitution, their rights, or the federal system of government. Instead of painting my optimistic picture of an engaged citizenry with a good understanding of how things really work, the same letters might as easily have been used to argue that the writers were so ill informed about official law that they failed at the basic tasks of well-functioning constitutional citizens.

I conclude by explaining why I have resisted such conclusions and believe that expansive and aspirational legal discourses can, at least sometimes, be a positive good. The letters writers' imaginative legal claims certainly suggest ignorance or extravagance if they are judged against the standard of official law. Writers expressed claims that legal authorities of their era were not willing to recognize as accurate statements of law. However, the same letters also provide some powerful reasons for rejecting the assumption that official law should be the baseline for evaluating the worthiness, quality, or even accuracy of citizen claims about law, particularly in a constitutional democracy that aspires to be guided by "We the People." The letters show that sometimes citizens can get things right and also that authorities often get it wrong when they declare that people's expressed legal aspirations are incorrect or extravagant.

The assumption that official law should be the baseline for evaluating popular legal and constitutional discourses is quite powerful in the scholarly literature. One indicator of its ubiquity is in the scholarly response to some recent proposals for an expanded public role in processes of constitutional interpretation. A few scholars, most notably Kramer (2004) and Tushnet (1999), have challenged the view that judges should be the ultimate interpreters of constitutional meaning and have argued instead for a popular constitutionalism that gives the people more direct involvement in processes of constitutional interpretation and constitutional development.[11] Other scholars have responded to such heretical suggestions by claiming that citizens simply lack the capacity to act responsibly as engaged constitutional citizens. Richard Posner (2004), for example, finds Kramer's idea of popular constitutionalism "barely intelligible." He writes, "I do not believe that many people are even interested in what the Constitution means" and accuses Kramer of a "stunning lack of realism in supposing that the average person is a competent interpreter of the Constitution" because "the average person has never read the Constitution."[12] The heart of such critiques is a belief that popular constitutionalism cannot work because Americans are not attentive enough to established law and Supreme Court doctrines. Constitutional law is thus best left to the experts.

While Posner offers no evidence for his assertions, they likely ring true for many legal scholars. His skepticism gets some support from studies of voter behavior that seem to show that most Americans are ill informed about and inattentive to politics and know very little about the Supreme Court. Some critics of popular constitutionalism have cited such studies as grounds for rejecting popular or political controls on the court (e.g., Devins 2007). There are, however, some important studies that provide good reason to question whether surveys actually show widespread ignorance of the court.[13] Moreover, even accepting, for the sake of argument, that Posner is correct, the measure of people's *capacity* to act as constitutional citizens should not be their ability to express to pollsters their interest in or knowledge of the Supreme Court. The more relevant test, for a theory like Kramer's, is whether people could develop a capacity to engage as constitutional citizens if they were presented with opportunities to have a meaningful say in constitutional processes. People today may not bother to learn about the Constitution, not because they are incapable, but because they so rarely have any meaningful voice in processes of constitutional interpretation or constitutional change.

The ability of citizens to understand the Constitution in a world where they have more direct say in constitutional processes cannot be observed directly. However, the letters to the CRS do provide some suggestive information. The letters reveal how people attempted to engage as constitutional citizens when they found themselves in difficult circumstances and looked to law or the Constitution as a potentially helpful resource. Many of the letters show that people in such situations found and read the Constitution and made good-faith efforts to articulate constitutional values and construct constitutional arguments.

Of course, skeptics like Posner might still insist that the arguments that people made in the letters simply confirmed their ignorance and incompetence. For example, writers who were drawn to the privileges and immunities clause revealed that they were unaware that the Supreme Court had rendered that clause a dead letter in 1873 (Slaughterhouse Cases, 83 US 36). More fundamentally, the mere fact that people wrote letters asking for help from federal officials showed their ignorance of the Supreme Court doctrines that limited federal power to protect rights.

Such skepticism makes sense only under the assumption that Supreme Court case law has to be the baseline for evaluating whether citizen interpretations of the Constitution are correct or valuable. The problem, however, is that the letters also provide some powerful reasons for rejecting such privileging of the Supreme Court. In hindsight, it is quite often the letter writers, and not legal authorities like judges, who got things right on the big constitutional questions. The vision of federal responsibility over rights that was voiced in many of the letters seems, by today's standards, more correct and much more attractive than the vision established at that time in official law. Moreover, writers did not simply demand an expanded federal role. The writers collectively illustrated the need for federal intervention by telling heartbreaking stories about the consequences of unchecked state power; including stories of unlawful detentions or brutality by corrupt police forces, arbitrary commitment to state mental hospitals, losing custody of children to state welfare officials, and abusive treatment in response to efforts to travel in search of work. Writers created a powerful record of the everyday difficulties caused by state and local officials' petty corruption, poor management, and lethal violence. They also drew attention to the inability of state governments to control their own abusive officials. Many writers concluded that such conditions gave federal officials a responsibility to exercise their unique capacity to check local abuses. In making their demands for an expanded federal role, the writers were indicating commitments to the core constitutional values expressed in the text of the Fourteenth Amendment.

According to the official legal standards of their era, the writers' insistence that the federal government needed to take seriously its constitutional responsibility to make promises of rights meaningful was "wrong." However, the views expressed by many writers have subsequently become widely accepted. The Supreme Court now recognizes that the Constitution gives the federal government broad power to provide redress for rights abuses by state actors. While there are still many constitutional controversies over the scope of federal power to protect rights, there is a broad consensus that the federal government cannot again abandon its role as a protector against rights violations perpetrated by state officials. The insistence of many letter writers that the Constitution gave the federal government responsibility to protect constitutional rights thus seems much less extravagant today than it did in 1939.[14]

Meanwhile, many of the constitutional and legal claims routinely offered by government authorities in 1939 have now been officially repudiated. The monotonous refrain of the CRS's claim that the federal government had no jurisdiction to intervene when states violated constitutional rights has not withstood the test of time. The Supreme Court's position has fared even worse. The opinions written in the CRS test cases show that Supreme Court justices, like relatively uninformed citizens, sometimes get things wrong. The justices also gave voice to imaginative, extravagant, and unrealistic claims. The most striking examples are in *Screws v. United States* (325 US 91 [1945]), the key CRS test case on police brutality that I discuss in chapter 2. In that case, the Supreme Court overturned the convictions of a murderous sheriff and two codefendants. The plurality opinion, which focused on an alleged technical problem with the jury instructions, is strained and disingenuous. (One telling indicator is that the criminal defendants had never objected to the jury instructions at any stage in the proceedings. The instructions became an issue for the first time after oral arguments as the divided justices searched for a way to dispose of the case.)[15] The justices' strained search for a constitutional problem that would allow them to reverse the conviction suggests that the real concerns motivating the justices' obstruction were not the ones they so implausibly articulated in their opinions. It was instead a more general concern about the CRS's effort to revive Reconstruction-era laws to conduct criminal prosecutions. Their concerns led them to transform a case about a murder perpetrated by a southern sheriff into a case about the pressing need to protect the rights of southern sheriffs. The seven justices who supported the ruling all gave great weight to their concern that the CRS could violate the rights of state officials through its quite minimal efforts to prevent law enforcement officials from murdering citizens.

Judged by today's constitutional understandings, the constitutional views expressed by most of the Supreme Court justices who participated in *Screws* seem, at best, wrong, and in some cases, repugnant. The most striking of the four *Screws* opinions was coauthored by Justices Roberts, Frankfurter, and Jackson. Those justices were not swayed by the Fourteenth Amendment's clear language expressing federal guarantees of rights and express grants of new enforcement powers to Congress. To justify the choices they made, they gave voice to ideas about state powers that matched the views of the slaveholders who lost the Civil War, not the ideas established by the framers of the reconstructed Constitution that emerged after the war ended.[16] The three justices also gave great weight to concerns about the rights of state officials who might be prosecuted under a CRS program that targeted only egregious rights violations. They gave voice to those concerns while failing to say anything meaningful about how their narrow reading of federal power affected the rights of the much larger group of people who would continue to be targeted by state law enforcement officials like Screws.

Those justices instead excoriated the Justice Department because it had "relieved" (139) the state of responsibility for prosecuting the sheriff

for his "local crime" (138). That claim, made by three Supreme Court justices, is as fantastical, unrealistic, and extravagant as any claim contained
in letters to the CRS. As the opinion itself notes, the Justice Department's
brief in the case established that the State of Georgia was unwilling to
prosecute Screws. The brief also explained department policies that mini-
mized the risk of supplanting state power. Those policies required CRS
attorneys to make efforts to convince state officials to act before initiating
any federal civil rights prosecutions and required that the CRS drop cases
if a state made any effort to investigate and prosecute a case.[17] Even without the documentation in the department's brief, the justices who wrote
the opinion would have known quite well that Georgia was not going to
prosecute Screws. Their recitation of their fantasy that the Justice Department "relieved" the state government of its responsibilities was not a
good-faith effort to address the underlying issues. (It is perhaps instructive that the same three justices referred to the man Screws murdered as
a "lad" [138]. Robert Hall was, in reality, an adult, a parent, a husband, a
skilled worker, and a constitutional citizen.)

To justify their obstruction of federal power in the *Screws* case, these
justices offered a remarkable reading of the Fourteenth Amendment. The
text of that amendment explicitly gives Congress new powers to pass legislation to fulfill the amendment's broad promises of equal protection, due
process, and basic rights of citizenship. The justices claimed: "By itself,
this Amendment is merely an instrument for striking down action by the
States in defiance of it" and "does not create rights and obligations actively
enforceable by federal law" (140). The justices also tellingly gave voice to
their hostility toward Reconstruction. Looking at the civil rights statute
used in the case, the justices claimed: "It is familiar history that much of
this legislation was born of that vengeful spirit which to no small degree
envenomed the Reconstruction era" (140). The historical underpinnings
of such critiques of Reconstruction have, of course, been demolished by
much subsequent scholarship.[18]

The position of the Supreme Court has, of course, changed since the
Screws case. However, the possibility that authorities will get things wrong
remains, as does the possibility that the people will sometimes be able
to do better than judges or government attorneys. It may be unrealistic
and exaggerated to claim a right "to earn our own living selling just good
food, ice cream, and pop," or an "inalienable right to earn my living as an
employe in my own business even though it is temporarily in charge of the
Government." But are such claims more laughable or self-serving than

Dick Cheney's claim that disclosure laws do not cover the vice president because he is not part of the executive branch? Are the citizens' claims in the letters less grounded in American history or the Constitution's text than the claim, made by purported "originalist" Clarence Thomas, that the Constitution is "color-blind"?[19]

Of course, recognizing that the government authorities can also exaggerate and get things wrong may not eliminate the urge to scorn letter writers for engaging in their own rhetorical excesses. Some letter writers also tried, perhaps deliberately or cynically, to make strained arguments about legal texts. Other writers just made things up and offered imagined or embellished legal claims. More important, even if the people sometimes got things right in the letters, there is no guarantee that the people will always articulate more attractive constitutional visions than legal authorities. In today's popular constitutional discourse, there is a frequent cry for a return of "states' rights" and withdrawal of much federal authority over local affairs. The content of the CRS letters has not led me to share in such nostalgia for an earlier era of unchecked state powers. Rather, the state government practices revealed in many of the CRS letters provide a useful reminder of why social movement activity eventually forced the federal government to develop capacities to check rights abuses by states.

Given that failures by legal authorities are inevitable and sometimes catastrophic, my more general conclusion is that authoritative pronouncements are not a suitable baseline for evaluating citizens' legal and constitutional claims. The fact that ordinary people might also sometimes produce some bad answers is not reason to scorn all popular engagement through legal and constitutional discourses. Of course, my argument is not that the people will always do better than judges. There are many letters that make disagreeable claims and some that express repulsive values. There are also important substantive arguments to be made against the positions taken by some letter writers. However, those arguments can be made quite powerfully on substantive grounds and without relying on the authority of the Supreme Court. The plausibility of a reading of constitutional text or the truth of a claim about history does not depend on what the Supreme Court happens to be saying. Moreover, a constitutional culture that encourages substantive engagement through argument seems preferable to one based on reflexive deference to judicial authority. Substantive arguments on the merits seems more likely to produce robust constitutional engagement.

The popular and official legal discourses on display in the CRS letters show that desire to eliminate "wrong" answers is not reason to discourage people from using legal discourses that allow them to express and communicate aspirations for a better and more just world. The boundaries of legitimate legal argument need not always be drawn at the border between government authorities and citizens. The now-rejected visions of rights expressed by government authorities in the *Screws* case and in the CRS reply letters may well have persisted if ordinary people had not been able to imagine and then develop commitments to more just constitutional ideals.[20]

The people do not always get what they need the first time they ask, but they would never get anything if they stopped looking for resonant ways of articulating novel demands. Many letters processed by the CRS demanded changes that eventually, after much too long a wait, became widely accepted features of the constitutional system. In these exchanges, government authorities proved less capable than the people of adopting legal rhetoric to express aspirations for a more just constitutional system, one based on greater fidelity to the text of the post–Civil War Constitution. With this in mind, it seems unfair to dismiss casually the constitutional visions expressed by ordinary people. Those visions can have value if the people who expressed them revealed that they did not fully understand the intricate doctrines promulgated by persons who temporarily occupied offices that gave them institutional authority to wield violence in the name of law. It also seems reasonable to hope, going forward, that ordinary people will continue to develop commitments to broad ideals of rights and will continue to imagine and express aspirations for legal entitlements that go beyond what official law is willing to recognize and support.

Appendix

Notes on the Archival Sources

The letters used in the book are preserved in correspondence files of the Department of Justice at the National Archives (Record Group 60, Entry 114, Classified Subject Files). Civil rights materials are in files beginning with 144 and are housed in boxes 17573–17608.

The Justice Department's routine correspondence files are not well preserved in the archives. Many of the files for particular states are missing entirely, and the files that are preserved often have materials missing. While there are quite a few routine letters from the first two years of CRS operations (1939–40) preserved in the correspondence files, there are only scattered letters over the next two years and almost none for subsequent years. The archives do have some of the case files for cases that the CRS began to pursue, as well as record slips that track paperwork processed by the department, including routine correspondence.

After spending time reviewing the available Justice Department materials on civil rights on the archives, I decided to use a sample of letters for my study. I used a scanner to copy over a thousand letters, together with any material regarding the replies made by the CRS or other agencies. The letters provide 879 cases (counting multiple letters from the same person as a single case).

The sample includes all the letters (188 cases) from a general correspondence file for civil rights (file 144-0). Those letters came from all over the country. The remaining cases come from separately organized state files from the same civil rights grouping. I sampled a group of states from the ones that were available and used all the letters from each of those state files. I selected states to get as much regional variation as possible.

The selection gives an adequate mix of urban and rural areas. The sample was Arkansas (144-9-0), California (144-11-0 and 144-12-0), Delaware (144-15-0), Florida (144-18-0), Illinois (144-23-0), Maryland (144-35-0), Missouri (144-42-0), and the District of Columbia (144-16-0). The state files for Deep South states (Georgia, Alabama, Mississippi, and Louisiana) were not available in the archives. I drew my sample by using entire state files rather than choosing a sample from within all the state files to make sure I could capture multiple letters on the same topic and multiple letters from the same person. The sample includes more than half of the letters from this era that are preserved in the archives. (Some of the letters in the Florida file were not coded as part of the sample because the scans became unavailable before I did the coding. I read the letters and have notes on the content but was not able to code them confidently without copies of the actual letters.)

The coded sample includes 710 cases where writers reported on or sought help with particular incidents. The other 169 cases involve people who commented on civil rights issues without reporting particular incidents. Letters in this group asked the president to veto some policy proposals related to civil rights, offered general praise for the CRS's efforts, or made comments or requests for general information about the CRS program. The comments about rights, law, and constitutionalism in the nonincident letters are often quite interesting. However, when I make quantitative claims related to responses made by the CRS, I do not include them, since most of the excluded cases did not receive any reply from the CRS.

The archived files contain the original letters and carbon copies of CRS reply letters. The available letters include many sent directly to the Justice Department as well as many letters sent to the White House and various other parts of the federal government and a few letters sent originally to Congress. The files also occasionally include internal documents like the routing slips that accompanied letters as they were passed to different Justice Department employees. In a few instances, the files contain drafts of responses that provide some information about how the CRS processed letters.

In addition to the bulk correspondence files, the archives also contain correspondence in case files for the 144 designation. The case files are numbered sequentially beginning with 1 (e.g., 144-16-1, 144-16-2, etc.). Most incidents that generated considerable CRS attention or that resulted in prosecutions were given case files, numbered in the order in which the files were created. The procedure for assigning a case file designation was not rigid. Some incidents that led to extended correspondence and investigatory activity were never assigned case files. Some of the case files are about incidents that never generated much activity beyond an initial letter or report. Many case files are missing. I read all the available case files from 1939–41 for the states that I use in my sample, as well as many other files from later years up to 1947. I did not find any instances where an individual complaint letter led to a criminal prosecution or some other significant form of help or attention from the department. There are some cases that the department did pursue that do have letters from individuals in the files. However, the letters do not appear to have been the initial source of the department's knowledge of the case. The cases that were investigated were high-profile cases that came to the department's attention through other sources (e.g., locally based US attorneys, the FBI, local government officials, the NAACP, the White House, or Justice Department employees who had seen newspaper stories).

The content of some of the missing letters can be tracked, albeit imperfectly, because the archives also contain a set of record slips (Entry 96) that Justice Department clerical staff created at the same time as replies were sent. Those records are typed on small index cards. They record information about records placed in department files. For the letters, the slips indicate the name and location of the letter writer and a very short description of the complaint that matches that summary of the complaint that appears in the corresponding CRS reply letter. The record slips provide *some* information about the content of letters that are missing, but could not substitute for the letters themselves for this study. As discussed in chapters 2 and 4, the CRS's expressed understanding of the subject of complaint letters was often very different from what was actually said in the letters. Moreover, my interest in precisely how writers expressed their demands makes it impossible to rely on the half-sentence summaries written by CRS staff in the card files. Through cross-checking, I also found that the record slips were not themselves complete. (There were some actual letters in the files that did not have corresponding record slips.)

I read all the letters and worked with two research assistants to code some basic information that could help me to make descriptive claims about the letters. I developed reliable codes for some broad descriptive categories in the letters and report that information in the text.

The missing letters in the archives and within files make it difficult to report information about some basic characteristics of the letters, such as regional variation in the content of the letters or changes in subject matter over time. Reporting such information would be misleading because of the materials missing from the archives. Such information would not capture the underlying reality of letters that were actually received by the Justice Department during the period covered here.

It is difficult to know exactly why letters are missing. Archivists (who were perpetually puzzled that I was interested in general correspondence rather than case files) informed me that Justice never transferred the missing state files to the archives. In response to a Freedom of Information Act request, the Justice Department informed me that the department no longer had any relevant files and that the department routinely destroys general correspondence after two years unless it leads to investigations or cases.

My reading of the archived materials, including comparison with the slip files, convinces me that the missing material is not the result of a deliberate effort. For example, there is nothing in the slip files or other material to suggest that the department avoided archiving embarrassing material. It may be that the accident is not that some letters are missing but that any of the letters were preserved.

I supplemented knowledge gained through the archival materials with material from broader historical studies of the CRS, particularly Goluboff (2007), Carr (1947), and Elliff (1967). I also read through the microform records of the President's Committee on Civil Rights published in 1948. Those records provide some summary information about the CRS correspondence but not detailed information about the content of any letters.

Letters Referenced in the Text

The following list covers the archival materials that I reference by date in the text and notes. The materials include letters and other items associated with the cases in my sample. Other archival materials that are not connected to my sample of cases are given full citations in the text and notes. The list is organized by complainant. For cases where I make reference to reply letters or other documents, the additional materials are listed chronologically under the initial item. Unless otherwise indicated, all the materials for each entry are located in the file indicated after the initial item.

James R. Allen to Frank Murphy, March 28, 1939. File 144-0.
   Assistant Attorney General Brien McMahon to Allen, April 6, 1939.
   Allen to Franklin Roosevelt, June 25, 1941. File 144-15-0.

Memorandum for Wendell Berge, May 24, 1941. File 144-15-0.

Memorandum for the Files, Re: James Allen, September 24, 1941. File 144-15-0.

"An alien with first paper waiting to become a Citizen" to Franklin Roosevelt, June 25, 1940. File 144-12-0.

Irving Amos to Frank Murphy, July 19, 1939. File 144-35-0.

Glenn Anderson, Coordinating Council, 46th Assembly District, to Franklin Roosevelt, October 20, 1939. File 144-0.

Allen Applegarth to Robert Jackson, March 19, 1939. File 144-11-0.

Edward Arps to Frank Murphy, March 28, 1939. File 144-0.

H. Bain to Frank Murphy, May 24, 1939. File 144-18-0.

Assistant Attorney General O. John Rogge to Bain, June 28, 1939.

Alford Baker to Department of Justice, March 30, 1939. File 144-0.

Assistant Attorney General Brien McMahon to Baker, April 6, 1939.

Bertha Baker to Attorney General, April 17, 1939. File 144-11-0.

Assistant Attorney General O. John Rogge to Baker, July 15, 1939.

Rogge to US Attorney Frank Hennessy, July 15, 1939.

Hennessy to Attorney General. July 24, 1939.

John S. Barbara Sr. to Department of Justice, April 2, 1939. File 144-0.

Antonio Bautista to Frank Murphy, February 18, 1939. File 144-0.

Murphy to Bautista, April 6, 1939.

Louis Becker to Department of Justice, October 9, 1939. File 144-23-0.

Becker to Division of Unemployment Compensation, Illinois, October 9, 1939.

Charles Bishop to Eleanor Roosevelt, August 1, 1940. File 144-42-0.

Assistant Attorney General O. John Rogge to US Attorney Harry Blanton, August 14, 1940.

Blanton to Rogge, August 16, 1940.

J. Edgar Hoover to Rogge, August 22, 1940.

Rogge to Hoover, August 27, 1940.

Rogge to Blanton, August 27, 1940.

Blanton to Rogge, September 10, 1940.

William Bork to Civil Liberties Division, Department of Justice, May 12, 1941. 144-12-0.

Bork to Civil Liberties Division, July 12, 1941.

Assistant Attorney General Wendell Berge to Bork, July 19, 1941.

Bork to Berge, July 28, 1941.

Norman Gould Boswell to Department of Justice, May 1, 1940. File 144-12-0.

W. Daniel Boyd to Frank Murphy, October 25, 1939. File 144-18-0.

Louise Bransten et al. to Franklin Roosevelt, July 1, 1940. File 144-11-0.

S. D. Brewton et al. to Attorney General, September 23, 1940. File 144-23.

Margaret Brophy, Henrietta Jeffries, Matilda Hammel, and Elsa Hotze to Frank Murphy, February 9, 1939. File 144-0.

Brien McMahon to Brophy, March 7, 1939.

Anna Mae Brown to Frank Murphy, March 29, 1939. File 144-37.

Florence Brown to Department of Justice, December 30, 1940. File 144-35..

Assistant Attorney General Wendell Berge to Brown, January 10, 1941.

Harold Brown to Frank Murphy, May 30, 1939. File 144-35-0.

Max Brown to US Attorney General, June 17, 1939. File 144-9-0.

Assistant Attorney General O. John Rogge to Brown, June 27, 1939.

Orval Brunk to Frank Murphy, September 9, 1939. File 144-0.

Emily Brunner to Frank Murphy, March 29, 1939, File 144-0.

Brien McMahon to Brunner, April 14, 1939.

Pearl Buffo to Franklin Roosevelt, July 9, 1940. File 144-11-0.

W. E. Bullard to Francis Biddle, September 22, 1941, File 144-0.

Senator Edward R. Burke to Frank Murphy, April 24, 1939. File 144-0.

Murphy to Burke, May 4, 1939.

Albert Campbell, Oil Workers International Union, to Franklin Roosevelt, October 19, 1939. File 144-12-0.

Harold Carlson to Frank Murphy, March 13, 1939. File 144-0.

Charles Carpenter to Frank Murphy, March 24, 1939. File 144-0.

L. E. Carpenter to Frank Murphy. November 29, 1939. File 144-12-0.

Carpenter to Ray Chesbro, Los Angeles City Attorney, November 29, 1939.

Carpenter to Murphy, December 16, 1939.

Carpenter to Murphy, December 28, 1939.

Eugene Causey to Frank Murphy, December 27, 1939. File 144-37-0.

Edward Kemp, Assistant to the Attorney General, to Causey, January 12, 1940.

Causey to Kemp, January 18, 1940.

Kemp to Assistant Attorney General O. John Rogge, January 27, 1940.

Kemp to Causey, February 14, 1940.

US Attorney John C. Lehr to Henry Schweinhaut, May 21, 1940.

Winton Church to Frank Murphy, July 12, 1939. File 144-37-0.

"A. Citizen" to Frank Murphy, March 27, 1939. File 144-0.

Joseph Clark to Robert Jackson, received February 20, 1940. File 144-37-2.

Joseph Patrick Coane to Frank Murphy, July 7, 1939. File 144-23-0.

Assistant Attorney General O. John Rogge to Coane, July 27, 1939.

Hattie Cochrane to Charles Murphy, received August 28, 1939. File 144-12-0.

Joseph Collier to Civil Liberties Division, August 4, 1940. File 144-23.

Assistant Attorney General O John Rogge to Collier, August 9, 1940.

Collier to Attorney General Robert Jackson, August 12, 1940.

V. T. Comer to Department of Justice, June 17, 1940. File 144-12-0.

M. F. Compart to Frank Murphy, September 9, 1939. File 144-23.

William S. Coombs to Frank Murphy, July 6, 1939. File 144-36-0.

J. T. Cooper to Franklin Roosevelt, May 20, 1940. File 144-0.

Ben Copean to US Attorney General, March 8, 1941. File 144-35-0.

Paul Cowles to Frank Murphy, October 9, 1939. File 144-11-0.

Frank Cox to Attorney General, September 24, 1940. File 144-12-0.

E. B. Croft to Attorney General, March 28, 1939. File 144-0.

Assistant Attorney General Brien McMahon to Croft, April 10, 1939.

David Curtis to US Attorney General, received June 22, 1939. File 144-23-0.

H. W. Dail to Frank Murphy, April 7, 1939. File 144-12.

Welly Hopkins to Dail, May 25, 1939.

Eugene Davidson to Crescent 5 and 10 Cent Store, December 11, 1939. File 144-16-0.

Mary Deming to Robert Jackson, June 15, 1940. File 144-37-0.

Assistant Attorney General O. John Rogge to Deming, August 8, 1940.

John Dew to Franklin Roosevelt, June 26, 1940. File 144-12-0.

F. B. Dodge to Frank Murphy, June 12, 1939. File 144-11-0.

Katherina von Dombrowski to Homer Cummings. November 29, 1939. File 144-36-0.

Harry Dollowing to Department of Justice, October 20, 1939. File 144-35-0.

Douglas Dorner to Frank Murphy, March 9, 1939. File 144-0.

Assistant Attorney General Brien McMahon to F. C. Harrington, WPA, March 17, 1939.

McMahon to Dorner, March 17, 1939.

Dorner to Murphy, June 23, 1939.

McMahon to Dorner, July 14, 1939.

Alvina Douglas to Franklin Roosevelt, February 12, 1940. File 144-37-0.

Assistant Attorney General O. John Rogge to Douglas, March 12, 1940.

Vinton Dowis to Franklin Roosevelt, February 14, 1940. File 144-37-0.
Virginia Dryer to Legal Department, Washington, DC, March 17, 1939.
    File 144-0.
Frank Duggan to John Rogge, October 26, 1940. File 144-35-0.
A. E. Elmer to Justice Department, January 14, 1940. File 144-23-0.
John Fewkes to Henry Schweinhaut, April 11, 1940. File 144-23-0.
Harry Flaharty to Frank Murphy, December 28, 1940. File 144-16-0.
John Flatley to Frank Murphy, received April 24, 1939. File 144-36-0.
G. R. Fox to Frank Murphy, August 20, 1939. File 144-42-0.
Royal Wilbur France to Frank Murphy, June 24, 1939. File 144-18-0.
    France to Orlando Police Chief William Smith, June 13, 1939.
    Assistant Attorney General O. John Rogge to France, August 4, 1939.
Burrill Freedman to Robert Jackson, June 26, 1940. File 144-23-0.
Nathan Fried to Justice Department, February 5, 1940. File 144-1-0.
Alex Gast to Franklin Roosevelt, December 31, 1940. File 144-0-42.
Lambert Gerin to Franklin Roosevelt, January 11, 1941. File 144-23-0.
William Gillespie to Eleanor Roosevelt, January 17, 1940. File 144-35-0.
Bernard Glick to Frank Murphy, March 30, 1939. File 144-0.
L. G. Goodrich to Frank Murphy, received June 8, 1939. File 144-37-0.
Robert Grant to Attorney General, March 26, 1940. File 144-12-0.
Frank Griffin to Franklin Roosevelt, March 12, 1939. File 144-0.
Mr. and Mrs. Leonard Griffin to Franklin Roosevelt, August 16, 1940.
    File 144-12-0.
Lonnie Griffith to Frank Murphy. March 30, 1939. File 144-0.
Fred Hall to Robert Jackson, June 3, 1940. File 144-12-0
Morris Hall to Frank Murphy, March 29, 1939. File 144-0.
    Assistant Attorney General Brien McMahon to Hall, April 8, 1939.
    Hall to Murphy, April 10, 1939.
    Assistant Attorney General Brien McMahon to Hall, May 6, 1939.
G. Haltzbander to Mrs. Roosevelt, February 10, 1941. File 144-9-0.
L. B. Hampton to Franklin Roosevelt, December 24, 1939. File 144-18-0.
    Assistant Attorney General O. John Rogge to Hampton, January 15,
    1940.
G. F. Harrington to Dept. of Education, February 25, 1940. File 144-11-0.
    Assistant Attorney General O. John Rogge to Harrington, March 25,
    1940.
C. C. Harris to Attorney General, June 1, 1941. File 144-12-0.
Roxanna Harris to Franklin Roosevelt, September 21, 1939. File 144-
    35-0.

Assistant Attorney General O. John Rogge to Harris, September 30, 1939.

Harris to Rogge, December 10, 1939.

William Harvey to Attorney General, August 7, 1939. File 144-12-0.

Snowden Haslup to US Attorney General, received July 24, 1939. File 144-35-0.

Ida Helpingstein, Workers Alliance Local 2052, to Franklin Roosevelt, October 19, 1939. File 144-12-0.

Anna Hopson to Franklin Roosevelt, January 12, 1940. File 144-23-0.

Horace Howard to Franklin Roosevelt, September 30, 1940. File 144-42-0.

Tillie Hubbard to Franklin Roosevelt, received March 31, 1939. File 144-0.

Mrs. Harry Hudspeth to Department of Justice, August 11, 1940. File 144-23-0.

Lulua Hughes to Frank Murphy, August 28, 1939. File 144-37-0.

Administrative Assistant to the Attorney General T. S. Quinn to Hughes, September 14, 1939.

W. A. C. Hughes to Victor Rotnem, December 3, 1943. File 144-35-4.

Assistant Attorney General Tom Clark to Hughes, December 10, 1943.

Clark to Barton Harrington, Assistant US Attorney, Baltimore, December 10, 1943.

Harrington to Clark, December 16, 1943.

US Attorney Bernard Flynn to Clark, December 16, 1943.

Clark to Flynn, December 21, 1943.

Clark to Hughes, December 22, 1943.

George W. Hurley to Sen. Sheridan Downey, January 15, 1941. File 144-12-0.

Marie James to Frank Murphy, June 19, 1939. File 144-11-0.

Aimo Jamsen, Finnish Workers Club, to Franklin Roosevelt, July 20, 1940. File 144-35-0.

Henry Johnson to Franklin Roosevelt, April 25, 1941. File 144-23.

Joseph H. Johnston to Nevada State Legislature, copy to Justice Department, March 4, 1939. File 144-0.

Jack Johnstone to John E. Cassidy, Attorney General of Illinois, August 12, 1940. File 144-23-0.

Charles Jones to Franklin Roosevelt, received February 7, 1940. File 144-12-0.

Lee Jones to FBI, September 22, 1940. File 144-9-0.

Martin W. Jones to Justice Department, April 20, 1940. File 144-16-0.

Thomas P. Jones to Frank Murphy, June 24, 1939. File 144-37-0.

Ever Joy to Franklin Roosevelt, March 9, 1939. File 144-0.

Assistant Attorney General Brien McMahon to Joy, March 27, 1939.

Joy to Murphy, April 6, 1939.

Anthony Jurich to Frank Murphy, September 25, 1939. File 144-12-1.

Viola Kendt to Franklin Roosevelt, September 19, 1940. File 144-23-0

Milton Kennedy to Franklin Roosevelt, March 6, 1939. File 144-0.

Jacob Kind to Franklin Roosevelt, April 13, 1939. File 144-0.

Samuel King to Frank Murphy, May 16, 1939. File 144-16-0.

Acting Assistant Attorney General Welly Hopkins to King, May 26, 1939.

William J. Kosma to Attorney General, February 20, 1940. File 144-37-0.

Henry N. Kost to Franklin Roosevelt, received November 6, 1941. File 144-18-0.

Assistant Attorney General Wendell Berge to Kost, November 14, 1941.

Kost to Berge, November 30, 1941.

Stuart Kroesch to Criminal Division, July 7, 1941. File 144-23-0.

Ermon Lachart and Letha Pelton to Franklin Roosevelt, February 25, 1940. File 144-12-0.

Virginia Lambert to Frank Murphy, April 7, 1939. File 144-0.

Layle Lane to Frank Murphy, June 1, 1939. File 144-18-0.

Acting Assistant Attorney General Welly Hopkins to Lane, June 9, 1939.

Lane to Hopkins, June 17, 1939.

Hopkins to Lane, June 24, 1939.

Lane to Hopkins, June 26, 1939.

Assistant Attorney General O. John Rogge to Lane, July 13, 1939.

Robert Laney and Sophie Laney to Justice Department, April 20, 1940. File 144-16-0.

"Laundry Employees" to Franklin Roosevelt, June 24, 1940. File 144-12-0.

Patricia Latimer to Frank Murphy, February 7, 1939. File 114-0.

Louise Leonard to Stephen Marley (White House), January 29, 1941. File 144-35-0.

Wendell Berge to Leonard, February 17, 1941.

Francois Leroseau III to Franklin Roosevelt, May 9, 1940. File 144-16-0.

Harry Levien to Whom It May Concern, January 10, 1940. File 144-16-0.

Morris Levin to Civil Liberties Section, September 3, 1940. File 144-42-0.

O. John Rogge to Harry Blanton, US Attorney, St. Louis. September 13, 1940.

Rogge to Levin. September 13, 1940

Maphtaly Levy to Frank Murphy, received December 28, 1939. File 144-36-0.

Thomas Lindsay to Robert Jackson, January 23, 1940. File 144-36-0.
> Assistant Attorney General O. John Rogge to Lindsay, February 2, 1940.

Erman Lockhart and Letha Pelton to Franklin Roosevelt, February 25, 1940. File 144-12-0.
> Assistant Attorney General O. John Rogge to Lockhart and Pelton, March 13, 1940.

Andrew W. Loewi to Frank Murphy, April 21, 1939. File 144-0.

Athol MacNair to Robert Jackson, March 21, 1940. File 144-16-0.

May Massing to Frank Murphy, May 19, 1939. File 144-42-0.

Sara K. McClure to Franklin Roosevelt, June 19, 1939. File 144-11-0.

Veronica McCormick to Edgar Hoover, August 5, 1941. File 144-12-0.
> McCormick to Franklin Roosevelt, April 9, 1941.
> McCormick to Eleanor Roosevelt, April 12, 1941.
> Assistant Attorney General Wendell Berge to McCormick, April 16, 1941.

Mrs. O. P. McCoy to Frank Murphy, March 31, 1939. File 144-0.

Frank McCulloch to Robert Jackson, June 26, 1941. File 144-23-0.

Mrs. Roy McDonald to Francis Biddle, October 11, 1944. File 144-10-7.

C. C. McGee to Frank Murphy, April 7, 1939. File 144-0.

Racene McGraw to Frank Murphy, June 17, 1939. File 144-16-0.

Thomas McHugh to Frank Murphy, September 16, 1939. File 144-11-0.
> Assistant Attorney General O. John Rogge to McHugh, October 6, 1939.

Raymond McKee to Frank Murphy, April 29, 1939. File 144-11-0.
> Assistant Attorney General Matthew McGuire to McKee, May 29, 1939.
> McKee to McGuire, June 7, 1939.

Frances McKoney to Robert Jackson, December 26, 1940. File 144-35-0.

Mrs. E. B. McMullen to Frank Murphy, January 13, 1940. File 144-18-0.
> Assistant Attorney General O. John Rogge to McMullen, February 9, 1940.
> McMullen to Murphy, February 15, 1940.
> Rogge to McMullen, March 12, 1940.

Eleanor Blake McNamara to Frank Murphy, August 23, 1939. File 144-16-0.
> Assistant Attorney General O. John Rogge to McNamara, September 8, 1939.

Frances McNutt to Franklin Roosevelt, August 23, 1939. File 144-12-0.
  Assistant Attorney General O. John Rogge to McNutt, September 11,
    1939.
John McVeigh to Franklin Roosevelt, March 22, 1939. File 144-0.
Carl Miller to Frank Murphy, March 28, 1939. File 144-0.
M. Mills to Attorney General, October 21, 1939. File 144-35-0.
James Minnis to Franklin Roosevelt, received September 15, 1939. File 144-
    23-0.
Pat Mohr to Frank Murphy, December 2, 1939. File 144-37-0.
Molly Mollison to Franklin Roosevelt, January 12, 1940. File 144-18-0.
Mary Moloney to Franklin Roosevelt, November 16, 1939. File 144-23.
  Moloney to Roosevelt, December 6, 1939.
  Assistant Attorney General O. John Rogge to Moloney, December 20,
    1939.
  Moloney to Roosevelt, December 31, 1939.
  Moloney to Roosevelt, April 16, 1940.
Dave Moore to Franklin Roosevelt, July 11, 1940. File 144-9-0.
  Assistant Attorney General O. John Rogge to Moore, July 22, 1940.
Zella Morrison to Brien McMahon, April 19, 1939. File 144-37-0.
  Brien McMahon to Morrison, May 2, 1939.
  Morrison to McMahon, May 5, 1939.
  Morrison to McMahon, May 31, 1939.
  Morrison to Franklin Roosevelt, June 6, 1939.
Charles Moussie to Attorney General, March 29, 1939. File 144-0.
S. J. Murphy to US Attorney J. Saxton Daniel, copy to Justice Department,
    received March 14, 1939. File 144-0.
  Assistant Attorney General Brien McMahon to S. J. Murphy, March
    28, 1939.
  Murphy to Attorney General Frank Murphy, April 4, 1939.
  Assistant Attorney General Brien McMahon to S. J. Murphy, April
    14, 1939.
Martha Nakielski to Frank Murphy, April 15, 1939. File 144-37-0.
Louis Nally to Frank Murphy, June 24, 1939. File 144-23-0.
Gertrude Notes to Eleanor Roosevelt, March 12, 1939. File 144-0.
Edward Olmstead to Sen. Arthur Vandenberg, October 7, 1939. File 144-
    37-0.
Pearl Squires Olsen to Frank Murphy, received March 11, 1939. File 144-0.
  Assistant Attorney General Brien McMahon to Olsen, March 21,
    1939.

Josephine O'Neal to Franklin Roosevelt, September 10, 1939. File 144-37-0.

Frank O'Neill to J. Edgar Hoover, August 27, 1940. File 144-11-0.

Hoover to Assistant Attorney General O. John Rogge, September 18, 1940.

O'Neill to Rogge, September 26, 1940.

Evangeline Pearson to Frank Murphy, March 6, 1939. File 144-0.

Assistant Attorney General Brien McMahon to Pearson, March 21, 1939.

Pearson to McMahon, March 1939.

McMahon to Pearson, March 30, 1939.

Pearson to McMahon, March 31, 1939.

McMahon to Pearson, April 13, 1939.

Pearson to Murphy, April 25, 1939.

Tyson Pearson to Franklin Roosevelt, October 12, 1940. File 144-12-0.

E. V. Pease to Franklin Roosevelt, March 18, 1940. File 144-15-0.

Pease to Attorney General Robert Jackson, March 18, 1940.

Assistant Attorney General O. John Rogge to Pease, March 27, 1940.

John Peters to Frank Murphy, April 29, 1939. File 144-42-0.

Peters to Frank Murphy, May 7, 1939.

Assistant Attorney General Welly Hopkins to Peters, May 25, 1939.

Peters to Hopkins, May 31, 1939.

Peters to Hopkins, June 12, 1939.

Hopkins to Peters, June 21, 1939.

Hopkins to K. P. Aldrich, Post Office Department, June 21, 1939.

Frank Murphy to Sen. Robert Taft, July 28, 1939.

Peters to Assistant Attorney General O. John Rogge, March 5, 1940.

Maeta Perry to Franklin Roosevelt, June 14, 1939. File 144-18-0.

Acting Assistant Attorney General Welly Hopkins to Perry, June 25, 1939.

Perry to Hopkins, December 7, 1940.

L. R. Pinckney to Frank Murphy, March 29, 1939. File 144-0.

Assistant Attorney General Brien McMahon to Pinckney, April 6, 1939.

Seth Plummer to President, received September 10, 1939. File 144-42-0.

Assistant Attorney General O. John Rogge to Plummer, September 23, 1940.

James H. Porter to Franklin Roosevelt, March 20, 1939. File 144-0.

Assistant Attorney General Brien McMahon to Porter, April 6, 1939.

Porter to McMahon, August 4, 1939.

Lucy Potter for Frank Murphy, July 16, 1939. File 144-23-0.

Lee Pressman, CIO, to Henry Schweinhaut, March 20, 1939. File 144-0.

C. C. Probert to Robert Jackson et al., July 22, 1940. File 144-37-0.

Bernard Ray to Franklin Roosevelt, June 24, 1940. File 144-23-0.

"A Reader" to Franklin Roosevelt, September 30, 1939. File 144-35-0.

Edna Reynolds to LaFollette Civil Liberties Committee, March 18, 1940. File 144-37-0.

Harry Reynolds to Franklin Roosevelt, received February 16, 1940. File 144-37-0.

Assistant Attorney General O. John Rogge to Reynolds, February 28, 1940.

Reynolds to Rogge, March 2, 1940.

Reynolds to Rogge March 14, 1940.

Reynolds to U.S. Senator J. Prentice Brown, March 14, 1940.

Rogge to Reynolds, March 22, 1940.

Reynolds to Rogge, March 24, 1940.

Reynolds to Franklin Roosevelt, September 23, 1940.

George Richter to Frank Murphy, June 16, 1939. File 144-0.

Thurman Reed Rigdon to Francis Biddle, May 2, 1942. File 144-35-0.

Memorandum for V. W. Rotnem, by John O'Brien, May 15, 1942.

Memorandum for Rotnem, by O'Brien, May 23, 1942.

J. B. Roarke to US Attorney Office, March 17, 1939. File 144-0.

Dorothy Rogers to Stewart Lynch, October 20, 1942. File 144-15.

Wendell Berge to Stewart Lynch, November 5, 1939.

George Rogers to US Department of Justice, received March 18, 1940. File 144-9.

Assistant Attorney General O. John Rogge to Rogers, March 28, 1940.

Rogge to Sam Rorex, US Attorney, Little Rock, March 29, 1940.

Rorex to Rogge, April 25, 1940.

Rogge to Rogers, May 18, 1940.

James Rogers to Franklin Roosevelt, June 16, 1940. File 144-37-0.

William Ross to Frank Murphy, April 26, 1939. File 144-36-0.

David Ruja to Robert Jackson, July 20, 1940. File 144-12-0.

George Runyan to Frank Murphy, December 28, 1939. File 144-37-0.

Assistant Attorney General O. John Rogge to Runyan, January 12, 1940.

Runyan to Rogge, April 2, 1940.

George Ruzicka to Franklin Roosevelt, received April 1939, File 144-0.
Assistant Attorney General Brien McMahon to Ruzicka, April 28, 1939.
Elsie Sanders to Frank Murphy, December 14, 1939. File 144-12-0.
Assistant Attorney General O. John Rogge to Sanders, December 28, 1939.
Sanders to Rogge, January 19, 1940.
Rogge to Sanders, February 8, 1940.
Roy B. Schwing to Frank Murphy, March 5, 1939. File 144-0.
Assistant Attorney General Brien McMahon to Schwing, May 16, 1939.
Marguerite Senour to Franklin Roosevelt, received June 5, 1940. File 144-12-0.
Herbert Shenkin to Victor Rotnem, Chief, Civil Liberties Unit, March 29, 1943. File 144-18-0.
Louis Sheppard to Court of Justice, September 11, 1940. File 144-11-0.
M. R. Silvernail to Frank Murphy, March 28, 1939. File 144-0.
A. P. Smith to Franklin Roosevelt, July 16, 1939. File 144-16-0.
F. J. Smith to Frank Murphy, March 20, 1939. File 144-0.
Harry Smith to Department of Justice, August 29, 1939. File 144-12-0.
Assistant Attorney General O. John Rogge to Smith, September 14, 1939.
Hattie Mae Smith to Franklin Roosevelt, July 18, 1940. File 144-0-23.
Julia Smith to Franklin Roosevelt, October 28, 1939. File 144-18-0.
Assistant Attorney General O. John Rogge to Smith, November 14, 1939.
William C. Smith to Robert Jackson, January 16, 1940. File 144-23-0.
Mrs. William H. Smith to Franklin Roosevelt, February 19, 1940. File 144-12-0.
Joseph Snyder to Justice Department, April 20, 1940. File 144-16-0.
Walter Spilky to Robert Jackson, July 8, 1940. File 144-23-0.
Nicolaas Steelink to Eleanor Roosevelt, received January 13, 1939. File 144-12-0.
Cecil Stevens to Eleanor Roosevelt, September 3, 1939. File 144-35-0.
John Stoddard to Frank Murphy, March 7, 1939. File 144-0.
Assistant Attorney General Brien McMahon to Stoddard, March 17, 1939.
C. E. Stutzman to Department of Justice, December 31, 1940. File 144-35-0.

Rev. B. Sumner to Department of Justice, April 3, 1939. File 144-0.

Brien McMahon to Sumner, April 29, 1939.

Richard Terry to Robert Jackson, May 20, 1940. File 144-12-0.

Charlie Thompson to Frank Murphy, November 30, 1939. File 144-18-0.

Assistant Attorney General O. John Rogge, to Herbert S. Phillips, US Attorney, Tampa, December 12, 1939.

Rogge to Post Office Department, December 12, 1939.

Rogge to K. P. Aldrich, Chief Inspector, Post Office Department, February 14, 1940.

R. A. Carlton, Post Office Inspector, to Phillips, February 6, 1940.

Thompson to Phillips, February 6, 1940 (telegram).

J. H. Tidwell et al. to Franklin Roosevelt, July 15, 1940. File 144-42-0.

C. B. Tippie to Attorney General, May 18, 1941. File 144-12-0.

Shelby Toombs to President, May 14, 1940. File 144-0.

Alice Townhill to J. E. Hoover, September 11, 1941. File 144-0.

George Trinckes to Department of Justice, April 3, 1939. File 144-0.

Assistant Attorney General Brien McMahon to Trinckes, April 25, 1939.

Earl Tucker to Attorney General, December 12, 1940. File 144-12-0.

Anton Vedral to Franklin Roosevelt, July 3, 1939. File 144-23-0.

William C. Uphoff to Franklin Roosevelt, August 26, 1939. File 144-23-0.

Edward Vocob to Frank Murphy, March 23, 1939. File 144-0.

Joseph Langhorne Walker to Department of Justice, July 13, 1939. File 144-16-0.

Regina Wallace to Frank Murphy, May 19, 1939. File 144-0.

Office of Mayor, New York City, to Wallace, September 22, 1939.

Wallace to Murphy, November 15, 1939.

Wallace to Franklin Roosevelt, January 11, 1940.

Wallace to H. W. Graf, Navy Department, February 14, 1940.

O. John Rogge to Wallace, January 24, 1940.

Wallace to Rogge, February 14, 1940.

Rogge to Wallace, February 29, 1940.

Wallace to Attorney General, March 27, 1940.

Eleanor Watjus to Franklin Roosevelt, February 10, 1941, File 144-23-0.

L. L. Wells to Department of Justice, April 6, 1939. File 144-0.

M. D. Willet to Franklin Roosevelt, October 27, 1940. File 144-9-0.

Georgiana Wines to Franklin Roosevelt, April 18, 1939. File 144-0.

Velva Wise to J. Edgar Hoover, January 16, 1942. File 144-9-0.

Hoover to Assistant Attorney General Wendell Berge, March 5, 1942.

Berge to Hoover, March 11, 1942.

Wise to Berge, June 24, 1942.

Wise to Berge, July 7, 1942.

Wise to Berge, July 13, 1942.

Wise to Berge, July 15, 1942.

Wise to Berge, August 12, 1942.

Wise to Berge, August 29, 1942.

Ruth Wood to Franklin Roosevelt, June 29, 1940. File 144-11-0.

Robert Wright to Franklin Roosevelt, October 28, 1941. File 144-35-0.

Wright to Franklin Roosevelt, November 13, 1941.

Assistant Attorney General Wendell Berge to US Attorney Bernard Flynn, November 26, 1941.

Y. Yamaguchi to Franklin Roosevelt, October 29, 1940. File 144-12-0.

Bernice Yendick to Franklin Roosevelt, October 10, 1939. File 144-37-0.

Bob Zagonel to U.S. Power Commission, February 14, 1939. File 144-0.

Notes

Chapter One

1. The CRS correspondence examined in this book comes from Justice Department files housed at the National Archives. The appendix provides details about the archival sources and a list of all the letters referenced in the text. In the pages that follow, I use the date and name to refer to the letters on that list.

2. I do not draw any conclusions about civil rights consciousness among African Americans or consciousness of discrimination based on the small number of race-related claims in the letters. I do not expect this pool of letters to the federal government provide a representative picture of African Americans' consciousness of rights. I point out that the number of race-related letters is small only because I have learned that readers will otherwise expect a study of civil rights complaints to the Roosevelt administration to be a book about racial discrimination. It is also important to note that the percentage of letters about race in my sample is likely lower than the percentage in the full population of letters processed by the CRS. Because I drew the sample from a general file designation for civil rights, it does not include letters complaining about peonage, which were also processed by the CRS. Many letters in the peonage files complained of near-slavery conditions in some agricultural workplaces in the South. See Goluboff (1999; 2007, chapter 2). In addition, some state files are missing from the archives, including all the states of the Deep South.

3. More than 70 percent of the letters presented themselves as being authored by a single individual, and many others were written by couples or a small group of similarly situated people who were not part of any formal organization.

4. Public Law 77-623. The CRS later became interested in using this provision to support its efforts to curtail abuses directed at the Jehovah's Witnesses by state officials (McMahon 2003, 140–41).

5. It is not clear what happened with Rogers's complaint. Assistant Attorney General Wendell Berge wrote to the US attorney in Delaware, Stewart Lynch,

requesting that he meet with school officials (November 5, 1942), but the file does not indicate whether Lynch participated in such a meeting. There is evidence in other cases that Rogers was correct to believe that local officials would sometimes back down if the Justice Department expressed concerns directly to local officials. For example, when Cumberland, Maryland, passed an ordinance banning picketing, the CRS asked the local US attorney to make an inquiry with local officials. The US attorney reported back that an assistant had met with the city's attorney, and the city had decided it would not enforce the law (Bernard Flynn to the attorney general, October 3, 1940, file 144-35-0).

6. Tocqueville may not have been correct in his observation. His famous claim that Americans of the early nineteenth century transformed all social conflicts into legal conflicts has recently been disputed by Graber (2004).

7. For overviews of the socio-legal literature on legal consciousness, see Silbey (2005); Marshall and Barclay (2006); McCann (2006). In addition to interview-based studies of legal consciousness, there are also numerous studies that document people's attitudes toward law using surveys of much larger samples of people. For example, social psychologist Tom Tyler and coauthors surveyed large samples of people on their ideas about compliance and trust in law (Tyler 1990; Tyler and Rasinski 1991; Tyler and Huo 2002). In addition, Gibson, Caldeira, and coauthors have conducted large-*n* surveys of public attitudes toward the Supreme Court as an institution and toward particular court decisions (see, e.g., Gibson 1989, 1991, 2007; Gibson and Caldeira 2009). These often revealing studies document how a representative sample responds to survey items probing attitudes toward law and rights. However, the gains in the sample come at the cost of a survey design that raises questions about whether such methods can access the political dimensions of legal discourses and ideology. (See discussion of this point in Silbey 2005, 337–38; Barclay and Silbey 2008.) Scholars have designed surveys to address questions about attitudes and dispositions toward law or legal institutions, but the surveys are not designed to document how people talk about law or use and construct legal discourses in their everyday lives.

8. Perspectives on the use and relative effectiveness of citizen letters as political participation can be found in Verba and Nie (1972); Kingdon (1989, 54–60). The conventional wisdom among political scientists is that letters to elected officials do not have significant effects on public policy unless they are combined with other forms of political activity.

9. See, for example, Alan Brinkley's (1982) account of Huey Long, the powerful Louisiana governor and senator, and Father Coughlin, the host of a popular radio show. Long in particular made attacks on some forms of concentrated wealth and advocated forms of redistribution. Arguably, Glenn Beck is a parallel figure to Coughlin, for he matches Coughlin by broadcasting wildly imaginative and occasionally anti-Semitic criticisms of a sitting president. Beck also channels Coughlin's fascistic cries that some betrayal ended a golden era that never actually existed. However, Beck does not follow Coughlin's (or Long's) economic populism.

10. Robert Gordon (1984) provides an insightful overview of historical work by scholars associated with the critical legal studies movements and a defense of their focus on judicial doctrine. Karl Klare (1978) provides an example of a scholar who tracks changes in legal consciousness by looking at appellate court opinions. Hendrik Hartog (1993) and Sally Merry (2000), in contrast, provide examples of historical studies of legal consciousness that look beyond pronouncements from judges and lawyers to also recover the voices of ordinary people from legal records.

11. See Levinson (1988, 29). On Levinson's other dimension, the *source* of doctrine, letter writers seemed to lean toward the Catholic position (both the text and established traditions) rather than the Protestant position (text alone as source of doctrine). However, as shown in chapter 4, the text itself was very important to many writers.

12. See Key (1966, 7).

13. On transposing and novel rights claims, see Polletta (2000, 379); Ewick and Silbey (1998, 40–41). Both sources cite Sewell (1992) as a foundational source.

14. I say "about" because there were eighty-nine letters from individuals that could not be coded for sex. Most were written by people who provided only initials rather than first names. The letters with only initials may include a substantial number of women. Some writers may have used initials if they felt they could add credibility by masking the fact that they were women, as sometimes happens when authors of children's books choose their nom de plume (e.g., J. K. Rowling and S. E. Hinton).

15. On the other hand, another feature of the study may counteract some of the bias created by the sample. The proliferation of rights bureaucracies and legally oriented interest organizations that has occurred since these letters were written may mean that people are now *more* willing to assert rights. Thus the resourcefulness with legal materials and general contentiousness of the letter writers in my sample may *under*state the extent to which people today are willing to deploy inventive legal claims.

16. Some studies that use public opinion polling to study attitudes toward law are cited above in note 7. Barclay and Silbey (2008) provide a compelling case for using different methods associated with legal consciousness to understand the political consequences of popular ideas about legal legitimacy. For more general examples of alternatives to polling methods for understanding political ideas among ordinary people, see Lane (1962); Walsh (2004).

17. Letters to the White House have also been an enduring source of scholarly and popular interest. For early scholarly perspectives, see Sussman (1956, 1959). There are several books that document letters sent to Franklin and Eleanor Roosevelt and to other federal agencies during Roosevelt's administration (Levine and Levine 2002; McElvaine 1983; Sussman 1963). Studies also show that presidents have used mail to gauge pubic opinion, particularly before the arrival of modern polling techniques and infrastructure (e.g., Rottinghaus 2006). There are also popular books of children's letters to presidents (e.g., Adler 1962; Adler and Adler

2009). Socio-legal scholars have also used letters to explore public ideas about law. For example, Michelson (2008) uses letters to a newspaper columnist in China to explore a more public and visible example the construction of legal meaning.

18. More generally, two works of historical synthesis have enhanced my understanding of the historical development of American ideas about rights and the Constitution and have helped me to situate the period I cover here. Kammen's (1994) broadly ranging historical inquiry into American constitutional culture gathers evidence that gets beyond elite views to the processes through which constitutional knowledge is created and shared, including accounts of popular celebrations of the Constitution and materials in school textbooks. Foner's *Story of American Freedom* (1998) offers a broad historical synthesis of work that looks at ideas about freedom and liberty in American history. See also Primus's (1999) valuable historical account of changing ideas about rights by key American political thinkers.

19. None of my claims about the value of the CRS letters are meant to establish that the letters to the CRS are a perfect or best source of data or even the best available. However, one other unique feature that made them attractive is that they were preserved and accessible. It is not easy to find collections that preserve protest letters to government regarding law and rights together with government responses. Much routine Justice Department correspondence that did not end up in case files was never archived. I learned in response to a Freedom of Information Act request that the Justice Department now routinely destroys citizen correspondence that does not lead to investigation or other official action.

20. Ninety percent of the cases in my sample were from 1939 and 1940. There are 413 from 1939, 375 from 1940, 75 from 1941, and 16 written from 1942 to 1944.

21. The states without letters are Colorado, Idaho, Montana, Nebraska, New Hampshire, North Carolina, North Dakota, Rhode Island, South Carolina, Utah, Vermont, and Wyoming.

22. Here I am echoing Robert Cover (1983), who points out that judges' interpretive decisions on the Constitution can be usefully understood as *jurispathic* (i.e., as an effort to kill off rival sources of meaning).

Chapter Two

1. Details on the Broadus killing are from the letter from W. A. C. Hughes Jr., (December 3, 1943) and from the following newspaper accounts in Baltimore's *Afro-American:* "Cop Kills Fort Meade Soldier, 26," (February 3, 1942); "Officer Bender Killed Man in 1940," (February 3, 1942); "Five Agencies Probe Death of Soldier" (February 7, 1942); "No Indictment of Officer Yet" (March 3, 1942); "Two Accused by Cop Face Trial Wed." (March 10, 1942); "Gov. Fails to Answer Plea for Hearing" (March 17, 1942).

2. On the march on Annapolis, see Cumberbatch (2009, 61, 68n59).

3. One case in 1939, four cases in 1940 (Elliff 1967, 104).

4. See, US Attorney Philips to Rogge, December 15, 1939. There was also no guarantee that the postal inspector's office would provide as much help as occurred in Charlie Thompson's case. In another case, the CRS forwarded a complaint from John Peters about mail fraud to the postal inspector's office (Welly Hopkins to K. P. Aldrich, Post Office Department, June 21, 1939). Peters wrote back to Justice repeatedly to complain that he had not received any help (May 31, 1939; June 12, 1939; July 21, 1939).

5. The fact that the cases the CRS pursued were reported in the press should not be taken as a sign that attention from the press drove CRS decision making. Press attention is an indicator of the seriousness of the incident, not just the level of public attention. Attention from the press certainly did not guarantee that the CRS would pursue a case. The murder of Broadus attracted considerable press attention and was also the impetus for a large political protest, but it did not get attention from federal prosecutors. Many writers included supportive press reports with their letters yet were refused help. Press attention was also not a necessary condition for CRS attention. Charlie Thompson's case does not appear to have attracted any public attention.

6. Bautista also sent a pamphlet about his organization that included a statement of the organization's objectives. The statement reveals that the civil libertarians of the Philippines had quite broad conceptions of rights and liberties. The objectives included such American-style rights as freedom of press, assembly, speech, and religion. But the list also included several other items that are not typically linked to "civil liberties" in the United States: "combat[ing] human exploitation in whatever form" and "help[ing] to enlighten those who are made to accept exploitation through ignorance," "elimination of monopolies from private hands," "elimination of unnecessary middlemen in the system of commodity distribution," and "revision of the system of taxation in order to make taxes correspond to capacity to pay, in order to restrict economic power of those most prone to exploit others."

7. The leading history of Reconstruction is Foner (1988). See also Amar (1998) on the transformative importance of the Civil War amendments in American constitutional law. On the processes that led to the Supreme Court's narrowing of the Reconstruction amendments, see Brandwein (2006, 2011). Nieman (1991) provides a broader historical overview of the relationship between constitutional development and African Americans. Litwack (1998) powerfully documents the horrors that resulted from this process of retrenchment.

8. In retrospect, another important marker of the court's growing interest in civil rights was the famous footnote 4 in *United States v. Carolene Products* (304 US 144 [1938]). However, the note did not attract much attention or have much impact until after the period covered here (Goluboff 2007, 47–49).

9. Carr (1947, chapter 3) provides a detailed overview of the available statutes,

their prior use, and the CRS's understanding of the legal problems that the statutes created.

10. The antipeonage statute was far from perfect. Ambiguities in the law created many unsettled questions about how the CRS could use it. See Carr (1947, 77–84).

11. Carr (1947, 57–74) provides a detailed discussion of the CRS's expectations about its ability to use existing statutes. Another concern for the CRS was that section 51 called for a fine of $5,000 and a prison sentence of up to ten years. The CRS worried that those strong penalties would make juries reluctant to convict. In contrast, section 52's penalty seemed too moderate for some types of cases: a maximum fine of $1,000 and a maximum sentence of one year (Carr 1947, 59–60).

12. The state action doctrine did not limit the power of state governments. Because the states retain broad police powers under the Constitution, states could, in theory, prosecute private actors for violations of rights under state laws. However, many state governments of that time period were not capable of, and usually not interested in, providing redress for many egregious rights violations. The manifest failure of state governments to protect rights was a primary reason for the growing interest in expanding federal protections. See Carr (1947, 106–7).

13. They were on solid constitutional ground. Brandwein (2011) argues that the text and history of the Fourteenth Amendment supports the view that it covers "state neglect" and that courts recognized the validity of such protection in its early case law on the amendment.

14. See, e.g., Brief for Petitioners, *Screws v. United States,* October Term 1944, no. 42, pp. 49–52.

15. On the CRS's pursuit of *Screws,* see Carr (1947, 106–15). The horror of the case is most powerfully captured in David Dante Troutt's short story "Never Was." The story is based on Troutt's research in the trial court records. It is reprinted in Troutt (1998, 97–132) and in Troutt (1999, 27–52).

16. See Carr (1947, 122–24).

17. Elliff's research on the early CRS documents show that political calculations around race were an important part of department decision making (1967, chapter 3). Elliff uses a series of internal department memos from the early 1940s to show how political appointees at Justice worked to contain dedicated attorneys at the CRS in order to prevent them from inflaming white elected officials in the South. When the CRS did take action, political officials were careful to reassure southern officials that the CRS would not be allowed to disrupt white southerners' "intimate relations with the Negro" (156). For detailed and more general accounts of the political conditions that made it impossible to take on civil rights issues more directly, see McMahon (2003). On the filibuster and other problems in Congress, see Zangrando (1980).

18. I do not mean to suggest here that the CRS was created purely or even primarily as an effort in symbolic politics. There is nothing in the records to sug-

gest that Murphy was not sincere. More tellingly, there is also nothing to suggest that the Justice Department tried to trumpet the creation of the CRS in order to please some African American constituency. If symbolic politics were the goal, it does not appear to have been very effective. For example, the important African American paper the *Chicago Defender* covered the creation of the CRS with a front-page story ("US May Dig into the Problem of Lynching," February 18, 1939) but did not mention the CRS the rest of that year. The formation of the CRS also did not merit mention in the *Defender*'s year-end list of the "20 Outstanding News Stories for 1939" (January 6, 1940). The NAACP's journal, the *Crisis*, also only rarely mentioned the CRS. Occasional correspondence between the NAACP and the CRS suggests that relations were mutually distrustful.

19. See note 17 above. The President's Committee on Civil Rights (1947) reported on difficulties with both US attorneys (120–22) and the FBI (122–26).

20. Brien McMahon, assistant attorney general, to Gordon McIntire, April 27, 1939: "[T]here is every indication that persons charged with enforcement of the law made every effort to protect the Negro from the mob." Brian McMahon, to Harvey Fields, US attorney, Shreveport, March 20, 1939; J. B. Thigpen to H. G. Fields, US attorney, Shreveport, April 6, 1939; Brien McMahon to Harvey Fields, April 27, 1939. The first letter to the US attorney refers to a letter from Gordon McIntire dated March 9, 1939, but the letter is not in the file (file 144-0).

21. The CRS also tried to keep the FBI out of Charlie Thompson's case. The department's initial letter to the US attorney in Florida specifically requested that he not inform the FBI of the department's interest in the case (Rogge to Herbert S. Phillips, December 12, 1939).

22. On the Quintar South case, see Elliff (1967, 109–11). See also Carr (1947, 105–8). Despite the failure to obtain a conviction, the US attorney in Atlanta reported that he thought the case had a positive effect on the policies of the Atlanta police (Carr 1947, 154).

23. David Blanton to Harry Blanton, June 26, 1939, file 144-42-0.

24. Harry Blanton to attorney general, September 29, 1939, file 144-42-0.

25. O. John Rogge to Harry Blanton, October 10, 1939, file 144-42-0.

26. "Civil Liberties," Murphy's nationally broadcast radio address, is reprinted in *United States Law Review* 73 (1939): 198–202. See also Murphy, "Civil Liberties and the Cities," address to the United States Conference of Mayors and National Institute of Municipal Law Officers, reprinted in *City Problems: The Annual Proceedings of the United States Conference of Mayors* (1939): 9–14.

27. It is difficult to determine the precise number of letters processed by the CRS. My sample is from letters given a civil rights designation and routed to the CRS. Most of the letters preserved in the archives are from 1939–41, and it is clear that there are many letters missing. (See appendix.) There are some published reports and estimates regarding the volume of letters processed by the CRS, but they are not entirely consistent. According to Carr (1947, 125) the attorney general

published figures on the number of letters handled by the CRS for 1942 (8,612) and 1943 (13,490). Carr himself estimated that about twenty thousand letters were processed in 1944. The President's Committee on Civil Rights (of which Carr was executive secretary) reported that the CRS processed between 1,500 and 2,500 civil rights "complaints" per year between 1939 and 1947, but the report is not clear about how "complaints" were distinguished from other correspondence (1947, 120).

28. The CRS did not typically reply to letters that simply urged the president to veto a law or to people who forwarded resolutions of organizations. There are some cases where the reply letters are not in the files but there is other evidence that a reply was sent. The actual replies are preserved only as carbon copies, and it is likely that some of the missing replies were lost and never archived. There are also cases where the file indicates that the CRS made a deliberate decision not to reply.

29. The note was written on an internal routing slip. Very few of the routing slips are preserved in the CRS correspondence files. I discuss Runyan's quite serious complaint in more detail in chapter 3 and his response to the CRS in chapter 4.

30. I discuss several examples in chapter 4.

31. An example is the letter sent to Patrick Coane, July 27, 1939.

32. September 11, 1939. There is no indication in the file of what happened to McNutt or her father.

33. A "Memorandum for the Files" (September 24, 1941) by two Justice Department officials reported the Allen had been "bombarding" the US attorney with "innumerable letters and complaints" for four years.

34. Not all Justice Department officials exhibited the patient attention that Lynch, Schweinhaut, and Rotnem gave to Mr. Allen. When the CRS inquired with the San Francisco US attorney about a letter writer named Bertha Baker, the attorney reported that his office simply ignored all letters sent from psychiatric institutions. He said that such letters "usually indicate mental conditions" and that "[f]rom experience in the past I have learned that to acknowledge receipt of most of these letters . . . is simply to invite a great many more, all to the same effect, and relating to matters over which even if true I would have no jurisdiction" (July 24, 1939). The CRS, on the other hand, routinely wrote back to people who wrote from psychiatric institutions.

35. There are a few instances where US attorneys sent letters or memos to the department reporting that a referred letter writer had visited, and those memos are written in ways that imply that such a report was routine if a person referred by the department approached a federal prosecutor. However, it is possible that there were other instances where US attorneys disposed of complainants without reporting it in writing to Washington. It is important to note also that the invitations in the reply letters were not very encouraging. The invitations came in letters that expressed general doubts about the legal authority of the federal government to

act, and the invitation to visit the US attorney was conditional on the person's being able to provide new information that would support a claim for federal jurisdiction. Such reply letters did not, however, tell complainants what a valid legal basis for federal jurisdiction might be. There are just nineteen cases in my sample where the Washington office directly contacted a US attorney about a complaint letter. None of those nineteen cases led to a prosecution.

36. The original letter was handled by Kemp, who worked as an assistant to Murphy, not for the CRS. However, after receiving Causey's second letter, Kemp sent a memo to John Rogge at the Criminal Division suggesting that the matter might "come within the scope of the Civil Liberties Unit" and asking that he prepare a second reply for Kemp to sign (January 27, 1940).

37. Kelli Kennedy, "Fla Homeless Woman Gets Help after Obama Question." Associated Press, Business News, February 12, 2009.

38. There is one case in my sample that shows that local governments also deployed contestable legal claims when responding to citizens. When Regina Wallace complained that she had been kidnapped and taken across state lines by officials of a public mental hospital in the Bronx (May 19, 1939), the CRS told her she should complain instead to local officials because the federal government had no jurisdiction. When Wallace wrote back to challenge that claim (November 15, 1939), she buttressed her position by including a copy of a letter she had received from the office of the mayor of New York. The mayor's letter stated that the city government had no jurisdiction to help because the case had to be handled in the courts (September 22, 1939).

39. The legal claims in the CRS replies might be characterized, following Bybee (2010), as an illustration of a link between legality and courtesy. Bybee provides a fascinating analysis of the normative claims and ritualized practices that support "the rule of law," claiming that the rule of law, like common courtesy, is a form of "acceptable hypocrisy." Interestingly, the link between courtesy and law may be even closer in these letters than in Bybee's account. The CRS's use of legal claims rather than more brutally honest replies can be read as a straightforward effort to remain courteous in a contentious exchange.

40. The letter writers' constitutional claims are discussed in more detail in chapter 4.

Chapter Three

1. It is not just letter writers' ideas about entitlements that seem unusual by today's standards but also their sense of what kinds of claims fit into categories like "civil rights" or "civil liberties." However, it is important to remember that such incongruity does not necessarily mean writers were confused or badly informed. Elite actors at that time, including government attorneys and judges, also defined

"civil rights" and "civil liberties" differently from the way experts define those terms today. Risa Goluboff (2007) has shown, for example, that "civil rights" was much more closely associated with issues of work and labor organizations at the time of the CRS founding than today. The different conceptions of the scope of rights at that time are also evident in some letters sent to the CRS by people who worked professionally on issues related to civil rights. An example is a letter from Oscar Heimlich, the owner and publisher of "Building America," a series of secondary school textbooks. Heimlich's letter asked the department for information and photographs to include in his new book series, "Civil Liberties." He enclosed an outline of the series that indicated that the series would devote as much space to "civil liberties and labor" and "civil liberties and education" as to issues related to racial minorities and First Amendment issues like censorship (March 7, 1939). Today, a series of school textbooks on civil liberties would likely be organized quite differently.

2. On the history and development of ideas about freedom of speech, see Graber (1991), Rabban (1997), Tsai (2008).

3. Sara K. McClure (June 19, 1930); Patricia Latimer (February 7, 1939); Joseph Johnston (March 4, 1939).

4. Memorandum for V. W. Rotnem, by John O'Brien, May 15, 1942, file 144-35-0.

5. Sixteen of the letters mentioning property rights did not provide any clear indication of the relative status of the writer.

6. Some political theorists have made similar claims about the scope of property rights. Waldron's (1988) account of the foundations of liberal property rights in political theory, and in particular his account of Locke's views, shows that there are alternatives to the received tradition of relatively narrow and conservative property rights.

7. Athol MacNair (February 21, 1940); Robert Laney and Sophie Laney (April 20, 1940); John Snyder (April 20, 1940); Martin Jones (April 20, 1940).

8. Resolution dated April 16, 1940, file 144-16-0.

9. France's letter revealed that he was a professor of economics at Rollins College but did not mention that he was a former attorney. See France (1957).

10. Lawrence Cramer to Francis Biddle, January 10, 1942; J. E. Hoover to Ugo Carusi, executive assistant to the attorney general, January 19, 1942; C. W. Palmer to Lawrence Cramer, January 22, 1941. All in file 144-23-7.

11. On the distinction between positive and negative freedom, see Berlin (1958). Many of the letters received by the CRS show how that distinction can break down as the topic shifts to the practical process of finding mechanisms for protecting rights. Many of the claims about negative rights, such as a right to be free from censorship or rights against police brutality, were expressed as claims about the inadequacy or inaccessibility of civil remedies. Positive entitlements to an adequately staffed and affordable civil justice system are necessary for protecting many negative rights. I do not attempt to provide a count of the number of positive

and negative rights claims because the distinction tends to break down in many of my cases.

12. Roosevelt introduced the Four Freedoms with his 1941 State of the Union address. That speech was the beginning of a renewed effort by government officials and elites to establish associations between "freedom" and government assistance. The administration's effort did not grab much popular attention until Norman Rockwell's famous paintings were published in 1943. By that time, the United States was deep into the war effort. See Foner (1998, 223–29) on the emergence and importance of the Four Freedoms. A much earlier example of Roosevelt's thinking on the changing role of government in ensuring economic freedom is his famous Address to the Commonwealth Club in September 1932. The speech is reprinted in Grafton (1999, 18–27).

13. Of course, efforts to use litigation campaigns to advance policy goals began long before *Brown*. The NAACP's campaign was novel only in that it was a high-profile campaign to advance a progressive rather than conservative cause. Business and antiunion interest groups had been using similar tactics for decades. See, for example, Ernst (1995).

14. O. John Rogge to Harry Blanton, September 13, 1940, file 144-42-0.

15. Coane's account is corroborated in some contemporaneous newspaper accounts. Coane included a clipping from the *People's Press* with his letter. See also "Policeman Ousted for Activities in Communist Party," *Chicago Daily Tribune,* February 4, 1937, 4; "Policeman Reinstated," *Chicago Daily Tribune,* January 19, 1938, 6.

16. Some other work-related letters dealt with relatively minor worker entitlements. For example, John Dew complained about cancellation of the Fourth of July holiday for Los Angeles County employees: "Other holidays are not discriminated against. We protest action as unprecedented and unpatriotic. What do you think?" (June 26, 1940). A group of "Laundry Employees" also complained about the loss of the holiday (June 24, 1940).

17. The quoted phrases are used in Bickel's seminal work on the countermajoritarian difficulty (Bickel 1962, 16). Lemieux and Watkins (2008) provide an overview of recent work revealing the shortcomings of Bickel's formulation.

18. E.g., Bickel (1962), Spann (1993).

Chapter Four

1. I am using "attention" as a general and neutral word that can cover a variety of goals. It can mean material assistance, or it can more mean only that the government official who reads the letter will give time and thought to the writer's message before setting it aside. I certainly do not mean it in a pejorative sense, as, for example, when one would say a misbehaving child "just wants some attention."

2. The Slaughterhouse Cases, 83 US 36. For perspectives on judicial and scholarly interpretations of the privileges and immunities clause and the surrounding history, see Brandwein (1999), Amar (1998). Disputes about the meaning of the clause and whether it should be resurrected continue to animate the Supreme Court today. See, for example, the disagreement between Justice Alito and Justice Thomas in *Chicago v. McDonald* (561 US 3025, 2010).

3. Boswell did not give information suggesting that he had any personal stake in this matter. His letterhead indicated that he was an artist and designer rather than a physician or healer.

4. Uphoff had been in trouble with the law earlier in connection with his business practices. See "Oil Men of St. Louis Get Victims Here," *Hayti Herald* (Hayti, Missouri), February 8, 1917, available at http://chroniclingamerica.loc.gov/lccn/sn89066651/1917-02-08/ed-1/seq-1/.

Chapter Five

1. Some readers might reject my claim that writers were aware of law's limitations by pointing out that people did not get any help. Doesn't that mean that letter writers were just wasting time? What kind of awareness is that? In response, I concede that some letter writers may have overestimated the likelihood of getting a favorable reply. However, it is a mistake to assume that people did not understand that it would be quite difficult to get attention from government officials. Moreover, the question of whether it was worth writing a letter hinges not just on the chances of getting help but also on whether there were alternative things that the writers could have done that would have been more likely to produce help. If people had nowhere else to turn, it could make sense to write even if the chances of getting help were exceedingly small. In addition, there are reasons to write besides just getting material redress—writers were able to exercise voice, register protest, and create a record of injustice. More generally, it would be a mistake to focus on an evaluation based on the quality of the writers' understanding of their chances. No goal-oriented analysis can provide a meaningful explanation or evaluation of all the choices made by the writers. It is impossible to determine what writers' goals were, and there is no reason to believe that all the writers had the same goals.

2. My findings here echo Ewick and Silbey (1998), who found that people expressed several different and seemingly contradictory stories about law in extended interviews about their daily experiences of social life. However, because I observe people engaged in more contentious and resistant interactions with government officials, I am led to different conclusions about how the apparent contradictions resolve themselves.

3. I do not attempt to provide a precise count of the number of writers who used extralegal claims. Such a number would not provide a meaningful measure of

how many people had faith in law. Most of the letters that could be coded as not making any extralegal claims were very short notes or telegrams that simply assert or inform the department about a problem or ask Roosevelt to veto a bill. Such writers may have betrayed a lack of faith if they had written more. In addition there are some conceptual problems that make it difficult to draw a precise line between legal and extralegal claims in some cases. I expect the basic distinction I am making to make sense to readers. In the case of rights that are expressed in absolute terms, it is usually easy to identify certain kinds of claims as irrelevant to a legal standard. For example, if all people (or citizens) have a right to sell ice cream, it should not matter that a person claiming the right is a teetotaler or is caring for a disabled relative. The line can be blurred in instances where the legal entitlement is more conditional. In addition, factual claims or claims about character can sometimes relate directly to legal standards for evidence and might thus be considered legal rather than extralegal. The kinds of claims I am making about legal and extralegal claims do not demand that I can provide a precise distinction that works on cases at the periphery. However, the difficulty of making a precise distinction is the reason I do not try to count the number of legal and extralegal claims.

4. File 144-1-21, Record Group 60, Entry 114, Box 17574. This case from 1945 is not part of my sample of letters. The CRS received notice of the case from the NAACP.

5. Levine and Levine (2002) collect a substantial number of letters from the public that were inspired by fireside chats.

Chapter Six

1. I am borrowing an analogy to "killing off" law from Robert Cover's (1983) description of judges as "jurispathic" officials whose rulings eliminate alternative expressions of law. Much of the rest of this concluding chapter is influenced and inspired by Cover's work, including the importance I give to "commitment" to constitutional values, my insistence that legal interpretation by nonauthoritative actors has value, and my refusal to privilege official versions of law. More generally, this book project has been inspired by Cover's imperative that "we ought to stop circumscribing the *nomos*; we ought to invent new worlds" (1983, 68).

2. Competing perspectives on the role of courts in rights protections are found in Rosenberg (1991) and McCann (1994). Both scholars conclude that judges are not typically able to advance rights on their own. My point is that legislation is also not a trouble-free alternative that allows people to avoid going through judges. New legislation that gives disempowered persons new legal claims of entitlement against powerful private interests almost never results in voluntary compliance. For example, employers massively resisted new rights given to workers by the Wagner Act in 1935 (Klare 1978). Reform occurs not with a single court ruling or the

passage of legislation but when the threat of legal sanction becomes credible enough to produce compliance (see Epp 2009).

3. Oliver Wendell Holmes, *Southern Pacific Company v. Jensen* (244 US 205, 222 [1917]).

4. For example, Francesca Polletta's (2000) fascinating study of novel civil rights claiming in the 1960s finds that the adoption of novel rights claims by activists was facilitated by some specific features of the organizational and social context. This study shows that individuals outside of movements can propagate novel and expansive legal and rights claims even in the absence of the supportive structural factors that Polletta identifies.

5. The seminal work for socio-legal studies of the "myth of rights" is, of course, Stuart Scheingold's *The Politics of Rights* (2004). In the first edition of that work, published in 1974, Scheingold himself acknowledged that his illuminating articulation of the myth was based largely on the work of political theorists and that there were few empirical studies demonstrating that people actually believed in the myth. In a separate article (2012), I review a variety of subsequent empirical studies that claim to link law and judicial institutions to widespread public perceptions of legitimacy. I find that there is considerable reason to question whether there is any widespread acceptance of legal ideals or a myth of rights.

6. No scholar would say that an instance where a lawyer called an incompetent judge "your honor" counted as evidence that the lawyer thought the judge was honorable. The same consideration should be given to ordinary people observed giving voice to legal ideals when addressing government officials in a position to help them. See also Bybee (2010), who portrays some of the ritualized practices that support the rule of law as "acceptable hypocrisies."

7. Wedeen's account of everyday resistance, like Ewick and Silbey's, resonates with Scott's pathbreaking scholarship on resistance (1985, 1990). See also Kelley (1994).

8. I do not mean to claim here that flexibility fully explains why legal discourses remain resonant. The pull of law, rights, and constitutionalism on Americans' political consciousness also both reflects and reinforces core features of the American state. The United States was slow among industrializing nations to develop a centralized bureaucratic mechanisms of governance. As a result, much regulation of economic activity was instead left to common-law judges (Skowronek 1982, Orren 1991). The federal government eventually developed greater administrative capacities, but law and legal processes of adversarial legalism continue to play an unusually important intermediary role between democratic politics and the development of regulatory policies (see, e.g., Kagan 2001; Haltom and McCann 2004; Epp 2009). Given the enduring structural importance of legal processes, it is not surprising that law saturates popular American political discourse.

9. Consider also Grant Gilmore's (1977) formulation of the idea that the existence of law indicates lack of consensus: "The better the society, the less law there

will be. In Heaven, there will be no law and the lion will lay down with the lamb. The values of an unjust society will reflect themselves in an unjust law. The worse the society, the more law there will be. In Hell, there will be nothing but law, and due process will be meticulously observed" (111).

10. I do not mean to imply that everyone faced the same threat or that the fear of such violence motivated everyone in the same way. A white college professor like Royal Wilbur France could confront a southern sheriff and challenge his racist practices without facing the same threat of violent retaliation as an African American soldier or mechanic. Nevertheless, the fear of extralegal violence comes through in a wide range of letters. Georgiana Wines, for example, mentioned her fear that she might be "gotten rid of" if Ford decided to retaliate against her efforts to organize a protest against the company.

11. Kramer and Tushnet both focus largely on making normative claims within constitutional theory rather than on building empirical evidence of how ordinary people understand and experience the Constitution. Kramer makes a historical argument that popular constitutionalism was the vision animating the original constitutional design. Tushnet supports his argument for "taking the Constitution away from the courts" by drawing attention to bad court decisions and doctrines. Tushnet's view that people support a "thin" constitution that articulates core values of equal treatment and basic rights, rather than a "thick" constitution of more technical provisions, gets some support in my findings here. Other perspectives on popular constitutionalism include Rosen's (2006) argument that the court can be a democratic and responsive institution and Levinson's (2006) call for a new constitutional convention to replace what he sees as a dangerously undemocratic American Constitution.

12. While Posner does say why he believes the things he says in the quoted passages, one passage in his review indicates the sympathies that motivate his contempt for popular constitutionalism: "The idea that lay people . . . are competent to deliver binding opinions on any legal question is wormwood, of course, to lawyers and judges. And not to them alone, but also to commercial interests and the propertied class: capital is secure only within a framework of reasonably clear rules and procedures administered by reasonably impartial professionals."

13. Gibson and Caldeira (2009) review survey findings and question the common claim of public ignorance of the Supreme Court. They also present evidence that people actually know quite a bit about the court and show that earlier findings that people are ignorant were the result of flawed survey design.

14. There are certainly some people who oppose the expansion of federal rights-protecting powers and who wish to return to days when state governments had more independence. However, I think such people would acknowledge that the argument for abandoning all federal protections has to be built on substance, not by citing current Supreme Court doctrine.

15. The fact that the Court acted *sua sponte* on the jury instructions issue is

acknowledged in the plurality opinion by Douglas (107) and in Rutledge's dissent (118).

16. On the link between competing interpretations of the Civil War amendments and competing understandings of slavery and the Civil War, see Brandwein (1999, chapters 2 and 3).

17. The justices discuss the brief at 159–61.

18. For recent perspectives on Reconstruction and constitutional change, see Foner (1988), Brandwein (1999, 2007), Amar (1998), Balkin (2010).

19. For example, *Parents Involved v. Seattle School District,* 551 US 701 (2006), 748, 772, 780.

20. Guidry and Sawyer (2003) provide a useful comparative and historical account of bottom-up mobilization for new entitlements as a core component of democracy.

Bibliography

Adler, Bill, ed. 1962. *Kids' Letters to President Kennedy*. New York: William Morrow.

Adler, Bill, and Bill Adler Jr., eds. 2009. *Kids' Letters to President Obama*. New York: Ballantine Books.

Amar, Akhil Reed. 1998. *The Bill of Rights: Creation and Reconstruction*. New Haven, CT: Yale University Press.

Anderson, Ellen A. 2004. *Out of the Closets and into the Courts: Legal Opportunity Structure and Gay Rights Litigation*. Ann Arbor: University of Michigan Press.

Balkin, Jack. 2010. "The Reconstruction Power." *New York University Law Review* 85:1801–61.

Barclay, Scott, and Susan S. Silbey. 2008. "Understanding Regime Change: Public Policy, Legitimacy, and Legal Consciousness." In Keith E. Whittington, R. Daniel Kelemen, and Gregory A. Caldeira, eds., *The Oxford Handbook of Law and Politics*. Oxford: Oxford University Press.

Barzilai, Gad. 2003. *Communities and Law: Politics and Cultures of Legal Identities*. Ann Arbor: University of Michigan Press.

Bell, Derrick A., Jr. 1980. "*Brown v. Board of Education* and the Interest-Convergence Dilemma." *Harvard Law Review* 93:518–533.

Berlin, Isaiah. 1958. *Two Concepts of Liberty*. Oxford: Clarendon.

Bickel, Alexander. 1962. *The Least Dangerous Branch: The Supreme Court at the Bar of Politics*. Indianapolis: Bobbs-Merrill.

Brandwein, Pamela. 1999. *Reconstructing Reconstruction: The Supreme Court and the Production of Historical Truth*. Durham, NC: Duke University Press.

———. 2006. "The *Civil Rights Cases* and the Lost Doctrine of State Neglect." In Ronald Kahn and Ken I. Kersch, eds., *The Supreme Court and American Political Development*. Lawrence: University Press of Kansas, 2004.

———. 2007. "A Judicial Abandonment of Blacks? Rethinking the 'State Action' Cases of the Waite Court." *Law and Society Review* 41:343–86.

———. 2011. *Rethinking the Judicial Settlement of Reconstruction*. New York: Cambridge University Press.

Brigham, John. 1996. *The Constitution of Interests: Beyond the Politics of Rights.* New York: New York University Press.

Brinkley, Alan. 1982. *Voices of Protest: Huey Long, Father Coughlin, and the Great Depression.* New York: Knopf.

———. 1995. *The End of Reform: New Deal Liberalism in Recession and War.* New York: Knopf.

Bumiller, Kristin. 1988. *The Civil Rights Society: The Social Construction of Victims.* Baltimore: Johns Hopkins University Press.

Bybee, Keith J. 2010. *All Judges Are Political—Except When They Are Not: Acceptable Hypocrisies and the Rule of Law.* Stanford, CA: Stanford University Press.

Caldeira, Gregory A., and James L. Gibson. 1992. "The Etiology of Public Support for the Supreme Court." *American Journal of Political Science* 36:635–64.

Carr, Robert K. 1947. *Federal Protection of Civil Rights: Quest for a Sword.* Ithaca, NY: Cornell University Press.

Cohen, Robert, ed. 2002. *Dear Mrs. Roosevelt: Letters from Children of the Great Depression.* Chapel Hill: University of North Carolina Press.

Coleman, Frank. 1944. "Freedom from Fear on the Home Front." *Iowa Law Review* 29:415–29.

Comaroff, Jean, and John L. Comaroff. 1997. *Of Revelation and Revolution.* Chicago: University of Chicago Press.

Cover, Robert M. 1975. *Justice Accused: Antislavery and the Judicial Process.* New Haven, CT: Yale University Press.

———. 1983. "The Supreme Court, 1982 Term—Foreword: Nomos and Narrative." *Harvard Law Review* 97:4–68.

———. 1986. "Violence and the Word." *Yale Law Review* 95:1601–29.

Crenshaw, Kimberle Williams. 1988. "Race, Reform, and Retrenchment: Transformation and Legitimation in Antidiscrimination Law." *Harvard Law Review* 101:1331–87.

Cumberbatch, Prudence. 2009. "What 'The Cause' Needs Is a 'Brainy and Energetic Woman': A Study of Female Charismatic Leadership in Baltimore." In Dayo F. Gore, Jeanne Theoharis, and Kozumi Woodward, eds., *Want to Start a Revolution? Radical Women in the Black Freedom Struggle.* New York: New York University Press.

Dalfiume, Richard M. 1968. "The 'Forgotten Years' of the Negro Revolution." *Journal of American History* 58:90–106.

Devins, Neal A. 2007. "The D'Oh! of Popular Constitutionalism." *Michigan Law Review* 105:1333–51.

Dudas, Jeffrey R. 2008. *The Cultivation of Resentment: Treaty Rights and the New Right.* Stanford, CA: Stanford University Press.

Dworkin, Ronald. 1977. *Taking Rights Seriously.* Cambridge, MA: Harvard University Press.

Edgerton, John. 1994. *Speak Now against the Day: The Generation before the Civil Rights Movement in the South.* Chapel Hill: University of North Carolina Press.

Elliff, John T. 1967. "The United States Department of Justice and Individual Rights, 1937–1962." PhD diss., Harvard University.

Engel, David M. 1984. "The Oven Bird's Song: Insiders, Outsiders, and Personal Injuries in an American Community." *Law and Society Review* 18:551–82.

Engel, David M., and Jaruwan S. Engel. 2010. *Tort, Custom, and Karma: Globalization and Legal Consciousness in Thailand.* Stanford, CA: Stanford University Press.

Engel, David M., and Frank Munger. 2003. *Rights of Inclusion: Law and Identity in the Life Stories of Americans with Disabilities.* Chicago: University of Chicago Press.

Epp, Charles R. 2009. *Making Rights Real: Activists, Bureaucrats, and the Creation of the Legalistic State.* Chicago: University of Chicago Press.

Ernst, Daniel R. 1995. *Lawyers against Labor: From Individual Rights to Corporate Liberalism.* Urbana: University of Illinois Press.

Ernst, E. Rose. 2007. "Move(ments) beyond Rights: Welfare Rights in an Era of Personal Responsibility." *Studies in Law, Politics, and Society* 40:79–101.

———. 2010. *The Price of Progressive Politics: The Welfare Rights Movement in an Era of Colorblind Racism.* New York: New York University Press.

Ewick, Patricia, and Susan S. Silbey. 1998. *The Common Place of Law: Stories from Everyday Life.* Chicago. University of Chicago Press.

———. 2003. "Narrating Social Structure: Stories of Resistance to Legal Authority." *American Journal of Sociology* 108:1328–72.

Foner, Eric. 1988. *Reconstruction: America's Unfinished Revolution, 1863–1877.* New York: Harper and Row.

———. 1998. *The Story of American Freedom.* New York: Norton.

Forbath, William E. 1991. *Law and the Shaping of the American Labor Movement.* Cambridge, MA: Harvard University Press.

France, Royal W. 1957. *My Native Grounds.* New York: Cameron and Associates.

Gabel, Peter, and Duncan Kennedy. 1984. "Roll Over, Beethoven." *Stanford Law Review* 36:1–55.

Galanter, Marc. 1974. "Why the Haves Come Out Ahead." *Law and Society Review* 9:95–160.

Garrow, David J. 1994. *Liberty and Sexuality: The Right to Privacy and the Making of* Roe v. Wade. Berkeley: University of California Press.

Gibson, James L. 1989. "Understandings of Justice: Institutional Legitimacy, Procedural Justice, and Political Tolerance." *Law and Society Review* 23:469–96.

———. 1991. "Institutional Legitimacy, Procedural Justice, and Compliance with Supreme Court Decisions: A Question of Causality." *Law and Society Review* 25:631–35.

———. 2007. "The Legitimacy of the US Supreme Court in a Polarized Polity." *Journal of Empirical Legal Studies* 4 (3): 507–38.

Gibson, James L., and Gregory. A. Caldeira. 2009. "Knowing the Supreme Court? A Reconsideration of Public Ignorance of the High Court." *Journal of Politics* 71 (2): 429–41.

Gilliom, John. 2001. *Overseers of the Poor: Surveillance, Resistance, and the Limits of Privacy.* Chicago: University of Chicago Press.

Gilmore, Grant. 1977. *The Ages of American Law.* New Haven, CT: Yale University Press.

Glendon, Mary Ann. 1991. *Rights Talk: The Impoverishment of Political Discourse.* New York: Free Press.

Goldberg-Hiller, Jonathan. 2004. *The Limits to Union: Same-Sex Marriage and the Politics of Civil Rights.* Ann Arbor: University of Michigan Press.

Goluboff, Risa L. 1999. "'Won't You Please Help Me Get My Son Home': Peonage, Patronage, and Protest in the World War II Urban South." *Law and Social Inquiry* 24:777–806.

———. 2007. *The Lost Promise of Civil Rights.* Cambridge, MA: Harvard University Press.

Gordon, Robert W. 1984. "Critical Legal Histories." *Stanford Law Review* 36: 57–125.

Graber, Mark A. 1991. *Transforming Free Speech: The Ambiguous Legacy of Civil Libertarianism.* Berkeley: University of California Press.

———.1993. "The Non-Majoritarian Difficulty: Legislative Deference to the Judiciary." *Studies in American Political Development* 7:35-73.

———. 2004. "Resolving Political Questions into Judicial Questions: Tocqueville's Thesis Revisited." *Constitutional Commentary* 21:485–545.

Grafton, John. 1999. *Great Speeches: Franklin Delano Roosevelt.* Mineola, NY: Dover Publications.

Greenhouse, Carol J. 1989. *Praying for Justice: Faith, Order, and Community in an American Town.* Ithaca, NY: Cornell University Press.

Gregory, James N. 2005. *The Southern Diaspora: How the Great Migration of Black and White Southerners Transformed America.* Chapel Hill: University of North Carolina Press.

Guidry, John A., and Mark Q. Sawyer. 2003. "Contentious Pluralism: The Public Sphere and Democracy." *Perspective on Politics* 1:273–89.

Haltom, William, and Michael J. McCann. 2004. *Distorting the Law: Politics, Media, and the Litigation Crisis.* Chicago: University of Chicago Press.

Hartog, Hendrik. 1993. "Abigail Bailey's Coverture: Law in a Married Woman's Consciousness." In Austin Sarat and Thomas R. Kearns, eds., *Law in Everyday Life.* Ann Arbor: University of Michigan Press.

Hoffman, Elizabeth A. 2003. "Legal Consciousness and Dispute Resolution: Different Disputing Behavior at Two Similar Taxicab Companies." *Law and Social Inquiry* 28:691–716.

————. 2005. "Dispute Resolution in a Worker Cooperative: Formal Procedures and Procedural Justice." *Law and Society Review* 39:51–82.

Hull, Kathleen E. 2006. *Same-Sex Marriage: The Cultural Politics of Love and Law.* New York: Cambridge University Press.

Kagan, Robert A. 2001. *Adversarial Legalism: The American Way of Law.* Cambridge, MA: Harvard University Press.

Kammen, Michael. 1994. *A Machine That Would Go of Itself: The Constitution in American Culture.* New York: St. Martin's.

Kelley, Robin D. G. 1994. *Race Rebels: Culture, Politics, and the Black Working Class.* New York: Free Press.

Kellogg, Peter J. 1979. "Civil Rights Consciousness in the 1940s." *Historian* 42: 18–41.

Key, V. O. 1966. *The Responsible Electorate: Rationality in Presidential Voting, 1936–1960.* Cambridge, MA: Harvard University Press.

Kingdon, John W. 1989. *Congressmen's Voting Decisions.* 3rd ed. Ann Arbor: University of Michigan Press.

Kirkland, Anna. 2008. "Think of the Hippopotamus: Rights Consciousness in the Fat Acceptance Movement." *Law and Society Review* 42:397–432.

Klare, Karl. 1978. "Judicial Deradicalization of the Wagner Act and the Origins of Modern Legal Consciousness, 1937–1941." *Minnesota Law Review* 62:265–339.

Klinker, Philip A., with Rogers Smith. 1999. *The Unsteady March: The Rise and Decline of Racial Equality in America.* Chicago: University of Chicago Press.

Kluger, Richard. 1975. *Simple Justice: The History of* Brown v. Board of Education *and Black America's Struggle for Equality.* New York: Knopf.

Korstad, Robert, and Nelson Lichtenstein. 1988. "Opportunities Found and Lost: Labor, Radicals, and the Early Civil Rights Movement." *Journal of American History* 75:786–811.

Kramer, Larry D. 2004. *The People Themselves: Popular Constitutionalism and Judicial Review.* New York: Oxford University Press.

Lane, Robert Edward. 1962. *Political Ideology: Why the Common Man Believes What He Does.* New York: Free Press.

Lee, Taeku. 2002. *Mobilizing Public Opinion: Black Insurgency and Racial Attitudes in the Civil Rights Era.* Chicago: University of Chicago Press.

Lemieux, Scott E., and George I. Lovell. 2008. "Understanding the Impact and Visibility of Ideological Change on the Supreme Court." *Studies in Law, Politics, and Society* 44:1–33.

————. 2010. "Legislative Defaults: Interbranch Power Sharing and Abortion Politics." *Polity* 42: 210–43.

Lemieux, Scott E., and David Watkins. 2008. "Beyond the 'Countermajoritarian Difficulty': Lessons from Contemporary Democratic Theory." *Polity* 41:30–62.

Leuchtenburg, William E. 2005. *The White House Looks South: Franklin D. Roosevelt, Harry S. Truman, Lyndon B. Johnson.* Baton Rouge: Louisiana State University Press.

Levine, Lawrence W., and Cornella R. Levine. 2002. *The People and the President: America's Conversation with FDR.* Boston: Beacon.

Levinson, Sanford. 1988. *Constitutional Faith.* Princeton, NJ: Princeton University Press.

———. 2006. *Our Undemocratic Constitution: Where the Constitution Goes Wrong (and How We the People Can Correct It).* New York: Oxford University Press.

Litwack, Leon F. 1998. *Trouble in Mind: Black Southerners in the Age of Jim Crow.* New York: Vintage.

Lovell, George I. 2003. *Legislative Deferrals: Statutory Ambiguity, Judicial Power, and American Democracy.* New York: Cambridge University Press.

———. 2012. "The Myth of the Myth of Rights." *Studies in Law, Politics, and Society* 59 (forthcoming).

Luker, Kristin. 1984. *Abortion and the Politics of Motherhood.* Berkeley: University of California Press.

Marshall, Anna-Maria. 2003. "Injustice Frames, Legality, and the Everyday Construction of Sexual Harassment." *Law and Social Inquiry* 28:659–89.

———. 2005. "Idle Rights: Employees' Rights Consciousness and the Construction of Sexual Harassment Policies." *Law and Society Review* 39: 83–124.

Marshall, Anna-Maria, and Scott Barclay. 2006. "In Their Own Words: How Ordinary People Construct the Legal World." *Law and Social Inquiry* 28: 617–28.

Martens, Allison M. 2007. "Reconsidering Judicial Supremacy: From the Counter-Majoritarian Difficulty to Constitutional Transformations." *Perspectives on Politics* 5:447–59.

Mather, Lynn, and Barbara Yngvesson. 1980–81. "Language, Audience, and the Transformation of Disputes." *Law and Society Review* 15:775.

Matsuda, Mari J. 1989. "When the First Quail Calls: Multiple Consciousness as Jurisprudential Method." *Women's Rights Law Reporter* 11:7-10.

McCann, Michael W. 1994. *Rights at Work: Pay Equity Reform and the Politics of Legal Mobilization.* Chicago: University of Chicago Press.

———. 2006. "On Legal Rights Consciousness: A Challenging Analytical Tradition." In Benjamin Fleury-Steiner and Laura Beth Nielsen, eds., *The New Civil Rights Research: A Constitutive Approach.* Aldershot, UK: Ashgate.

McCann, Michael W., and William Haltom. 2004. *Distorting the Law: Politics, Media, and the Litigation Crisis.* Chicago: University of Chicago Press.

McElvaine, Robert S., ed. 1983. *Down and Out in the Great Depression: Letters from the "Forgotten Man."* Chapel Hill: University of North Carolina Press.

McMahon, Kevin J. 2003. *Reconsidering Roosevelt on Race: How the Presidency Paved the Road to Brown.* Chicago: University of Chicago Press.

Merry, Sally Engle. 1990. *Getting Justice and Getting Even: Legal Consciousness among Working-Class Americans.* Chicago: University of Chicago Press.

———. 2000. *Colonizing Hawaii: The Cultural Power of Law.* Princeton, NJ: Princeton University Press.

———. 2006. *Human Rights and Gender Violence: Translating International Law into Local Justice.* Chicago: University of Chicago Press.

Mezey, Susan Gluck. 2005. *Disabling Interpretations: The Americans with Disabilities Act in Federal Court.* Pittsburgh: University of Pittsburgh Press.

———. 2007. *Queers in Court: Gay Rights Law and Public Policy.* New York: Rowman and Littlefield.

Michelson, Ethan. 2008. "Dear Lawyer Bao: Everyday Problems, Legal Advice, and State Power in China." *Social Problems* 55:43–71.

Nielson, Laura Beth. 2004. *License to Harass: Law, Hierarchy, and Offensive Public Speech.* Princeton, NJ: Princeton University Press.

Nieman, Donald G. 1991. *Promises to Keep: African Americans and the Constitutional Order, 1776 to the Present.* New York: Oxford University Press.

Noonan, John T., Jr. 2002. *Narrowing the Nation's Power: The Supreme Court Sides with the States.* Berkeley: University of California Press.

O'Reilly, Kenneth. 1995. *Nixon's Piano: Presidents and Racial Politics from Washington to Clinton.* New York: Free Press.

Orren, Karen. 1976. "Standing to Sue: Interest Group Conflict in the Federal Courts." *American Political Science Review* 70:723–41.

———. 1991. *Belated Feudalism: Labor, the Law, and Liberal Development in the United States.* New York: Cambridge University Press.

Polletta, Francesca. 2000. "The Structural Context of Novel Rights Claims: Southern Civil Rights Organizing, 1961–1966." *Law and Society Review* 34:367–406.

Posner, Richard A. 2004. "The People's Court." Review of *The People Themselves: Popular Constitutionalism and Judicial Review*, by Larry Kramer. *New Republic*, July 19, 32.

Powe, Lucas A., Jr. 2000. *The Warren Court and American Politics.* Cambridge, MA: Harvard University Press.

President's Committee on Civil Rights. 1948. *To Secure These Rights: Report of the President's Committee on Civil Rights.* New York: Simon and Schuster.

Prejean, Helen. 1993. *Dead Man Walking: An Eyewitness Account of the Death Penalty in the United States.* New York: Random House.

Primus, Richard A. 1999. *The American Language of Rights.* New York: Cambridge University Press.

Rabban, David M. 1997. *Free Speech in Its Forgotten Years.* New York: Cambridge University Press.

Rosen, Jeffrey. 2006. *The Most Democratic Branch: How the Courts Serve America.* Oxford: Oxford University Press.

Rosenberg, Gerald N. 1991. *The Hollow Hope: Can the Courts Bring About Social Change?* Chicago: University of Chicago Press.

Rotnem, Victor W. 1942. "Clarifications of Civil Rights States." *Bill of Rights Review* 2:260–61.

———. 1943. "The Federal Civil Right 'Not to Be Lynched.'" *Washington University Law Quarterly* 28:57–73.

Rottinghaus, Brandon. 2006. "'Dear Mr. President': The Institutionalization and Politicization of Public Opinion Mail in the White House." *Political Science Quarterly* 121:451–76.

Sarat, Austin. 1990. "The Law Is All Over: Power, Resistance and the Legal Consciousness of the Welfare Poor." *Yale Journal of Law and the Humanities* 2:343.

———. 2001. *When the State Kills: Capital Punishment and the American Condition.* Princeton, NJ: Princeton University Press.

Sarat, Austin, and Thomas R. Kearns. 1995. "Beyond the Great Divide: Forms of Legal Scholarship and Everyday Life." In Austin Sarat and Thomas R. Kearns, eds., *Law in Everyday Life.* Ann Arbor: University of Michigan Press.

Sarat, Austin, and Stuart Scheingold, eds. 2006. *Cause Lawyers and Social Movements.* Stanford, CA: Stanford University Press.

Schattschneider, E. E. 1960. *The Semisovereign People: A Realist's View of Democracy in America.* New York: Holt, Rinehart and Winston.

Scheingold, Stuart. 2004. *The Politics of Rights: Lawyers, Public Policy, and Political Change.* 2nd ed. Ann Arbor: University of Michigan Press.

Schierenbeck, Jake. 2000. "Lost and Found: The Incredible Life and Times of (Miss) Layle Lane" *American Educator* 24:4-19.

Schuck, Peter H. 1983. *Suing Government: Citizen Remedies for Official Wrongs.* New Haven, CT: Yale University Press.

Scott, James C. 1985. *Weapons of the Weak: Everyday Forms of Peasant Resistance.* New Haven, CT: Yale University Press.

———. 1990. *Domination and the Arts of Resistance: Hidden Transcripts.* New Haven, CT: Yale University Press.

Sewell, William H. 1992. "A Theory of Structure: Duality, Agency, and Transformation." *American Journal of Sociology* 98:1–29.

Silbey, Susan S. 2005. "After Legal Consciousness." *Annual Review of Law and Social Science* 1:323–68.

Silverstein, Helena. 1996. *Unleashing Rights: Law, Meaning, and the Animal Rights Movement.* Ann Arbor: University of Michigan Press.

Sitkoff, Harvard. 1978. *A New Deal for Blacks: The Emergence of Civil Rights as a National Issue.* New York: Oxford University Press.

Skowronek, Stephen. 1982. *Building a New American State: The Expansion of Administrative Capacities.* Cambridge: Cambridge University Press.

Spann, Girardeau. 1993. *Race against the Court: The Supreme Court and Minorities in Contemporary America.* New York: New York University Press.

Sussman, Leila A. 1956. "Communication to the Policy-Maker: Petition and Pressure." *Public Opinion Quarterly* 20:5–16.

———. 1959. "Mass Political Letter Writing in America: The Growth of an Institution." *Public Opinion Quarterly* 23:203–12.

———. 1963. *Dear FDR: A Study of Political Letter Writing.* New York: Bedminster.

Teles, Steven Michael. 2008. *The Rise of the Conservative Legal Movement: The Battle for Control of the Law*. Princeton, NJ: Princeton University Press.

Troutt, David Dante. 1998. *The Monkey Suit, and Other Short Fiction on African Americans and Justice*. New York: New Press.

———. 1999. "Screws, Koon, and Routine Aberrations: The Use of Fictional Narratives in Federal Police Brutality Prosecutions." *New York University Law Review* 74:18-122.

Tsai, Robert. L. 2008. *Eloquence and Reason: Creating a First Amendment Culture*. New Haven, CT: Yale University Press.

Tushnet, Mark V. 1984. "An Essay on Rights." *Texas Law Review* 62:1363–1403.

———. 1987. *The NAACP's Legal Strategy against Segregated Education, 1925–1950*. Chapel Hill: University of North Carolina Press.

———. 1999. *Taking the Constitution Away from the Courts*. Princeton, NJ: Princeton University Press.

———. 2003. *The New Constitutional Order*. Princeton, NJ: Princeton University Press.

Tyler, Tom R. 1990. *Why People Obey the Law*. New Haven, CT: Yale University Press.

Tyler, Tom R., and Yuen J. Huo, 2002. *Trust in the Law: Encouraging Public Cooperation with the Police and Courts*. New York: Russell Sage Foundation.

Tyler, Tom R., and Kenneth Rasinski. 1991. "Procedural Justice, Institutional Legitimacy, and the Acceptance of Unpopular US Supreme Court Decisions: A Reply to Gibson." *Law and Society Review* 25:621–30.

Verba, Sidney, and Norman H. Nie. 1972. *Participation in America: Political Democracy and Social Equality*. New York: Harper and Row.

Waldron, Jeremy. 1988. *The Right to Private Property*. Oxford: Oxford University Press.

———. 1996. "Rights and Needs: The Myth of Disjunction." In Austin Sarat and Thomas R. Kearns, eds., *Legal Rights: Historical and Philosophical Perspectives*. Ann Arbor: University of Michigan Press.

Walsh, Katherine Cramer. 2004. *Talking about Politics: Informal Groups and Social Identity in American Life*. Chicago: University of Chicago Press.

Wechsler, Herbert. 1959. "Toward Neutral Principles of Constitutional Law." *Harvard Law Review* 73:1–35.

Wedeen, Lisa. 1999. *Ambiguities of Domination: Politics, Rhetoric, and Symbols in Contemporary Syria*. Chicago: University of Chicago Press.

Williams, Patricia A. 1991. *The Alchemy of Race and Rights*. Cambridge, MA: Harvard University Press.

Yngvesson, Barbara. 1993. *Virtuous Citizens, Disruptive Subjects: Order and Complaint in a New England Court*. New York: Routledge.

———. 1994. "Making Law at the Doorway: The Clerk, the Court, and the Construction of Community in a New England Town." In Carol Greenhouse,

Barbara Yngvesson, and David Engel, eds., *Law and Community in Three American Towns*. Ithaca, NY: Cornell University Press.

Zangrando, Robert L. 1980. *The NAACP Crusade against Lynching, 1909–1950*. Philadelphia: Temple University Press.

Zemans, Frances Kahn. 1983. "Legal Mobilization: The Neglected Role of the Law in the Political System." *American Political Science Review* 77:690–703.

Index

THE CHICAGO SERIES IN LAW AND SOCIETY

Edited by John M. Conley and Lynn Mather